RIDING THE WAVES OF CULTURE

Second Edition

RIDING THE WAVES OF CULTURE

UNDERSTANDING CULTURAL DIVERSITY IN BUSINESS

FONS TROMPENAARS AND
CHARLES HAMPDEN-TURNER

NICHOLAS BREALEY
PUBLISHING

LONDON

This new edition first published by
Nicholas Brealey Publishing Limited in 1997

Reprinted with corrections 1998, 1999

36 John Street
London
WC1N 2AT, UK
Tel: +44 (0)171 430 0224
Fax: +44 (0)171 404 8311

1163 E. Ogden Avenue, Suite 705-229
Naperville
IL 60563-8535, USA
Tel: (888) BREALEY
Fax: (630) 428 3442

http://www.nbrealey-books.com

Text © 1993, 1997 Intercultural Management Publishers NV
Charts © 1993, 1997 Nicholas Brealey Publishing Ltd

The rights of Fons Trompenaars and Charles Hampden-Turner to be
identified as the authors of this work have been asserted in accordance
with the Copyright, Designs and Patents Act 1988.

ISBN 1-85788-176-1

British Library Cataloguing in Publication Data
A catalogue record for this book is available from the
British Library.

Printed in Finland by Werner Söderström Oy.

CONTENTS

PREFACE TO THE SECOND EDITION

Since the first edition of this book was published we have carried out a great deal more work for our database and it now consists of 30,000 participants who have completed our questionnaire. This new material has enabled us to refine and develop our ideas and we have included our latest thinking in this revised edition.

In addition to updating the original research findings, we have added three new chapters and a revised appendix. Chapter 13 analyses a methodology for reconciling cultural dilemmas and developing transcultural competence. Chapters 14 and 15 discuss diversity *within* rather than *between* countries, describing ethnic differences in South Africa and the USA and also considering the effect on culture of gender, age, functional background and organisational structure. Appendix 2 outlines our research methodology in more detail.

The first edition of this book took over ten years to complete. Many people whose paths Fons crossed during that time were very helpful. He would like to do justice to them all in chronological order, since he has a sequential approach to time:

I am deeply indebted professionally to Frits Haselhoff for his insights into management and strategy. He also helped me to obtain a scholarship and to defend my PhD thesis in Philadelphia.

Thank you, too, Erik Bree and Rei Torres from the Royal Dutch/Shell Group for your sponsorship, both in money and in research opportunity during the difficult first years of my project.

I am also very grateful to the two gurus in my professional life. First of all Hasan Ozbekhan, who taught me the principles of systems theory in such a profound and stimulating way that most of the thoughts on which this book are based are drawn directly from his excellent mind. Second, Charles Hampden-Turner, who helped me to develop thinking about culture as a way of solving dilemmas. His creative mind encourages me continuously to stretch existing ideas to new levels. He made a major editorial contribution to the first edition of this book, while always respecting what I was trying to communicate. The additions to this second edition are so significantly influenced by Charles's way of thinking that I invited him to become co-author.

I am very much obliged to Giorgio Inzerilli for his solid – at times provocative – translations from deep anthropological thinking to management applications. His way of communicating the link between practice and concept has been very important not only to this book but also to the way my colleagues and I present workshops. Many of the examples used are directly or indirectly due to him, and he also put me on the track of defining the seven dimensions of culture.

I am grateful to our colleagues Kevan Hall, Philip Merry and Leonel Brug for help in developing more effective relationships with clients. They are some of the few people I trust to make presentations on major points of this book without feeling too anxious.

Many thanks to my colleagues in the Trompenaars Hampden-Turner Intercultural Management Group (formerly the Centre for International Business Studies/United Notions), Tineke Floor, Naomi de Groot, Vincent Merk, Oscar van Weerdenburg and Peter Prud'homme, for their continuous support and positive criticism.

We would also like to thank Martin Gillo from Advanced Micro Devices and RS Moorthy for their guidance in the applicability of our thoughts.

A great deal of work was done for the revised edition by Professor Peter Woolliams of the University of East London. His help was not limited to the production of our interactive educational tools but extended to complex statistical analysis of our database. His insights have been very enlightening. Thank you, Peter.

Chapter 14 on South Africa came to fruition with the significant help of Louis van de Merwe (Trompenaars Group South Africa) and Peter Prud'homme (United Notions in Amsterdam). Thank you, Louis and Peter.

Chapter 15 on diversity in the USA was very much improved by the comments of Dina Raymond of Motorola. We needed her female sensitivity to check our male conclusions. Thank you Dina.

And obviously we could not be stimulated more than by the comments of Geert Hofstede. He introduced Fons to the subject of intercultural management some 20 years ago. We do not always agree, but he has made a major contribution to the field, and was responsible for opening management's eyes to the importance of the subject. By defending his 25-year-old model, we found an extra impetus to go beyond "plotting" differences, to develop a method of taking advantage of these differences through reconciliation.

We also want to thank Nicholas Brealey Publishing for their support, in particular Sally Lansdell who edited the revised edition.

Fons Trompenaars
Charles Hampden-Turner
September 1997

1

AN INTRODUCTION TO CULTURE

This book is about cultural differences and how they affect the process of doing business and managing. It is not about how to understand the French (a sheer impossibility) or the British (try, and you will soon give up). It is our belief that you can never understand other cultures. Those who are married know that it is impossible ever completely to understand even people of your own culture. The Dutch author became interested in this subject before it grew popular because his father is Dutch and his mother is French. It gave him an understanding of the fact that if something works in one culture, there is little chance that it will work in another. No Dutch "management" technique his father tried to use ever worked very effectively in his French family.

This is the context in which we started wondering if any of the American management techniques and philosophy we were brainwashed with in many years of the best business education money could buy would apply in the Netherlands or the UK, where we came from, or indeed in the rest of the world.

Both authors have been studying the effect of culture on management for many years. This book describes much of what we have discovered. The different cultural orientations described result from 15 years of academic and field research. Many of the anecdotes and cases used in the text have come up in the course of more than 1000 cross-cultural training programmes we have given in over 20 countries. The names of the companies used in most of the cases are disguised.

Apart from the training programme material, 30 companies, with departments spanning 50 different countries, have contributed to the research. These include AKZO, AMD, AT&T, BSN, Eastman Kodak, Elf Aquitaine, SGS/Thomson, CRA, Glaxo, Heineken, ICI, Lotus, Mars, Motorola, Philips, Royal Dutch Airlines KLM, the Royal Dutch/Shell Group, Sematech, TRW, Van Leer, Volvo and Wellcome, to name a few. In order to gather comparable samples, a minimum of 100 people with similar backgrounds and occupations were taken in each of the countries in which the companies operated. Approximately 75% of the participants belong to management (managers in operations, marketing, sales and so on), while the remaining 25% were general admin-istrative staff (typists, stenographers, secretaries). The database now num-bers 30,000 participants. This is twice as much as four years ago when the first edition was published. The empirical results are, however, just an illus-tration of what we are trying to say.

This book attempts to do three things: dispel the notion that there is "one best way" of managing and organising; give readers a better under-standing of their own culture and cultural differences in general, by learn-ing how to recognise and cope with these in a business context; and provide some cultural insights into the "global" versus "local" dilemma facing international organisations. Possibly the most important aspect of the book is the second of these. I believe understanding our own culture and our own assumptions and expectations about how people "should" think and act is the basis for success.

The impact of culture on business

Take a look at the new breed of international managers, educated accord-ing to the most modern management philosophies. They all know that in the SBU, TQM should reign, with products delivered JIT, where CFTs distribute products while subject to MBO. If this is not done appropriately we need to BPR. (SBU = strategic business unit; TQM = total quality management; JIT = just-in-time; CFT = customer first team; MBO = management by objectives; BPR = business process reengineering.)

But just how universal are these management solutions? Are these "truths" about what effective management really is: truths that can be applied anywhere, under any circumstances?

Even with experienced international companies, many well-intended "universal" applications of management theory have turned out badly. For example, pay-for-performance has in many instances been a failure on the African continent because there are particular, though unspoken, rules about the sequence and timing of reward and promotions. Similarly, man-agement-by-objectives schemes have generally failed within subsidiaries of multinationals in southern Europe, because managers have not wanted to conform to the abstract nature of preconceived policy guidelines.

Even the notion of human-resource management is difficult to translate to other cultures, coming as it does from a typically Anglo-Saxon doctrine. It borrows from economics the idea that human beings are "resources" like physical and monetary resources. It tends to assume almost unlimited capacities for individual development. In countries without these beliefs, this concept is hard to grasp and unpopular once it is understood.

International managers have it tough. They must operate on a number of different premises at any one time. These premises arise from their culture of origin, the culture in which they are working and the culture of the organisation which employs them.

In every culture in the world such phenomena as authority, bureaucracy, creativity, good fellowship, verification and accountability are experienced in different ways. That we use the same words to describe them tends to make us unaware that our cultural biases and our accustomed conduct may not be appropriate, or shared.

There is a theory that internationalisation will create, or at least lead to, a common culture worldwide. This would make the life of international managers much simpler. People point to McDonald's or Coca-Cola as examples of tastes, markets and hence cultures becoming similar everywhere. There are, indeed, many products and services becoming common to world markets. What is important to consider, however, is not what they are and where they are found physically, but **what they mean to the people in each culture**. As we will describe later, the essence of culture is not what is visible on the surface. It is the shared ways groups of people understand and interpret the world. So the fact that we can all listen to Walkmans and eat hamburgers tells us that there are some novel products that can be sold on a universal message, but it does not tell us what eating hamburgers or listening to Walkmans means in different cultures. Dining at McDonald's is a show of status in Moscow whereas it is a fast meal for a fast buck in New York. If business people want to gain understanding of and allegiance to their corporate goals, policies, products or services wherever they are doing business, they must understand what those and other aspects of management mean in different cultures.

In addition to exploring why universal applications of western management theory may not work, we will also try to deal with the growing dilemma facing international managers known as "glocalisation".

As markets globalise, the need for standardisation in organisational design, systems and procedures increases. Yet managers are also under pressure to adapt their organisation to the local characteristics of the market, the legislation, the fiscal regime, the socio-political system and the cultural system. This balance between consistency and adaptation is essential for corporate success.

Paralysis through analysis: the elixir of the management profession

Peters and Waterman in *In Search of Excellence* hit the nail on the head with their critique of "the rational model" and "paralysis through analysis". Western analytical thinking (taking a phenomenon to pieces) and rationality (reckoning the consequences before you act) have led to many international successes in fields of technology. Indeed, technologies do work by the same universal rules everywhere, even on the moon. Yet the very success of the universalistic philosophy now threatens to become a handicap when applied to interactions between human beings from different cultures.

Man is a special piece of technology and the results of our studies, extensively discussed in this book, indicate that the social world of the international organisation has many more dimensions to deal with.

Some managers, especially in Japan, recognise the multi-dimensional character of their company. They seem able to use a logic appropriate to machines (analytic–rational) **and** a logic more appropriate to social relations (synthetic–intuitive), switching between these as needed.

In the process of internationalisation the Japanese increasingly take the functioning of local society seriously. They were not the first to observe "When in Rome, do as the Romans do", but they seem to act on this more than westerners do. The Japanese have moreover added another dimension: "When in Rome, understand the behaviour of the Romans, and thus become an even more complete Japanese."

In opposition to this we have our western approach, based on American business education, which treats management as a profession and regards emotionally detached rationality as "scientifically" necessary. This numerical, cerebral approach not only dominates American business schools, but other economic and business faculties. Such schools educate their students by giving them the right answers to the wrong questions. Statistical analysis, forecasting techniques and operational studies are not "wrong". They are important technical skills. The mistake is to assume that technical rationality should characterise the human element in the organisation. No one is denying the existence of universally applicable scientific laws with objective consequences. These are, indeed, culture-free. But the belief that human cultures in the workplace should resemble the laws of physics and engineering is a **cultural**, not a scientific belief. It is a universal assumption which does not win universal agreement, or even come close to doing so.

The internationalisation of business life requires more knowledge of cultural patterns. Pay-for-performance, for example, can work out well in the cultures where these authors have had most of their training: the USA, the Netherlands and the UK. In more communitarian cultures like France, Germany and large parts of Asia it may not be so successful, at least not the Anglo-Saxon version of pay-for-performance. Employees may not accept that individual members of the group should excel in a way that reveals the shortcomings of other members. Their definition of an "outstanding individual" is one who benefits those closest to him or her. Customers in more communitarian cultures also take offence at the "quick buck" mentality of the best sales people; they prefer to build up relationships carefully, and maintain them.

How proven formulas can give the wrong result

Why is it that many management processes lose effectiveness when cultural borders are crossed?

Many multinational companies apply formulas in overseas areas that are derived from, and are successful in, their own culture. International management consulting firms of Anglo-Saxon origin are still using similar methods to the neglect of cultural differences.

An Italian computer company received advice from a prominent international management consulting firm to restructure to a matrix organisation. It did so and failed; the task-oriented approach of the matrix structure challenged loyalty to the functional boss. In Italy bosses are like fathers, and you cannot have two fathers.

Culture is like gravity: you do not experience it until you jump six feet into the air. Local managers may not openly criticise a centrally developed appraisal system or reject the matrix organisation, especially if confrontation or defiance is not culturally acceptable to them. In practice, though, beneath the surface, the silent forces of culture operate a destructive process, biting at the roots of centrally developed methods which do not "fit" locally.

The flat hierarchy, SBUS, MBO, matrix organisations, assessment centres, TQM, BPR and pay-for-performance are subjects of discussion in nearly every bestseller about management, and not only in the western world. Reading these books (for which managers happily do not have much time any more) creates a feeling of euphoria. "If I follow these ten commandments, I'll be the **modern leader**, the **change master**, the **champion**." A participant from Korea told us in quite a cynical tone that he admired the USA for solving one of the last major problems in business, i.e. how to get rid of people in the process of reengineering. The fallacy of the "one best way" is a management fallacy which is dying a slow death.

Although the organisational theory developed in the 1970s introduced the environment as an important consideration, it was unable to kill the dream of the one best way of organising. It did not measure the effects of national culture, but systematically pointed to the importance of the market, the technology and the product for determining the most effective methods of management and organisation.

If you study similar organisations in different cultural environments, they often turn out to be remarkably uniform by major criteria: number of functions, levels of hierarchy, degree of specialisation and so on. Instead of proving anything, this may mean little more than that uniformity has been imposed on global operations, or that leading company practices have been carefully imitated, or even that technologies have their own imperatives. Research of this kind has often claimed that this "proves" that the organisation is culture free. But the wrong questions have been asked. The issue is not whether a hierarchy in the Netherlands has six levels, as does a similar company in Singapore, but what the hierarchy and those levels mean to the Dutch and Singaporeans. Where the meaning is totally different, for example, a "chain of command" versus "a family", then human-resource policies developed to implement the first will seriously miscommunicate in the latter context.

In this book we examine the visible and invisible ways in which culture impacts on organisations. The more fundamental differences in culture and their effects may not be directly measurable by objective criteria, but they will certainly play a very important role in the success of an international organisation.

Culture is the way in which people solve problems

A useful way of thinking about where culture comes from is the following: **culture is the way in which a group of people solves problems and reconciles dilemmas**.[1] The particular problems and dilemmas each culture must resolve will be discussed below. If we focus first on what culture is, perhaps it is easiest to start with this example.

Imagine you are on a flight to South Africa and the pilot says, "We have some problems with the engine so we will land temporarily in Burundi" (for those who do not know Burundi, it is next to Rwanda). What is your first impression of Burundi culture once you enter the airport building? It is not "what a nice set of values these people have", or even "don't they have an interesting shared system of meaning". It is the concrete, observable things like language, food or dress. Culture comes in layers, like an onion. To understand it you have to unpeel it layer by layer.

On the outer layer are the products of culture, like the soaring skyscrapers of Manhattan, pillars of private power, with congested public streets between them. These are expressions of deeper values and norms in a society that are not directly visible (values such as upward mobility, "the more-the-better", status, material success). The layers of values and norms are deeper within the "onion", and are more difficult to identify.

But why do values and norms sink down into semi-awareness and unexamined beliefs? Why are they so different in different parts of the world?

A problem that is regularly solved disappears from consciousness and becomes a basic assumption, an underlying premise. It is not until you are trying to get rid of the hiccups and hold your breath for as long as you possibly can that you think about your need for oxygen. These basic assumptions define the meaning that a group shares. They are implicit.

Take the following discussion between a medical doctor and a patient. The patient asks the doctor: "What's the matter with me?" The doctor answers: "Pneumonia." "What causes pneumonia?" "It is caused by a virus." "Interesting," says the patient, "what causes a virus?" The doctor shows signs of severe irritation and the discussion dies. Very often that is a sign that the questioner has hit a basic assumption, or in the words of Collingwood,[2] an absolute presupposition about life. What is taken for granted, unquestioned reality: this is the core of the onion.

National, corporate and professional culture

Culture also presents itself on different levels. At the highest level is the culture of a **national** or regional society, the French or west European versus the Singaporean or Asian. The way in which attitudes are expressed within a specific organisation is described as a **corporate** or organisational culture. Finally, we can even talk about the culture of particular functions within organisations: marketing, research and development, personnel. People within certain functions will tend to share certain **professional** and ethical orientations. This book will focus on the first level, the differences in culture at a national level.

Cultural differences do not only exist with regard to faraway, exotic countries. In the course of our research it has become increasingly clear that there are at several levels as many differences between the cultures of West Coast and East Coast America as there are between different nations (although for the purposes of this book most American references are averaged). All the examples show that there is a clear-cut cultural border between the north-west European (analysis, logic, systems and rationality) and the Euro-Latin (more person-related, more use of intuition and sensitivity). There are even significant differences between the neighbouring Dutch and Belgians.

The average Belgian manager has a family idea of the organisation. He or she experiences the organisation as paternalistic and hierarchical, and, as in many Latin cultures, father decides how it should be done. The Belgian sees the Dutch manager as overly democratic: what nonsense that everybody consults everybody. The Dutch manager thinks in a way more consistent with the Protestant ethic than the Belgian, who thinks and acts in a more Catholic way. Most Dutch managers distrust authority, while Belgian managers tend to respect it.

Nearly all discussions about the unification of Europe deal with techno-legal matters. But when these problems are solved, the real problem emerges. Nowhere do cultures differ so much as inside Europe. If you are going to do business with the French, you will first have to learn how to lunch extensively. The founder of the European Community, Jean Monnet, once declared: "If I were again facing the challenge to integrate Europe, I would probably start with culture." Culture is the context in which things happen; out of context, even legal matters lack significance.

The basis of cultural differences

Every culture distinguishes itself from others by the specific solutions it chooses to certain problems which reveal themselves as dilemmas. It is convenient to look at these problems under three headings: those which arise from our relationships with other people; those which come from the passage of time; and those which relate to the environment. Our research, to be described in the following chapters, examines culture within these three categories. From the solutions different cultures have chosen to these universal problems, we can further identify seven fundamental dimensions of culture. Five of these come from the first category.

Relationships with people
There are five orientations covering the ways in which human beings deal with each other. We have taken Parsons's five relational orientations as a starting point.[3]

Universalism versus particularism. The universalist approach is roughly: "What is good and right can be defined and always applies." In particularist cultures far greater attention is given to the obligations of relationships and unique circumstances. For example, instead of assuming that the one good way must always be followed, the particularist reasoning is that friendship has special obligations and hence may come first. Less attention is given to abstract societal codes.

Individualism versus communitarianism. Do people regard themselves primarily as individuals or primarily as part of a group? Furthermore, is it more important to focus on individuals so that they can contribute to the community as and if they wish, or is it more important to consider the community first since that is shared by many individuals?

Neutral versus emotional. Should the nature of our interactions be objective and detached, or is expressing emotion acceptable? In North America and north-west Europe business relationships are typically instrumental and all about achieving objectives. The brain checks emotions because these are believed to confuse the issues. The assumption is that we should resemble our machines in order to operate them more efficiently. But further south and in many other cultures, business is a human affair and the whole gamut of emotions deemed appropriate. Loud laughter, banging your fist on the table or leaving a conference room in anger during a negotiation is all part of business.

Specific versus diffuse. When the whole person is involved in a business relationship there is a real and personal contact, instead of the specific relationship prescribed by a contract. In many countries a diffuse relationship is not only preferred, but necessary before business can proceed.

In the case of one American company trying to win a contract with a South American customer (see Chapter 7), disregard for the importance of the relationship lost the deal. The American company made a slick, well-thought-out presentation which it thought clearly demonstrated its superior product and lower price. Its Swedish competitor took a week to get to know the customer. For five days the Swedes spoke about everything except the product. On the last day the product was introduced. Though somewhat less attractive and slightly higher priced, the diffuse involvement of the Swedish company got the order. The Swedish company had learned that to do business in particular countries involves more than overwhelming the customer with technical details and fancy slides.

Achievement versus ascription. Achievement means that you are judged on what you have recently accomplished and on your record. Ascription means that status is attributed to you, by birth, kinship, gender or age, but also by your connections (who you know) and your educational record (a graduate of Tokyo University or Haute Ecole Polytechnique).

In an achievement culture, the first question is likely to be "**What** did you study?", while in a more ascriptive culture the question will more likely be "**Where** did you study?". Only if it was a lousy university or one they do not recognise will ascriptive people ask what you studied; and that will be to enable you to save face.

Attitudes to time

The way in which societies look at **time** also differs. In some societies what somebody has achieved in the past is not that important. It is more important to know what plan they have developed for the future. In other societies you can make more of an impression with your past accomplishments than those of today. These are cultural differences that greatly influence corporate activities.

With respect to time, the American Dream is the French Nightmare. Americans generally start from zero and what matters is their present performance and their plan to "make it" in the future. This is *nouveau riche* for the French, who prefer the *ancien pauvre*; they have an enormous sense of the past and relatively less focus on the present and future than Americans.

In certain cultures like the American, Swedish and Dutch, time is perceived as passing in a straight line, a sequence of disparate events. Other cultures think of time more as moving in a circle, the past and present together with future possibilities. This makes considerable differences to planning, strategy, investment and views on home-growing your talent, as opposed to buying it in.

Attitudes to the environment

An important cultural difference can also be found in the attitude to the **environment**. Some cultures see the major focus affecting their lives and the origins of vice and virtue as residing within the person. Here, motivations and values are derived from within. Other cultures see the world as more powerful than individuals. They see nature as something to be feared or emulated.

The chairman of Sony, Mr Morita, explained how he came to conceive of the Walkman. He loves classical music and wanted to have a way of listening to it on his way to work without bothering any fellow commuters. The Walkman was a way of not imposing on the outside world, but of being in harmony with it. Contrast that to the way most westerners think about using the device. "I can listen to music without being disturbed by other people."

Another obvious example is the use of face masks that are worn over the nose and mouth. In Tokyo you see many people wearing them, especially in winter. When you inquire why, you are told that when people have colds or a virus, they wear them so they will not "pollute" or infect other people by breathing on them. In London they are worn by bikers and other athletes who do not want to be "polluted" by the environment.

Structure of the book

This book will describe why there is no "one best way of managing", and how some of the difficult dilemmas of international management can be mediated. Throughout, it will attempt to give readers more insight into their own culture and how it differs from others.

Chapters 2–8 will initiate the reader into the world of cultural diversity in relations with other people. How do cultures differ in this respect? In what ways do these differences impact on organisations and the conduct of international business? How are the relationships between employees affected? In what different ways do they learn and solve conflicts?

Chapters 9 and 10 discuss variations in cultural attitudes to time and the environment, which have very similar consequences for organisations.

Chapter 11 discusses how general cultural assumptions about man, time and the environment affect the culture of organisations. It identifies the four broad types of organisation which have resulted, their hierarchies, relationships, goals and structures.

Chapter 12 considers how managers can prepare the organisation for the process of internationalisation through some specific points of intervention. This chapter is intended to deal in a creative way with the dilemmas of internationalisation, and to repeat the message that an international future depends on achieving a balance between any two extremes.

What will emerge is that the whole centralisation versus decentralisation debate is really a false dichotomy. What is needed is the skill, sensitivity and experience to draw upon all the decentralised capacities of the international organisation.

Chapter 13 analyses the different steps which people need to take to reconcile cultural dilemmas. This is done through a case study which elicits the various problems that occur when professional people from different cultures meet.

Chapter 14 and 15 discuss the diversity we find within cultures. Research findings illustrate ethnic differences within the USA and South Africa and the effect on culture of gender, age, functional background and type of industry. We will conclude that the cultures of nations are an important factor in defining the meaning which people assign to their environment, but that other factors should not be ignored.

What this book attempts to make possible is the genuinely international organisation, sometimes called the transnational, in which each national culture contributes its own particular insights and strengths to the solution of worldwide issues and the company is able to draw on whatevcr it is that nations do best.

References
1 Schein, E., *Organisational Culture and Leadership*, Jossey-Bass, San Francisco, 1985.
2 Collingwood, R.G., *Essay on Metaphysics*, Gateway, Chicago, 1974.
3 Parsons, T., *The Social System*, Free Press, New York, 1951.

2
THE ONE BEST WAY OF
ORGANISING DOES NOT EXIST

However objective and uniform we try to make organisations, they will not have the same meaning for individuals from different cultures. The meanings perceived depend on certain cultural preferences, which we shall describe. Likewise the meaning that people give to the organisation, their concept of its structure, practices and policies, is culturally defined.

Culture is a shared system of meanings. It dictates what we pay attention to, how we act and what we value. Culture organises such values into what Geert Hofstede[1] calls "mental programmes". The behaviour of people within organisations is an enactment of such programmes.

Each of us carries within us the ways we have learnt of organising our experience to mean something. This approach is described as phenomenological, meaning that the way people perceive phenomena around them is coherent, orderly and makes sense.

A fellow employee from a different culture makes one interpretation of the meaning of an organisation while we make our own. Why? What can we learn from this alternative way of seeing things? Can we let that employee contribute in his or her own way?

This approach to understanding an international organisation is in strong contrast to the traditional approach, in which managers or researchers decide unilaterally how the organisation should be defined. Traditional studies have been based on the physical, verifiable characteristics of organisations, which are assumed to have a common definition for all people, everywhere, at all times. Instead of this approach, which looks for laws and common properties among "things" observed, we shall look for consistent ways in which cultures structure the perceptions of what they experience.

What the gurus tell us

Management gurus like Frederick Taylor, Henri Fayol, Peter Drucker, Mike Hammer, James Champy and Tom Peters have one thing in common: they all gave (two are dead) the impression, consciously or unconsciously, that there was one best way to manage and to organise. We shall be showing how very American and in the case of Fayol, how French, these assumptions were. Not much has changed in this respect over the last century. Is it not desirable to be able to give management a box of tools that will reduce the complexities of managing? Of course it is. We see the manager reach for the tools to limit complexity, but unfortunately the approach tends to limit innovation and intercultural success as well.

Studies in the 1970s, though, did show that the effectiveness of certain methods does depend on the environment in which we operate.

More recently, most so-called "contingency" studies have asked how the major structures of the organisation vary in accordance with major variables in the environment. They have tended to show that if the environment is essentially simple and stable then steep hierarchies survive, but if it is complex and turbulent, flatter hierarchies engage it more profitably. Such studies have mainly been confined to one country, usually the USA. Both structure and environment are measured and the results explain that X amount of environmental turbulence evokes Y amount of hierarchical levels, leading to Z amount of performance. The fact that Japanese corporations engage in very turbulent environments with much steeper hierarchies has not as a rule been addressed.

We should note that these contingency studies are still searching for one best way in specified circumstances. They still believe their universalism is scientific, when in fact it is a cultural preference. "One best way" is a yearning, not a fact. Michel Crozier, the French sociologist, working in 1964,[2] could find no studies that related organisations to their socio-cultural environments. Of course those who search for sameness will usually find it and if you stick to examining common objects and processes, like refining oil according to chemical science, then pipes will be found to have the same function the world over. If the principles of chemical engineering are the same, why not all principles? It seems a plausible equation.

Talcott Parsons,[3] an American sociologist, has however suggested that organisations have to adapt not simply to the environment but also to the views of participating employees. It has only been in recent years that this consideration of employee perceptions, and differing cultures, has surfaced in management literature.

Neglect of culture in action

Take the following meeting of a management team trying to internationalise a company's activities. This case is a summary of an interview with a North American human-resource manager, a case history which will be referred to throughout the book. Although the case is real, the names of the company and the participants are fictitious.

The Missouri Computational Company (MCC)

MCC, founded in 1952, is a very successful American company. It develops, produces and sells medium-size and large computers. The company currently operates as a multinational in North and South America, Europe, South-East Asia, Australia and the Middle East. Sales activities are regionally structured. The factories are in St Louis and Newark (NJ); the most important research activities take place in St Louis.

Production, R&D, personnel and finance are co-ordinated at the American head office. Business units handle the regional sales responsibilities. This decentralised structure does have to observe certain centralised limitations regarding logos, letter types, types of products and financial criteria. Standardisation of labour conditions, function classification and personnel planning is co-ordinated centrally, whereas hiring is done by the regional branches. Each regional branch has its own personnel and finance departments. The management meets every two weeks, and this week is focusing on globalisation issues.

Internationalisation. Mr Johnson paid extra attention in the management meeting. As vice-president of human resources worldwide he could be facing serious problems. Management recognises that the spirit of globalisation is becoming more active every day. Not only do the clients have more international demands, but production facilities need to be set up in more and more countries.

This morning a new logo was introduced to symbolise the worldwide image of the company. The next item on the agenda was a worldwide marketing plan.

Mr Smith, the CEO, saw a chance to bring forward what his MBA taught him to be universally applicable management tools. In addition to global images and marketing, he saw global production, finance and human-resources management as supporting the international breakthrough.

Johnson's hair started to rise as he listened to his colleague's presentation. "The organisation worldwide should be flatter. An excellent technique for this would be to follow the project approach that has been so successful in the USA." Johnson's question about the acceptance of this approach in southern Europe and South America was brushed aside with a short reply regarding the extra time that would be allotted to introduce it in these cultures. The generous allocation of six months would be provided to make even the most unwilling culture understand and appreciate the beauty of shorter lines of communication.

Finally, all of this would be supported by a strong pay-for-performance system so that in addition to more effective structures, the employees would also be directed towards the right goals.

Johnson's last try to introduce a more "human" side to the discussion concerning the implementation of the techniques and policy instruments was useless. The finance manager, Mr Finley, expressed the opinion of the entire management team: "We all know that cultural differences are decreasing with the increasing reach of the media. We should be world leaders and create a future environment that is a microcosm of Missouri."

Mr Johnson frowned at the prospect of next week's international meeting in Europe.

Mr Johnson knew from experience there would be trouble in communicating this stance to European human-resource managers. He could empathise with the Europeans, while knowing that central management did not really intend to be arrogant in extending a central policy worldwide. What could he do to get the best outcome from his next meeting? We shall follow this through in Chapter 4.

Culture as a side dish?

Culture still seems like a luxury item to most managers, a dish on the side. In fact, culture pervades and radiates meanings into every aspect of the enterprise. Culture patterns the whole field of business relationships. The Dutch author remembers a conversation he had with a Dutch expatriate in Singapore. He was very surprised when questioned about the ways in which he accommodated to the local culture when implementing management and organisation techniques. Before answering, he tried to find out why he should have been asked such a stupid question. "Do you work for personnel by any chance?" Then he took me on a tour through the impressive refinery. "Do you really think the products we have and the technology we use allow us to take local culture into consideration?"

Indeed, it would be difficult for a continuous-process company to accommodate to the wishes of most Singaporeans to be home at night. In other words, reality seems to show us that variables such as product, technology and markets are much more of a determinant than culture is. In one sense this conclusion is correct. Integrated technologies have a logic of their own which operates regardless of where the plant is located. Cultures do not compete with or repeal these laws. They simply supply the social context in which the technology operates. A refinery is indeed a refinery but the culture in which it is located may see it as an imperialist plot, a precious lifeline, the last chance for an economic takeoff, a prop for a medieval potentate or a weapon against the West. It all depends on the cultural context.

It is quite possible that organisations can be the same in such objective dimensions as physical plant, layout or product, yet totally different in the meanings which the surrounding human cultures read into them. We once interviewed a Venezuelan process operator, showing him the company organigram and asking him to indicate how many layers he had above and below him. To our surprise he indicated more levels than there were on the chart. We asked him how he could see these. "This person next to me," he explained, "is above me, because he is older."

One of the exercises we conduct in our workshops is to ask participants to choose between the following two extreme ways to conceive of a company, asking them which they think is usually true, and which most people in their country would opt for.

A   One way is to see a company as a system designed to perform functions and tasks in an efficient way. People are hired to perform these functions with the help of machines and other equipment. They are paid for the tasks they perform.

B   A second way is to see a company as a group of people working together. They have social relations with other people and with the organisation. The functioning is dependent on these relations.

Figure 2.1 (page 18) shows the wide range of national responses. Only a little over a third of French, Korean or Japanese managers see a company as a system rather than a social group, whereas the British and Americans are fairly evenly divided, and there is a large majority in favour of the system in Russia and several countries of eastern Europe.

These differing interpretations are important influences on the interactions between individuals and groups. Formal structures and management techniques may appear uniform. Indeed they imitate hard technologies in order to achieve this, but just as plant and equipment have different cultural meanings, so do social technologies.

An alternative approach

All organisational instruments and techniques are based on **paradigms** (sets of assumptions). An assumption often taken for granted is that social

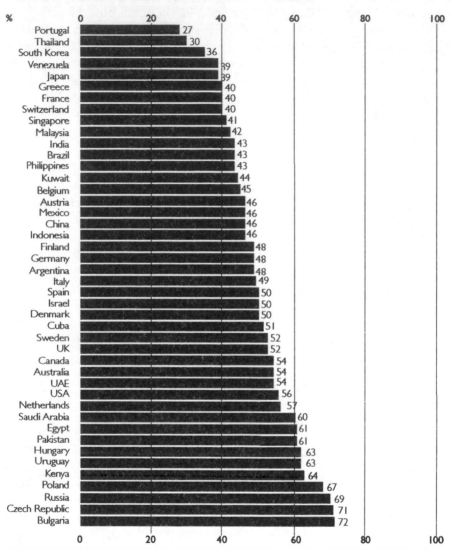

Figure 2.1 **Which kind of company is normal?**
Percentage of respondents opting for a system rather than a social group

%	Value
Portugal	27
Thailand	30
South Korea	36
Venezuela	39
Japan	39
Greece	40
France	40
Switzerland	40
Singapore	41
Malaysia	42
India	43
Brazil	43
Philippines	43
Kuwait	44
Belgium	45
Austria	46
Mexico	46
China	46
Indonesia	46
Finland	48
Germany	48
Argentina	48
Italy	49
Spain	50
Israel	50
Denmark	50
Cuba	51
Sweden	52
UK	52
Canada	54
Australia	54
UAE	54
USA	56
Netherlands	57
Saudi Arabia	60
Egypt	61
Pakistan	61
Hungary	63
Uruguay	63
Kenya	64
Poland	67
Russia	69
Czech Republic	71
Bulgaria	72

reality is "out there", separated from the manager or researcher in the same way as the matter of a physics experiment is "out there". The physics researchers can give the physical elements in their experiments any name they want. Dead things do not talk back and do not define themselves.

The human world, however, is quite different. As Alfred Shutz[4] pointed out, when we encounter other social systems they have already given names to themselves, decided how they want to live and how the world is to be interpreted. We may label them if we wish but we cannot expect them to understand or accept our definitions, unless these correspond to their own. We cannot strip people of their common sense constructs or routine ways of seeing. They come to us as whole systems of patterned meanings and understandings. We can only try to understand, and to do so means starting with the way they think and building from there.

Hence organisations do not simply react to their environment as a ship might to waves. They actively select, interpret, choose and create their environments.

SUMMARY

We cannot understand why individuals and organisations act as they do without considering the **meanings** they attribute to their environment. "A complex market" is not an objective description so much as a cultural perception. Complex to whom? To an Ethiopian or to an American? Feedback sessions where people explore their mistakes can be "useful feedback" according to American management culture and "enforced admissions of failure" in a German management culture. One culture may be inspired by the very thing that depresses another.

The organisation and its structures are thus more than objective reality; they comprise fulfilments or frustrations of the mental models held by real people.

Rather than there being "one best way of organising" there are several ways, some very much more culturally appropriate and effective than others, but all of them giving international managers additional strings to their bow if they are willing and able to clarify the reactions of foreign cultures.

References
1 Hofstede, G., *Culture's Consequences*, Sage, London, 1980.
2 Crozier, M., *The Bureaucratic Phenomenon*, University of Chicago Press, 1964.
3 Parsons, T., *The Social System*, Free Press, New York, 1951.
4 Schutz, A., *On Phenomenology and Social Relations*, University of Chicago Press, 1970.

3

THE MEANING OF CULTURE

A fish only discovers its need for water when it is no longer in it. Our own culture is like water to a fish. It sustains us. We live and breathe through it. What one culture may regard as essential, a certain level of material wealth for example, may not be so vital to other cultures.

The concept of culture

Social interaction, or meaningful communication, presupposes common ways of processing information among the people interacting. These have consequences for doing business as well as managing across cultural boundaries. The mutual dependence of the actors is due to the fact that together they constitute a connected system of meanings: a shared definition of a situation by a group.

How do these shared beliefs come about and what is their influence on the interactions between members of an organisation? An absolute condition for meaningful interaction in business and management is the existence of mutual expectations.

On a cold winter night in Amsterdam the Dutch author sees someone enter a cigar shop. His Burberry coat and horn spectacles reveal him to be well off. He buys a pack of cigarettes and takes a box of matches. He then visits the newspaper stand, purchases a Dutch newspaper and quickly walks to a wind-free corner near the shopping gallery. I approach him and ask if I can smoke a cigarette with him and whether he would mind if I read the second section of his paper. He looks at me unbelievingly and says, "I need this corner to light my paper". He throws me the pack of cigarettes because he does not smoke. When I stand back, I see that he lights the newspaper and holds his hands above the flames. He turns out to be homeless, searching for warmth and too shy to purchase a single box of matches without the cigarettes.

In this situation my expectations are not met by the individual observed. My expectations about the behaviour of the man say more about myself than about him. What I expect depends on where I come from and the meanings I give to what I experience. Expectations occur on many different levels, from concrete, explicit levels to implicit and subconscious ones. I am misled not only by the "meaning" of the man's clothing and appearance, but also on the simple level of the newspaper and cigarettes. When we observe such symbols they trigger certain expectations. When the expectations of who we are communicating with meet our own, there is mutuality of meaning.

The existence of mutual beliefs is not the first thing that comes to mind when you think about culture. In cultural training workshops we often start by asking participants: "What does the concept of culture mean to you? Can you differentiate a number of components?" In 20 years we have seldom encountered two or more groups or individuals with identical suggestions regarding the concept of culture. This shows the inclusiveness of the concept. The more difficult question is perhaps: "Can you name anything that is **not** encompassed by the concept of culture?"

The layers of culture

The outer layer: explicit products

Go back to the temporary flight detour to Burundi from Chapter 1. What are the first things you encounter on a cultural level? Most likely it is not the strange combination of norms and values shared by the Burundis (who actually consist of Hutus and Tutsis, two very different tribes) that catches your attention first. Nor is it the sharing of meanings and value-orientations. An individual's first experience of a new culture is the less esoteric, more concrete factors. This level consists of **explicit** culture.

Explicit culture is the observable reality of the language, food, buildings, houses, monuments, agriculture, shrines, markets, fashions and art. They are the symbols of a deeper level of culture. Prejudices mostly start on this symbolic and observable level. We should never forget that, as in the Burberry coat example, each opinion we voice regarding explicit culture usually says more about where **we** come from than about the community we are judging.

If we see a group of Japanese managers bowing, we are obviously observing explicit culture as the sheer act of bending. However, if we ask the Japanese "Why do you bow?", a question they may not welcome, we penetrate the next layer of culture.

The middle layer: norms and values

Explicit culture reflects deeper layers of culture, the norms and values of an individual group. **Norms** are the mutual sense a group has of what is

Figure 3.1 **A model of culture**

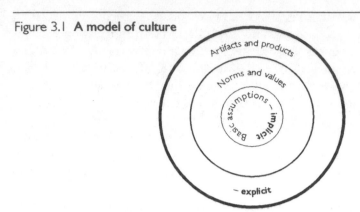

"right" and "wrong". Norms can develop on a formal level as written laws, and on an informal level as social control. **Values,** on the other hand, determine the definition of "good and bad", and are therefore closely related to the ideals shared by a group.

A culture is relatively stable when the norms reflect the values of the group. When this is not the case, there will most likely be a destabilising tension. In eastern Europe we have seen for years how the norms of Communism failed to match the values of society. Disintegration is a logical result.

While the norms, consciously or subconsciously, give us a feeling of "this is how I normally **should** behave", values give us a feeling of "this is how I **aspire** or **desire** to behave". A value serves as a criterion to determine a choice from existing alternatives. It is the concept an individual or group has regarding the desirable. For instance, in one culture people might agree with the value: "Hard work is essential to a prosperous society." Yet the behavioural norm sanctioned by the group may be: "Do not work harder than the other members of the group because then we would all be expected to do more and would end up worse off." Here the norm differs from the value.

Some Japanese might say that they bow because they like to greet people: that is a value. Other might say they don't know why except that they do it because the others do it too. Then we are talking about a norm.

It takes shared meanings of norms and values that are stable and salient for a group's cultural tradition to be developed and elaborated.

Why have different groups of people, consciously or subconsciously, chosen different definitions of good or bad, right or wrong?

The core: assumptions about existence

To answer questions about basic differences in values between cultures it is necessary to go back to the core of human existence.

The most basic value people strive for is survival. Historically, and presently, we have witnessed civilisations fighting daily with nature: the Dutch with rising water; the Swiss with mountains and avalanches; the Central Americans and Africans with droughts; and the Siberians with bitter cold.

Each has organised themselves to find the ways to deal most effectively with their environments, given their available resources. Such continuous problems are eventually solved automatically. "Culture" comes from the same root as the verb "to cultivate", meaning to till the soil: the way people act upon nature. The problems of daily life are solved in such obvious ways that the solutions disappear from our consciousness. If they did not we would go crazy. Imagine having to concentrate on your need for oxygen every 30 seconds. The solutions disappear from our awareness, and become part of our system of absolute assumptions.

The best way to test if something is a basic assumption is when the question provokes confusion or irritation. You might, for example, observe that some Japanese bow deeper than others. Again, if you ask why they do it the answer might be that they don't know but that the other person does it too (norm) or that they want to show respect for authority (value). A typical Dutch question that might follow is: "Why do you respect authority?" The most likely Japanese reaction would be either puzzlement or a smile (which might be hiding their irritation). When you question basic assumptions you are asking questions that have never been asked before. It might lead to deeper insights, but it also might provoke annoyance. Try in the USA or the Netherlands to raise the question of why people are equal and you will see what we mean.

Groups of people organise themselves in such a way that they increase the effectiveness of their problem-solving processes. Because different groups of people have developed in different geographic regions, they have also formed different sets of logical assumptions.

We see that a specific organisational culture or functional culture is nothing more than the way in which groups have organised themselves over the years to solve the problems and challenges presented to them. Changes in a culture happen because people realise that certain old ways of doing things do not work any more. It is not difficult to change culture when people are aware that the survival of the community is at stake, where survival is considered desirable.

From this fundamental relationship with the (natural) environment man, and after man the community, takes the core meaning of life. This deepest meaning has escaped from conscious questioning and has become self-evident, because it is a result of routine responses to the environment. In this sense culture is anything but nature.

Culture directs our actions

Culture is beneath awareness in the sense that no one bothers to verbalise it, yet it forms the roots of action. This made one anthropologist liken it to an iceberg, with its largest implicit part beneath the water.

Culture is man-made, confirmed by others, conventionalised and passed on for younger people or newcomers to learn. It provides people with a meaningful context in which to meet, to think about themselves and face the outer world.

In the language of Clifford Geertz, culture is the means by which people "communicate, perpetuate, and develop their knowledge about attitudes towards life. Culture is the fabric of meaning in terms of which human beings interpret their experience and guide their action".[1]

Over time, the habitual interactions within communities take on familiar forms and structures, which we will call **the organisation of meaning**. These structures are imposed upon the situations which people confront and are not determined by the situation itself. For example, the wink of an eye. Is it a physical reflex from dust in the eye? Or an invitation to a prospective date? Or could it be someone making fun of you to others? Perhaps a nervous tick? The wink itself is real, but its meaning is attributed to it by observers. The attributed meaning may or may not coincide with the intended meaning of the wink. Effective social interaction, though, depends on the attributed meaning and intended meaning coinciding.

Cultures can be distinguished from each other by the differences in shared meanings they expect and attribute to their environment. Culture is not a "thing", a substance with a physical reality of its own. Rather, it is made by people interacting, and at the same time determining further interaction.

Culture as a "normal distribution"

People within a culture do not all have identical sets of artifacts, norms, values and assumptions. Within each culture there is a wide spread of these. This spread does have a pattern around an average. So, in a sense, the variation around the norm can be seen as a normal distribution. Distinguishing one culture from another depends on the limits we want to make on each side of the distribution.

In principle, each culture shows the total variation of its human components. So while the USA and France have great variations, there are also many similarities. The "average", or "most predictable" behaviour, as depicted by Figure 3.2, will be different for these two countries.

Figure 3.2 **Culture as a normal distribution**

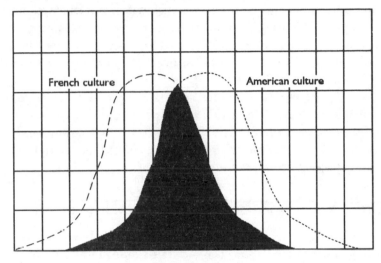

Norms and values

Figure 3.3 **Culture and stereotyping**

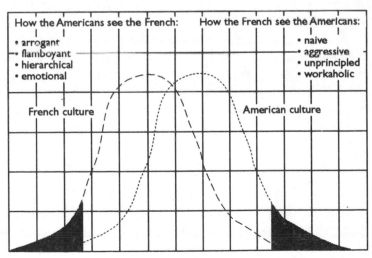

Norms and values

Cultures whose norms differ significantly tend to speak about each other in terms of extremes (Figure 3.3). Americans might describe the French as having the behavioural characteristics shown in section A in the graph, or the tail of the normal distribution. The French will use a similar caricature, section Z, for the Americans. This is because it is differences rather than sameness which we notice.

Using extreme, exaggerated forms of behaviour is **stereotyping**. It is, quite understandably, the result of registering what surprises us, rather than what is familiar. But there are dangers in doing this. First, a stereotype is a very limited view of the average behaviour in a certain environment. It exaggerates and caricatures the culture observed and, unintentionally, the observer.

Second, people often equate something different with something wrong. "Their way is clearly different from ours, so it cannot be right." Finally, stereotyping ignores the fact that individuals in the same culture do not necessarily behave according to the cultural norm. Individual personality mediates in each cultural system.

Cultures vary in solutions to common problems and dilemmas

To explain variations in the meaning organisations have for people working in them, we need to consider variations in meanings for different cultures. If we can identify and compare categories of culture that affect organisations, this will help us understand the cultural differences that must be managed in international business.

In every culture a limited number of general, universally shared human problems need to be solved. One culture can be distinguished from another by the specific solution it chooses for those problems. The anthropologists, F. Kluckhohn and F.L. Strodtbeck,[2] identify five categories of problems, arguing that all societies are aware of all possible kinds of solution but prefer them in different orders. Hence in any culture there is a set of "dominant", or preferred, value orientations. The five basic problems mankind faces, according to this scheme, are as follows:

1 What is the relationship of the individual to others? (relational orientation)
2 What is the temporal focus of human life? (time orientation)
3 What is the modality of human activity? (activity orientation)
4 What is a human being's relation to nature? (man-nature orientation)
5 What is the character of innate human nature? (human nature orientation)

In short, Kluckhohn and Strodtbeck argue that mankind is confronted with universally shared problems emerging from relationships with fellow beings, time, activities and nature. One culture can be distinguished from another by the arrangement of the specific solutions it selects for each set of problem situations. The solutions depend on the meaning given by people to life in general, and to their fellows, time and nature in particular.

In our research we have distinguished seven dimensions of culture (see Chapter 1), also based on societies' differing solutions to relationships with other people, time and nature. The following chapters will explain these dimensions and how they affect the process of managing across cultures.

Instead of running the risk of getting stuck by perceiving cultures as static points on a dual axis map, we believe that cultures **dance** from one preferred end to the opposite and back. In that way we do not risk one cultural category excluding its opposite, as has happened in so many similar studies, of which Hofstede's five mutually exclusive categories are the best known. Rather, we believe that one cultural category seeks to "manage" its opposite and that value dimensions self-organize in systems to generate new meanings. Cultures are circles with preferred arcs joined together. In this revised edition we have therefore introduced new questions which measure the extent to which managers seek to **integrate and reconcile** values. And we are testing the hypothesis that cultures which have a natural tendency to reconcile seemingly opposing values have a better chance of being successful economically than cultures which lack that inclination. All cultures are similar in the dilemmas they confront, yet different in the solutions they find, which creatively transcend the opposites.

SUMMARY

This chapter described how common meanings arise and how they are reflected through explicit symbols. We saw that culture presents itself to us in layers. The outer layers are the products and artifacts that symbolise the deeper, more basic values and assumptions about life. The different layers are not independent from one another, but are complementary.

The shared meanings that are the core of culture are man-made, are incorporated into people within a culture, yet transcend the people in the culture. In other words, the shared meanings of a group are within them and cause them to interpret things in particular ways, but are also open to be changed if more effective "solutions" to problems of survival are desired by the group.

The solutions to three universal problems that mankind faces distinguish one culture from another. The problems – people's relationship to time, nature and other human beings – are shared by mankind; their solutions are not. The latter depend on the cultural background of the group concerned. The categories of culture that emerge from the solutions cultures choose will be the subject of the next seven chapters. Their significance to work-related relationships, management instruments and organisational structures will also be explored.

References
1 Geertz, C., *The Interpretation of Cultures*, Basic Books, New York, 1973.
2 Kluckhohn, F. and Strodtbeck, F.L., *Variations in Value Orientations*, Greenwood Press, Westport, Conn., 1961.

4

RELATIONSHIPS AND RULES

People everywhere are confronted with three sources of challenge. They have relationships with other people, such as friends, employees, customers and bosses. They must manage time and ageing. And they must somehow come to terms with the external nature of the world, be it benign or threatening.

We have already identified the five dimensions of how we relate to other people. It is easiest to summarise these in abstract terms which may seem rather abstruse. I list them again with some translations in brackets.

1 Universalism versus particularism (rules versus relationships).
2 Communitarianism versus individualism (the group versus the individual).
3 Neutral versus emotional (the range of feelings expressed).
4 Diffuse versus specific (the range of involvement).
5 Achievement versus ascription (how status is accorded).

These five value orientations greatly influence our ways of doing business and managing as well as our responses in the face of moral dilemmas. Our relative position along these dimensions guides our beliefs and actions through life. For example, we all confront situations in which the established rules do not quite fit a particular circumstance. Do we do what is deemed "right" or do we adapt to the circumstances of the situation? If we are in a difficult meeting do we show how strongly we feel and risk the consequences, or do we show "admirable restraint"? When we encounter a difficult problem do we break it apart into pieces to understand it, or do we see everything as related to everything else? On what grounds do we show respect for someone's status and power, because they have achieved it or because other circumstances (like age, education or lineage) define it? These are all dilemmas to which cultures have differing answers. Part of the purpose of culture is to provide answers and guide behaviour in otherwise vexatious situations.

Before discussing the first dimension – universal versus particular forms of relating to other people – let us rejoin the perplexed Mr Johnson of the Missouri Computational Company (MCC) from Chapter 2. He is due to preside over an international human resources meeting in which 15 national representatives are expected to agree on the uniform implementation of a pay-for-performance system. Here is some background on MCC and a summary of its main policy directives.

Since the late 1970s MCC has been operating in more than 20 countries. As its foreign sales have grown, top management has become increasingly concerned about international co-ordination. Overseas growth, while robust, has been unpredictable. The company has therefore decided to co-ordinate the processes of measuring and rewarding achievement worldwide. Greater consistency in managing country operations is also on the agenda. There is not a complete disregard for national differences; the general manager worked in Germany for five years, and the marketing manager spent seven years in the Singapore operation.

It has been agreed to introduce a number of policy principles which will permeate MCC plants worldwide. They envisage a shareable definition of "How we do things in MCC" to let everyone in MCC , wherever they are in the world, know what the company stands for. Within this, there will be centrally co-ordinated policies for human resources, sales and marketing.

This would benefit customers since they, too, are internationalising in many cases. They need to know that MCC could provide high levels of service and effectiveness to their businesses, which increasingly cross borders. MCC needs to achieve consistent, recognisable standards regardless of the country in which it is operating. There is already a history of standardising policies.

The reward system. Two years ago, confronted with heavy competition, the company decided to use a more differentiated reward system for the personnel who sold and serviced mid-size computers. One of the reasons was to see whether the motivation of the American sales force could be increased. In addition, the company became aware that the best sales people often left the firm for better-paying competitors. They decided on a two-year trial with the 15 active sales people in the St Louis area.

Experiment with pay-by-performance. The experiment consisted of the following elements.

- A bonus was introduced which depended on the turnover figures each quarter for each sales person: 100% over salary for the top sales person; 60% for the second best; 30% for numbers three and four; and no bonus for the remainder.

- The basic salary of all sales people of mid-size computers was decreased by 10%.

During the first year of the trial period there were continuous discussions among the affected employees. Five sales people left the company because they were convinced the system treated them unjustly. Total sales did not increase as a result of all this. Despite this disaster, management continued the experiment because they believed that this kind of change was necessary and would take time to be accepted.

The universal versus the particular

MCC in the USA is of course operating in a universalist culture. But even here a universalist solution has run into particularist problems. This first dimension defines how we judge other people's behaviour. There are two "pure" yet alternative types of judgment. At one extreme we encounter an obligation to adhere to standards which are universally agreed to by the culture in which we live. "Do not lie. Do not steal. Do unto others as you would have them do unto you" (the Golden Rule), and so on. At the other extreme we encounter particular obligations to people we know. "X is my dear friend, so obviously I would not lie to him or steal from him. It would hurt us both to show less than kindness to one another."

Universalist, or rule-based, behaviour tends to be abstract. Try crossing the street when the light is red in a very rule-based society like Switzerland or Germany. Even if there is no traffic, you will still be frowned at. It also tends to imply equality in the sense that all persons falling under the rule should be treated the same. But situations are ordered by categories. For example, if "others" to whom you "do unto" are not categorised as human, the rules may not apply. Finally, rule-based conduct has a tendency to resist exceptions that might weaken that rule. There is a fear that once you start to make exceptions for illegal conduct the system will collapse.

Particularist judgments focus on the exceptional nature of present circumstances. This person is not "a citizen" but my friend, brother, husband, child or person of unique importance to me, with special claims on my love or my hatred. I must therefore sustain, protect or discount this person **no matter what the rules say**.

Business people from both societies will tend to think each other corrupt. A universalist will say of particularists, "they cannot be trusted because they will always help their friends"; a particularist, conversely, will say of universalists, "you cannot trust them; they would not even help a friend".

In practice we use both kinds of judgment, and in most situations we encounter they reinforce each other. If a female employee is harassed in the workplace we would disapprove of this because "harassment is immoral and against company rules" and/or because "it was a terrible experience for Jennifer and really upset her". The universalist's chief objection, though, will be the breach of rules; "women should not have to deal with harassment in the workplace; it is wrong". The particularist is likely to be more disapproving of the fact that it caused distress to poor Jennifer.

Problems are not always so easily agreed upon as this one. Sometimes rules of supposed universal application do not cover a case of particular concern very well. There are circumstances much more complex than the rules appear to have envisaged. Consider the further adventures of the Missouri Computational Company, with its head office in St Louis intent on imposing general policy guidelines on employees of many nations.

MCC has recently acquired a small but successful Swedish software company. Its head founded it three years ago with his son Carl, and was joined by his newly graduated daughter Clara and his youngest son Peter 12 months ago. Since the acquisition MCC has injected considerable capital and also given the company its own computer distribution and servicing in Sweden. This has given a real boost to the business.

MCC is now convinced that rewards for sales people must reflect the increasing competition in the market. It has decreed that at least 30% of remuneration must depend on individual performance. At the beginning of this year Carl married a very rich wife. The marriage is happy and this has had an effect on his sales record. He will easily earn the 30% bonus, though this will be small in relation to his total income, supplemented by his wife's and by his share of the acquisition payment.

Peter has a less happy marriage and much less money. His only average sales figures will mean that his income will be reduced when he can ill afford it. Clara, who married while still in school, has two children and this year lost her husband in an air crash. This tragic event caused her to have a weak sales year.

At the international sales conference national MCC managers present their salary and bonus ranges. The head of the Swedish company believes that performance should be rewarded and that favouritism should be avoided; he has many non-family members in his company. Yet he knows that unusual circumstances in the lives of his children have made this contest anything but fair. The rewards withheld will hurt more deeply than the rewards bestowed will motivate. He tries to explain the situation to the American HR chief and the British representative, who both look sceptical and talk about excuses. He accedes to their demands.

His colleagues from France, Italy, Spain and the Middle East, who all know the situation, stare in disbelief. They would have backed him on the issue. His family later say they feel let down. This was not what they joined the company for.

This episode from our ongoing MCC case shows that universalist and particularist points of view are not always easy to reconcile. The culture you come from, your personality, religion and the bonds with those concerned lead you to favour one approach more than another.

Universalist versus particularist orientations in different countries

Much of the research into this cultural dimension has come from the USA, and is influenced by American cultural preferences. The emerging consensus among these researchers, though, is that universalism is a feature of modernisation per se, of more complex and developed societies. Particularism, they argue, is a feature of smaller, largely rural communities in which everyone knows everyone personally. The implication is that universalism and sophisticated business practice go together and all nations might be better off for more nearly resembling the USA.

We do not accept this conclusion. Instead, we believe that cultural dilemmas need to be reconciled in a process of understanding the advantages of each cultural preference. The creation of wealth and the development of industry should be an evolving process of discovering more and better universals covering and sustaining more particular cases and circumstances.

The story below, created by Stouffer and Toby (Americans),[1] is another exercise used in our workshops. It takes the form of a dilemma which measures universal and particularist responses.

> You are riding in a car driven by a close friend. He hits a pedestrian. You know he was going at least 35 miles per hour in an area of the city where the maximum allowed speed is 20 miles per hour. There are no witnesses. His lawyer says that if you testify under oath that he was only driving 20 miles per hour it may save him from serious consequences.
> What right has your friend to expect you to protect him?

33

Ia My friend has a definite right as a friend to expect me to testify to the lower figure.

Ib He has some right as a friend to expect me to testify to the lower figure.

Ic He has no right as a friend to expect me to testify to the lower figure.

What do you think you would do in view of the obligations of a sworn witness and the obligation to your friend?

Id Testify that he was going 20 miles an hour.

Ie Not testify that he was going 20 miles an hour.

Figure 4.1 shows the result of putting these questions to a variety of nationalities. The percentage represents those who answered that the friend had no right or some right and would then not testify (c or b+e). North Americans and most north Europeans emerge as almost totally universalist in their approach to the problem. The proportion falls to under 75% for the French and Japanese, while in Venezuela two-thirds of respondents would lie to the police to protect their friend.

Time and again in our workshops, the universalists' response is that, as the seriousness of the accident increases, the obligation to help their friend decreases. They seem to be saying to themselves, "the law was broken and the serious condition of the pedestrian underlines the importance of upholding the law". This suggests that universalism is rarely used to the exclusion of particularism, rather that it forms the first principle in the process of moral reasoning. Particular consequences remind us of the need for universal laws.

Particularist cultures, however, are rather more likely to support their friend as the pedestrian's injuries increase. They seem to reason, "my friend needs my help more than ever now that he is in serious trouble with the law". Universalists would regard such an attitude as corrupt. What if we all started to lie on behalf of those close to us? Society would fall apart. There is indeed something in this argument. But particularism, which is based on a logic of the heart and human friendship, may also be the chief reason that citizens would not break laws in the first place. Do you love your children or present them with a copy of the civil code? And what if the law becomes a weapon in the hands of a corrupt elite? You can choose what you call corruption.

In a workshop we were giving some time ago we presented this dilemma. There was one British woman, Fiona, among the group of French participants. Fiona started the discussion of the dilemma by ask-

Figure 4.1 **The car and the pedestrian**
Percentage of respondents opting for a universalist system rather than a particular social group (answers c or b+e)

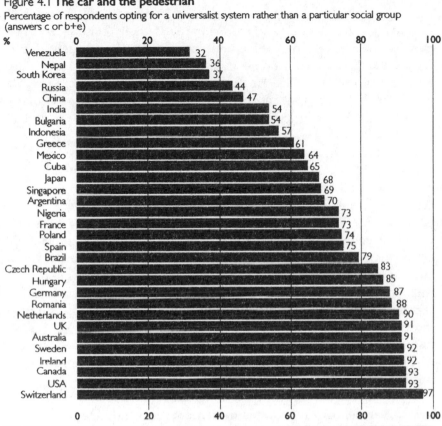

ing about the condition of the pedestrian. Without that information, she said, it would be impossible to answer the question. When the group asked her why this information was so indispensable, Dominique, an employee of a French airline, interjected: "Naturally it is because if the pedestrian is very seriously injured or even dead, then my friend has the absolute right to expect my support. Otherwise, I would not be so sure." Fiona, slightly irritated but still laughing, said: "That's amazing. For me it is absolutely the other way around."

This illustration shows that we "anchor" our response in one of the two principles. All nations might agree that universals and particulars should ideally be resolved, that is, that all exceptional cases be judged by more humane rules. What differs are their starting points.

As Figure 4.1 shows, universalists are more common in Protestant cultures, where the congregation relates to God by obedience to His written laws. There are no human intermediaries between God and His adherents, no one with the discretion to hear particular confessions, forgive sins or make special allowances. Predominantly Catholic cultures retained these features of religion, which are more relational and particularist. People can break commandments and still find compassion for their unique circumstances. God for the Catholics is like them, moreover; He will probably understand that you were lying for your friend, particularly one who had the bad luck to have the stupid pedestrian crossing in front of his or her car.

Countries with strongly universalist cultures try to use the courts to mediate conflicts. A recently released American book on automobile insurance is called *Hit Me I Need the Money*. Indeed the USA, credited with being the most litigious society on earth, has considerably more lawyers per head of population than relatively particularist Japan. The more universal the country, the greater the need for an institution to protect the truth. There is also incidentally a strong correlation between universalism and expenditure per head on pet food. This is not the same as pet ownership; particularist France has more dogs than universalist Germany, but French dogs are integrated into the family and eat leftovers. It has nothing to do with what lawyers eat, either; the reason is the lack of trust in humanity in a universalist society. Dogs, like lawyers, are the institution needed for protection, and one of the ways mistrust in people can be combatted.

However, countries may be more or less universalist depending on what the rules are **about**. French and Italian managers, who were particularist on the traffic accident, believe that when writing on a subject as important as food you have a universal obligation to truth. Consider the following scenario, described by Stouffer and Toby.

> You are a newspaper journalist who writes a weekly review of new restaurants. A close friend of yours has sunk all her savings in a new restaurant. You have eaten there and you really think the restaurant is no good.
> What right does your friend have to expect you to go easy on her restaurant in your review?
>
> 1a She has a definite right as a friend to expect me to go easy on her restaurant in my review.
> 1b She has some right as a friend to expect me to do this for her.
> 1c She has no right as a friend to expect me to do this for her.

Figure 4.2 **The bad restaurant**

Percentage of respondents who would not write a false review or give no right to the friend to expect to be helped (answers c or b+e)

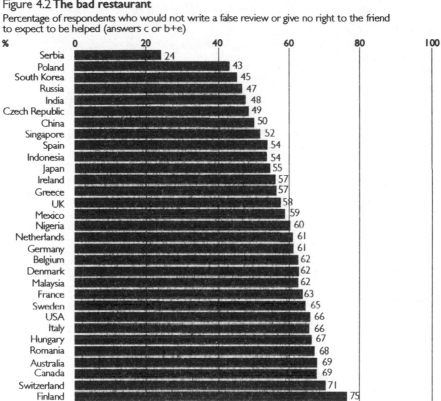

	%
Serbia	24
Poland	43
South Korea	45
Russia	47
India	48
Czech Republic	49
China	50
Singapore	52
Spain	54
Indonesia	54
Japan	55
Ireland	57
Greece	57
UK	58
Mexico	59
Nigeria	60
Netherlands	61
Germany	61
Belgium	62
Denmark	62
Malaysia	62
France	63
Sweden	65
USA	66
Italy	66
Hungary	67
Romania	68
Australia	69
Canada	69
Switzerland	71
Finland	75

Would you go easy on her restaurant in your review given your obligations to your readers and your obligation to your friend?

1d Yes.

1e No.

In this second example, a universalist's view is that as a journalist you are writing for everyone, the universe of readers, not for your friend. Your obligation is to be "truthful and unbiased". In some cultures, then, it seems more important to universalise good taste than legal procedure. For them it is easier to leave the pedestrian in trouble than to judge the quality of food wrongly. (See Figure 4.2.)

A third dilemma we use to explore this dimension has to do with the rule of confidentiality concerning the secret deliberations of a business.

You are a doctor for an insurance company. You examine a close friend who needs more insurance. You find he is in pretty good shape, but you are doubtful on one or two minor points which are difficult to diagnose.

What right does your friend have to expect you to tone down your doubts in his favour?

1a My friend has a definite right as a friend to expect me to tone down my doubts in his favour.

1b He has some right as a friend to expect me tone down my doubts in his favour.

1c He has no right as a friend to expect me to tone down my doubts in his favour.

Would you help your friend in view of the obligations you feel towards your insurance company and your friend?

1d Yes.

1e No.

There are some interesting differences here between the scores on this dilemma and the previous two. The Japanese and Indonesians, especially, jump from the situational ethics they showed previously to a strongly universalistic stance on corporate confidentiality. Quite possibly this occurs because the situation is broader than a particular friend; at stake here is loyalty to a group or corporation versus loyalty to an individual outside that group.

This dilemma may also be presenting issues of communitarianism versus individualism, to be considered in Chapter 5. As these dimensions are related as well as relational, we must be careful in interpreting the meaning different national groups give them.

Universalism versus particularism in international business

When companies go global there is an almost inevitable move towards universalist ways of thinking. After all, products and services are being offered to a wider and wider universe of people. Their willingness to buy is "proof" of a universal appeal. It follows that the ways of producing the product, managing those who make it and distributing it to customers should also be universalised. Let us consider the following examples of some of the areas where the universalist versus particularist dilemma shows up:

Figure 4.3 **The doctor and the insurance company**
Percentage of respondents who would not tone down their doubts in favour
of their friend (answers c or b+e)

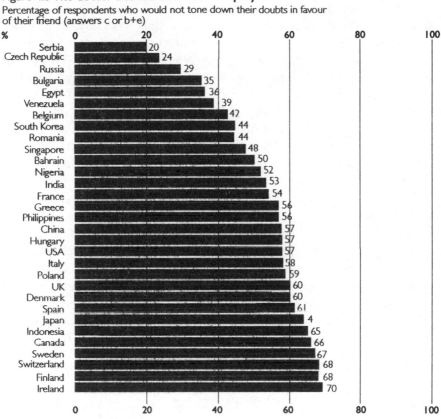

Serbia	20
Czech Republic	24
Russia	29
Bulgaria	35
Egypt	36
Venezuela	39
Belgium	42
South Korea	44
Romania	44
Singapore	48
Bahrain	50
Nigeria	52
India	53
France	54
Greece	56
Philippines	56
China	57
Hungary	57
USA	57
Italy	58
Poland	59
UK	60
Denmark	60
Spain	61
Japan	4
Indonesia	65
Canada	66
Sweden	67
Switzerland	68
Finland	68
Ireland	70

- the contract;
- timing a business trip;
- the role of head office;
- job evaluations and rewards.

The contract

Weighty contracts are a way of life in universalist cultures. A contract serves to record an agreement on principle and codifies what the respective parties have promised to do. It also implies consent to the agreement and provides recourse if the parties do not keep to their side of the deal. Introducing lawyers into the process of negotiation puts the parties on notice that any breach could be costly and that promises made initially must be kept, even if these prove inconvenient.

How might a legal contract be perceived by a more particularist business partner? There is another reason why people tend to keep their promises. They have a personal relationship with their colleague, whom they hold in particular regard. If you introduce contracts with strict requirements and penalty clauses, the implied message is that one party would cheat the other if not legally restrained from doing so. Those who feel they are not trusted may accordingly behave in untrustworthy ways. Alternatively they may terminate their relationship with a universalist business partner because that partner's precautions offend them and the contract terms are too rigid to allow a good working relationship to evolve.

One serious pitfall for universalist cultures in doing business with more particularist ones is that the importance of the relationship is often ignored. The contract will be seen as definitive by the universalist, but only as a rough guideline or approximation by the particularist. The latter will want to make the contract as vague as possible and may object to clauses that tie them down. This is not necessarily a sign of impending subterfuge, but a preference for mutual accommodation. Given the rise of Japanese economic power, the automatic superiority of the universalist position can no longer be assumed. Good customer relationships and good employee relationships may involve doing **more** than the contract requires. Moreover, relationships have a flexibility and durability which contracts often lack. Asian, Arab and Latin business people may expect contracts to be qualified where circumstances have changed.

In a ten-year contract between a Canadian ball-bearing producer and an Arabic machine manufacturer, a minimum annual quantity of ball-bearings was agreed upon. After about six years the orders from the Middle East stopped coming in. The Canadians' first reaction was: "This is illegal."

A visit to the customer only increased their confusion. The contract had apparently been cancelled unilaterally by the Arabs because the Canadian contract-signer had left the company. The so-called universally applicable law was not considered relevant any more in the eyes of the Arabs. What could the Canadians say against this logic, especially when they discovered that the ball-bearings were never even used? It turned out that the product was purchased solely out of the particular loyalty to the Canadian contract-signer, not because of a felt legal obligation.

Timing a business trip

A universalist business person – a North American, British, Dutch, German or Scandinavian – is wise to take much longer than usual when visiting a particularist culture. Particularists get suspicious when hurried. At least twice the time normally necessary to establish a contractual agreement is necessary to forge what has to be a closer relationship. It is important to create a sound relational and trustworthy basis that equates the quality of the product with the quality of the personal relationship. Rolls-Royce recently gave Toyota a deadline to make an acquisition offer and Toyota promptly withdrew. Something similar happened in negotiations between Samsung and Fokker, when after a Dutch deadline Samsung pulled out. This process takes a considerable amount of time, but for particularists, the time taken to grow close to your partner is saved in the avoidance of trouble in the future. If you are not willing to take time now, the relationship is unlikely to survive vicissitudes.

The role of head office

In those western countries which are high in universalism, the head office tends to hold the keys to global marketing, global production and global human-resource management. Our own experience, though, is that, within more particularist national cultures, the writ of the head office fails to shape local ways of operating. Different groups develop their own local standards which become the basis of their solidarity and resistance to centralised edicts. Stratified boundaries are created by the national subsidiary between itself and head office and differentiation is deliberately sought.

Particularist groups seek gratification through relationships, especially relationships to the leader. Generally, the more particularist, the greater the commitment between employer and employee. The employer in these cultures strives to provide a broad array of satisfactions to employees: security, money, social standing, goodwill and socio-emotional support. Relationships are typically close and long-lasting. Job turnover is low and commitments to the labour force long-term. The local chief wishes all this to redound to his or her own credit, not that of the foreign owner. Research done in an American bank with branches in Mexico found Mexican staff to be far more particularist, with a tendency to distance themselves as far as possible from head office in the USA in order to minimise universalist pressures.[2]

What frequently occurs is that foreign-based subsidiaries will **pretend** to comply with head office directives, which leads to a kind of ritualistic "corporate rain dance". They will go through the motions so long as they are under scrutiny, but they do not believe that rain will result. As soon as the attention of head office is diverted to other matters, normal life proceeds.

Job evaluations and rewards

Head office policies in the human-resource area often lay down systems that all expatriate managers are required to apply locally. The logic of this universal system – that all jobs should be described, all candidates should have their qualifications compared with these descriptions and all job occupants should have their performance evaluated against what their contracts specified they would do – is surely "beyond culture". It seems a demonstrably fair and universal way of managing. This general system sprang up in the post-war years when companies, especially American multinationals, saw very rapid growth. Thousands of employees within the USA needed fair methods of appraisal and promotion and before long this spread to the rest of the developed world. Labour unions often gave their support to these methods, seeing them as protection from arbitrary discipline or anti-union activity. A worker could only be fired for demonstrable failure to do a defined piece of work. In such regulations there was, indeed, protection for many employees. Managers had to behave consistently. They could not take harsh steps in one instance and be lenient in another.

A system designed by Colonel Hay of the American army, called the HAY job evaluation system, is now widely used in businesses to evaluate what base salaries should be for the performance of various functions. Each function and job within it is scored with the help of the employee, his or her direct superior and a panel which includes people doing similar jobs elsewhere. This helps to maintain internal consistency and facilitates transfers between different subsidiaries throughout a company's network without changes in salary or training. Minor concessions are usually made to local conditions by way of a cost-of-living allowance, but otherwise uniformity is maintained. All this sounds highly plausible. All such procedures may appear to be working with the paperwork duly completed. But what in fact happens in more particularist societies?

The following incident occurred in a multinational oil company. During a presentation to a group of Venezuelan managers, representatives from head office were explaining new developments in the HAY function assessment system for R&D functions. They explained that the function would be less clearly separated from the function-holder, and that there would now be "benchmarks" determining the level of the function. The Venezuelans showed the pro forma response by concluding the presentation with a loud round of applause.

After a good lunch and a third glass of wine, a few of the Venezuelan managers became quite talkative. They asked whether the visiting group would be interested in hearing about the Venezuelan way of assessing functions in the laboratory. "Would you like to hear what we say we do or what we really do?" they asked. Already aware of what their "party line" was, the head office representatives asked for what really went on.

Reality turned out to be much simpler than the complex system. Each year, they explained, the six-person management team got together after the assessment round. In the meeting this group decided on the most appropriate candidates for promotion. The employees selected were then rushed to the HR department in order to set up the function-description required by head office. HR had already been informed of what the score was to be for the particular functions.

This is an interesting example of reverse causality. Instead of the job description and evaluation "choosing" the person that best filled it, the person was first informally and intuitively chosen and then wrote their own description and evaluation.

This begs the question of whether a process in which universals guide particulars is necessarily better than a process in which particular people guide and choose their universals. As the local Venezuelan boss put it: "Who decides on the promotion of **my** subordinates, Colonel Hay or me?" The same kind of question and circularity will arise when we consider performance and achievement in Chapter 8.

Reconciling universalism and particularism

In all the seven cultural dichotomies we have identified, of which universalism versus particularism is the first, the two extremes can always in a sense be found in the same person. The two horns of the dilemma are very close to each other, as it is easy to realise if, as a universalist, you substitute your father or daughter for the friend who is driving the car. In fruitful cross-cultural encounters both sides avoid pathological excesses. Figure 4.4, whose methodology is explained in Chapter 13, illustrates this.

This figure shows the beginnings of a **vicious** circle. If you follow the logic of the flow, you see that the universalist approach at best helps us to avoid the pathologies of particularism taken too far; and the particularist position needs to be taken to avoid the pathologies of universalism taken too far. In fact, the universalist position is encouraging opposition from the particularist position.

When the two are working effectively together we talk about a **virtuous** circle. Here cross-cultural encounters can synergise and come out on a level much higher than any of the cultures could achieve on their own.

In one case the resolution brought a company to a higher level. A group of European microprocessor sales people were complaining that they lost a large part of their potential market because American headquarters could not produce the adaptations which different European clients were requesting. When interviewing the HQ in California, the Americans said that they couldn't understand why their European col-

Figure 4.4 **Reconciling universalism and particularism**

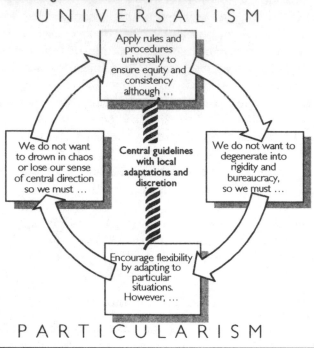

UNIVERSALISM

Apply rules and procedures universally to ensure equity and consistency although ...

We do not want to drown in chaos or lose our sense of central direction so we must ...

Central guidelines with local adaptations and discretion

We do not want to degenerate into rigidity and bureaucracy, so we must ...

Encourage flexibility by adapting to particular situations. However, ...

PARTICULARISM

leagues could not grasp the loss of economies of scale and the gross under-capacity which their chips facilities experienced. It is obviously not enough simply to map the problematic nature of a dilemma as two horns, one opposing the other, as in Figure 4.5.

When approaching this dilemma between the two extremes, we may seek a compromise. However, a compromise is frequently worse than just choosing between one of the two horns. It could mean, for example, going for two chips instead of one universal chip. By doing this you would lose both economies of scale and most of your clients. The best approach is to frame the dilemmas as two axes, X and Y, and then try to find a 10/10 solution. This means that the drive for the universal chip needs to be connected in some way to the process of fulfilling the particular need in Europe.

In our workshop the Americans proposed to invite the R&D people from some of their clients to co-develop the next (universal) chip. The Europeans, in turn, thought it would be preferable to get American R&D people over to work with local R&D people in Europe. The principle was the same, but the starting point was different. The Americans preferred to start from a universal position and have some input from the particular needs of the client. The Europeans felt more at home with first testing the

Figure 4.5 **A vicious circle**

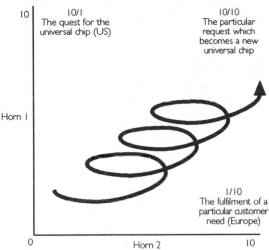

value of their particular need by some universal Californian rules. But both were aiming for the creation of a unique, particular, customised microprocessor that might lead to a renewed spate of "universal sales".

The case of the pharmaceutical joint venture

Mr Geddy Teok, an American-Chinese (second generation) employee of a large New Jersey pharmaceutical firm, was based in Tokyo, Japan. His main aim was to get a major joint venture going with one of the largest Japanese pharmaceutical manufacturers. After four years of negotiating the supreme moment had come for signing contracts. Obviously the lawyers from HQ in New Jersey were well prepared and sent the contract to Geddy one week before the "ceremony".

After four years of Japanese experience, Geddy was shocked when he received the document from the USA. He told us: "I could not even count the number of pages. There were just too many. But I remember the number of inches it measured when laying it on the table. I would guess that with every inch one of the Japanese would leave the room in despair. I hope they will come with a group of ten. Then at least I will keep one person to talk to. The Japanese will sign contracts, but you should not take it too far."

Geddy Teok decided to call HQ and ask for some help. The legal department said that the relationship was so complex that the contract needed to cover many possible instances. Moreover, a consultancy firm that advised them regularly said that Asians in general and Japanese in particular had a reputation of being quite loose in defining what was developed by them and what came from the USA: "We better have some pain now and be clear in the terms of our relationship, than to run into problems later because of miscommunication. If they sign it at least they show they are serious."

Geddy was in despair, but he only had a day to decide what to do. The meeting was tomorrow. Should he perhaps call the Japanese CEO, with whom he had built up quite a relationship? Or should he just go for it? Geddy framed his dilemma quite clearly to us: "Whatever I would do, it would hurt my career. If I insist on the Japanese partners signing the contract they will see it as proof of how little trust has been developed over the years of negotiation. This might mean a postponement of the discussions and in the worst case the end of the deal. If I reduce the contract to a couple of pages and present it as a 'letter of intent', HQ in general and even worse the whole legal department will jump on me, jeopardizing my career."

If you were Geddy, what would you do?

Being aware of the cultural dynamics does not really help you (don't forget that if you were not aware of the cultural differences between the Japanese and the Americans your situation would be even worse). It is not enough to say that the Americans tend to be universalist so they believe the Japanese should sign the contract. Nor does it suffice to say that the Japanese tend to be particularist in their approach. Transcultural effectiveness is not only measured by the degree to which you are able to grasp the opposite value. It is measured by your competence in reconciling the dilemmas, i.e. the degree to which you are able to make both values work together, as in the microprocessor case.

It might be advisable for Geddy to ask what the logic of the typical universalist would be in order to have the contract signed. In fact, the Americans' position is: "Our trust in the other party is not sufficient so we need the backing of a binding contract." For the Japanese, who do frequently sign contracts, the logic would be: "I'll only sign the contract if I have trust in the other party and they see this as a sign of respect for our relationship. Where the relationship is good enough we can easily change the details of the contract later, e.g. if the particular circumstances have changed."

We would advise Geddy to do the following. First, make culture a point of discussion and tell the Japanese counterpart what kind of problem you are facing: "Our American headquarters have sent me a 1100-page contract. Obviously this is normal practice in the US, but it was not meant to insult you." By doing this you are sharing the dilemma. Try to establish and respect the Japanese logic by asking: "What would you do in my case?"

The actual Japanese response was another question: "How long would you stay here, Mr Teok?" Geddy's answer was honest and brilliant at the same time: "Until the job is done, Mr Samamoto." "In that case I'll sign the contract," replied the Japanese.

Test yourself
In order to measure the degree to which individuals and cultures tend to reconcile we have developed a series of questions that not only measure the degree to which you identify with one of the opposing values, but also your tendency to reconcile. We are currently testing the hypothesis that the creation of wealth is highly correlated with people's capacity to reconcile. In the first dimension the questions would be the following:

Six months after the ABC mining company had signed a long-term contract with a foreign buyer to buy bauxite in 10 annual instalments, the world price of bauxite collapsed. Instead of paying $4 a tonne below world market price, the buyer now faced the prospect of paying $3 above.
The buyer faxed ABC to say it wished to renegotiate the contract. The final words of the fax read: "You cannot expect us as your new partner to carry alone the now ruinous expense of these contract terms."
ABC negotiators had a heated discussion about this situation. Several views were offered:

1 A contract is a contract. It means precisely what its terms say. If the world price had risen we would not be crying, nor should they. What partnership are they talking about? We had a deal. We bargained. We won. End of story.
2 A contract symbolises the underlying relationship. It is an honest statement of original intent. Where circumstances transform the mutual spirit of that contract, then terms must be renegotiated to preserve the relationship.
3 A contact symbolises the underlying relationship. It is an honest statement of original intent But such rigid terms are too brittle to withstand turbulent environments. Only tacit forms of mutuality have the flexibility to survive.
4 A contract is a contract. It means precisely what the terms say. If the world price had risen we would not be crying, nor should they. We would, however, consider a second contract whose terms would help offset their losses.

> Allocate "1" to the approach you prefer and "2" to your second choice. Similarly, indicate what you believe would be favoured by your closest colleagues at work.

This type of question is asked in order to assess participants' preference for a full universalist answer (1); a full particularist answer (2); a particularist answer reconciled with the universal orientation (3); and a universalist answer reconciled with the particular relationship (4). Our current research is trying to find support for the hypothesis that answers 3 and 4 are more effective in successful transcultural relationships.

Finally we should return to Mr Johnson of MCC.

- What do you think will happen when he tries to introduce pay-for-performance worldwide, especially in particularistic cultures?
- Do you believe that bonuses of 30%, 60% and 100% over salary, taken from the salaries of other employees, will be deemed fair?
- Will high performers be encouraged or discouraged in their work by those whose salaries have been cut in order to pay them?
- Will local management co-operate wholeheartedly in this change or find ways of getting around it?
- Does local management have it in its power to organise sales territories so that it can choose who performs well for particular areas?

Practical tips for doing business in universalist and particularist cultures

Recognising the differences

Universalist	Particularist
1 Focus is more on rules than relationships.	1 Focus is more on relationships than on rules.
2 Legal contracts are readily drawn up.	2 Legal contracts are readily modified.
3 A trustworthy person is the one who honours their word or contract.	3 A trustworthy person is the one who honours changing mutualities.
4 There is only one truth or reality, that which has been agreed to.	4 There are several perspectives on reality relative to each participant.
5 A deal is a deal.	5 Relationships evolve.

Tips for doing business with:

Universalists (for particularists)	Particularists (for universalists)
1 Be prepared for "rational", "professional" arguments and presentations that push for your acquiescence.	1 Be prepared for personal "meandering" or "irrelevancies" that do not seem to be going anywhere.
2 Do not take impersonal, "get down to business" attitudes as rude.	2 Do not take personal, "get to know you" attitudes as small talk.
3 Carefully prepare the legal ground with a lawyer if in doubt.	3 Carefully consider the personal implications of your legal "safeguards".

When managing and being managed

Universalists	Particularists
1 Strive for consistency and uniform procedures.	1 Build informal networks and create private understandings.
2 Institute formal ways of changing the way business is conducted.	2 Try to alter informally accustomed patterns of activity.
3 Modify the system so that the system will modify you.	3 Modify relations with you, so that you will modify the system.
4 Signal changes publicly.	4 Pull levers privately.
5 Seek fairness by treating all like cases in the same way.	5 Seek fairness by treating all cases on their special merits.

References
1 Stouffer, S.A. and Toby, J., "Role Conflict and Personality", *American Journal of Sociology*, LUI-5, 1951, pages 395–406.
2 Zurcher, L.A., Meadows, A. and Zurcher, S.L., "Value Orientations, Role Conflict and Alienation from Work: a Cross-Cultural Study", *American Sociological Review*, No. 30, 1965, pages 539–48.

5

THE GROUP AND THE INDIVIDUAL

The conflict between what each of us wants as an individual, and the interests of the group we belong to, is the second of our five dimensions covering how people relate to other people. Do we relate to others by discovering what each one of us individually wants and then trying to negotiate the differences, or do we place ahead of this some shared concept of the public and collective good?

Individualism has been described (Parsons and Shils[1]) as "a prime orientation to the self", and communitarianism as "a prime orientation to common goals and objectives". Just as for our first dimension, cultures do typically vary in putting one or the other of these approaches first in their thinking processes, although both may be included in their reasoning. The 30,000 managers who have answered the following question show this, although the division here is not quite so sharp as for the universal versus the particular example.

> Two people were discussing ways in which individuals could improve the quality of life.
>
> **A** One said: "It is obvious that if individuals have as much freedom as possible and the maximum opportunity to develop themselves, the quality of their life will improve as a result."
> **B** The other said: "If individuals are continuously taking care of their fellow human beings the quality of life will improve for everyone, even if it obstructs individual freedom and individual development."
>
> Which of the two ways of reasoning do you think is usually best, A or B?

As Figure 5.1 shows, the highest scoring individualists are the Romanians, Nigerians and Canadians, closely followed by the Americans, Czechs and Danish, all over 65% in favour of A. Some of the lowest scoring Europeans are the French at 41%. This may come as a surprise. But remember that the French all take vacations in August, on the same date. They join the Club Méditerranée in order to be together. In the Netherlands we spread our holiday dates (otherwise we might meet one of our relations). For the French the community is France and the family. They become individualists in other social encounters. That the Japanese are not significantly more group oriented in their answers to this question than the French is particularly interesting; also that the Chinese score, though only slightly, as more individualist than the Indians.

Figure 5.1 **The quality of life**

Percentage of respondents opting for individual freedom (answer a)

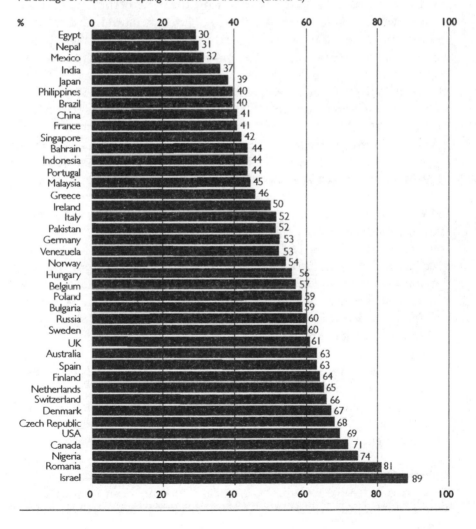

Concepts of individualism and communitarianism

Individualism is often regarded as the characteristic of a modernising society, while communitarianism reminds us of both more traditional societies and the failure of the Communist experiment. We shall see, though, that the success of the "Five Dragons", Japan, Hong Kong, Singapore, South Korea and Taiwan, raises serious questions about both the success and the inevitability of individualism.

As in the case of universalism and particularism, it is probably truer to say that these dimensions are complementary, not opposing, preferences. They can each be effectively reconciled by an integrative process, a universalism that learns its limitations from particular instances, for example, and by the individual voluntarily addressing the needs of the larger group.

International management is seriously affected by individualist or communitarian preferences within various countries. Negotiations, decision-making and motivation are the most critical areas. Practices such as promotion for recognised achievements and pay-for-performance, for example, assume that individuals seek to be distinguished within the group and that their colleagues approve of this happening. They also rest on the assumption that the contribution of any one member to a common task is easily distinguishable and that no problems arise from singling him or her out for praise. None of this may, in fact, be true in more communitarian cultures.

Most of our received wisdom on this subject derives from the individualistic West, especially from theorists writing in English. The capital letter "I" is one of the most used capitals in the English language. So the idea that rising individualism is a part of the rise of civilisation itself needs to be treated as a cultural belief rather than a fact beyond dispute. Clearly, however, it took many centuries for the individual to emerge from the surrounding community. It is generally believed that the essence of the relationship between the individual and society, at least in the West, has changed considerably since the Renaissance. In earlier societies individuals were defined primarily in terms of their surrounding community: the family, the clan, the tribe, the city-state or the feudal group.

Individualism was very much to the fore during the periods of intense innovation such as the Renaissance, the Age of Exploration, the Netherlands' Golden Age, the French Enlightenment, and the industrial revolutions of Britain and the USA. A whole range of causes and effects have been offered to explain this.

Individualism and religion
There is considerable evidence that individualism and communitarianism follows the Protestant–Catholic religious divide. Calvinists had contracts

or covenants with God and with one another for which they were personally responsible. Each Puritan worshipper approached God as a separate being, seeking justification through works. Roman Catholics have always approached God as a community of the faithful. Research has found that Catholics score higher on group choices and Protestants significantly lower. Geert Hofstede's research[2] confirms this; as do our own findings that Latin Catholic cultures, along with Asian cultures of the Pacific Rim, score lower on individualism than the Protestant West, for instance, the UK, Scandinavia (as a rule), the Netherlands, Germany, the USA and Canada.

Individualism and politics
Individualism has been adopted or opposed by different political factions in the history of countries, and the strength of that ethic today depends greatly on the fortune of its advocates. It triumphed in the USA, but is still strongly opposed by the French Catholic tradition. Eighteenth-century France, though, was exposed to the pleasures of individualism by Voltaire and Rousseau. Later, in the nineteenth century, the French socialists pointed to the positive effects of individualism, while outlining a new independence from traditional structures and rejecting the authority of religious, economic and intellectual hierarchies. French business may have been affected forever by the fact that the pro-business French liberal party was in power when France fell suddenly to the Nazis in 1940. The fortunes of British individualism, at least in commerce, have been affected by Mrs Thatcher and her revolution.

Does modernisation imply individualism?

That individualism, or self-orientation, is a crucial element of modern society has been argued by Ferdinand Tönnies.[3] He suggested that in modernising we emerge from *Gemeinschaft*, a family-based intimate social context in which the person is not sharply differentiated, into *Gesellschaft*, a workplace of individual tasks and separated responsibilities. Adam Smith, too, saw the division of labour as individualising.[4] Max Weber saw many meanings in individualism: dignity, autonomy (meaning "self-rule"), privacy and the opportunity for the person to develop.[5]

We take it for granted in many western countries that individual geniuses create businesses, invent new products, deserve high salaries and shape our futures. But do they? How much credit is due to them and how much due to the patterns of organised employees? Why are Nobel Prizes for science awarded to single individuals becoming the exception? If a creative genius combines ideas, where did such ideas come from if not the community? Are we really self-made or did our parents, teachers, families and friends have a hand in it?

The following dilemma, which explores this dimension, shows that people from different cultures make different choices about appropriate ways of working.

> Which kind of job is found more frequently in your organisation?
>
> **A** Everybody works together and you do not get individual credit.
> **B** Everybody is allowed to work individually and individual credit can be received.

Figure 5.2 shows the results of these answers. It differs from the previous illustrations of responses to dilemmas in that nationals are much more divided in their approach; the highest score choosing B is 88%. However, the range between countries remains very great. Only 43% of the Japanese believe that a job is where one is allowed to work individually, whereas at the other extreme this is the experience of approximately 90% of Czechs, Poles, Bulgarians, Hungarians and Russians. This of course has a strong relationship with recent political organisation in the latter countries.

Which community?

Individuals are either self- or community-oriented, though we must be careful in generalising about which "community" a particular culture identifies with. The high internal variation of scores in our research, we believe, has to do with the numerous communities with which different cultures choose to identify. Take, for example, the following question.

> A defect is discovered in one of the installations. It was caused by negligence of one of the members of a team. Responsibility for this mistake can be carried in various ways.
>
> **A** The person causing the defect by negligence is the one responsible.
> **B** Because he or she happens to work in a team the responsibility should be carried by the group.
>
> Which one of these two ways of taking responsibility do you think is usually the case in your society, A or B?

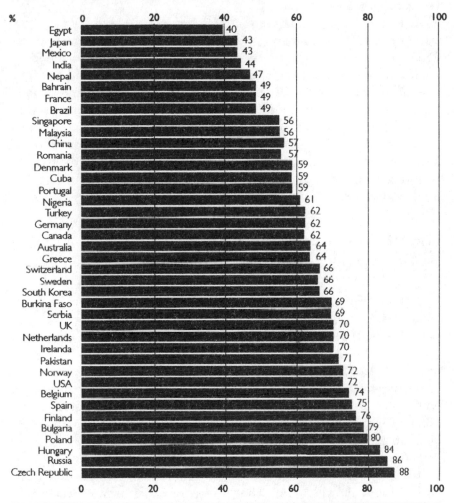

Figure 5.2 **Which kind of job?**
Percentage of respondents where individual credit is received

Country	%
Egypt	40
Japan	43
Mexico	43
India	44
Nepal	47
Bahrain	49
France	49
Brazil	49
Singapore	56
Malaysia	56
China	57
Romania	57
Denmark	59
Cuba	59
Portugal	59
Nigeria	61
Turkey	62
Germany	62
Canada	62
Australia	64
Greece	64
Switzerland	66
Sweden	66
South Korea	66
Burkina Faso	69
Serbia	69
UK	70
Netherlands	70
Irelanda	70
Pakistan	71
Norway	72
USA	72
Belgium	74
Spain	75
Finland	76
Bulgaria	79
Poland	80
Hungary	84
Russia	86
Czech Republic	88

This question triggers a number of scores which are consistent with the previous question, but we can also identify a number of shifts. This has to do with the heterogeneity of the concept of "community" or "group". For each single society, it is necessary to determine the group with which individuals have the closest identification. They could be keen to identify with their trade union, their family, their corporation, their religion, their profession, their nation or the state apparatus. The French tend to identify with *la France, la famille, le cadre*; the Japanese with the corporation; the former eastern bloc with the Communist Party; and Ireland with the

Roman Catholic Church. Communitarian goals may be good or bad for industry depending on the community concerned, its attitude and relevance to business development.

As Figure 5.3 shows, the impact of Communist organisation on Russian and east European managers has in this respect been extremely limited. They score highest on the individual responsibility assumption. Americans are just above the middle of the range at 54%, rather below several European countries. Japan scores at 32% individualist, while Indonesia takes the communitarian crown with 16%. The approach to the situation will of course differ in relation to third parties; if Americans are criticised there is a good chance that Bill will put an elbow into the stomach of Pete, while asking whose rotten idea it was, while the Italians will walk out as having suffered a group insult, regardless of the fact that it was Giorgio who did it.

Is individualism a corporate requirement?

While the French experience individualism more negatively, the more optimistic philosophy of Germany sees, in the words of Simmel, "an organic unity of individual and society".[6] The USA, with its vast acreage available to migrating individuals, is often seen as the world's major exponent of individualism and indeed scores highest, or nearly so, on most of our research instruments. De Tocqueville, the nineteenth-century French aristocrat, described Americans as exhibiting "a strong confidence in self, or reliance upon one's own exertion and resources". The "Commission of National Goals" reporting to President Eisenhower claimed that the possibility of individual self-realisation was the central goal of American civilisation.

Yet there are dissenting voices on the usefulness of individualism even in the USA. The Harvard sociologist, Daniel Bell, has accused consumerist-type individualism, what he terms modernism, of weakening America's industrial infrastructure.[7] As the information society develops, those with a communitarian ethos disseminate information faster. Information is shareable in a way physical products are not. Bell and Nelson see a shift from "tribal brotherhood" which excludes individuality, to "universal otherhood" that includes it, while still focusing upon superordinate group goals.[8]

A visionary call for the integration of individualism and communitarianism came from Emile Durkheim, the nineteenth-century French sociologist. He saw communitarianism taking both primitive and more modern forms. In its primitive form the society has a communitarian conscience

Figure 5.3 **Whose fault was it?**
Percentage of respondents opting for individual responsibility

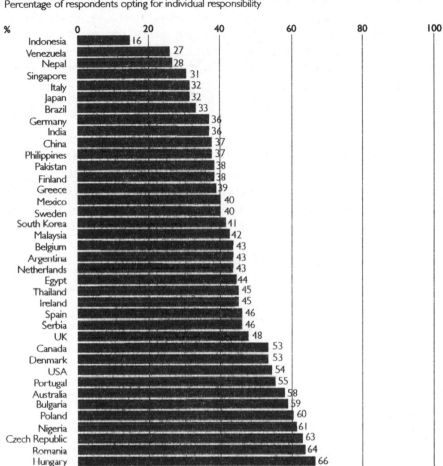

from which none dare deviate. The individual is dominated by the community. Durkheim called this mechanical solidarity which he saw as losing ground because industry requires a division of labour, which mechanical solidarity is slow to accommodate. This would help explain the early economic success of individualist (and Protestant) nations.

But Durkheim also saw a later, more sophisticated form of voluntary integration among sovereign beings which he called organic solidarity. The extension of the division of labour would cause the individual to share fewer and fewer characteristics with other individuals in the same society and would call for a new form of social integration. This involved biological-type integration as found in developing organisms, which are both differentiated and integrated. In 1965 Paul Lawrence and Jay Lorsch[9] found that highly creative plastics companies, prospering in turbulent environments, were both more highly differentiated and more highly integrated. It was a vindication of the model of organic growth, and pointed to an increasingly necessary synthesis of individualism and communitarianism in increasingly complex, differentiated and interdependent societies. We see the issue as essentially circular, with two "starting points"(see Figure 5.4).[10]

We all go through these cycles, but starting from different points and conceiving of them as means or ends. The individualist culture sees the individual as "the end" and improvements to communal arrangements as the means to achieve it. The communitarian culture sees the group as its end and improvements to individual capacities as a means to that end. Yet if the relationship is truly circular, the decision to label one element as an end and another as a means is arbitrary. By definition circles never end. Every "end" is also means to another goal.

Figure 5.4 **Reconciling individualism and communitarianism**

This is closer to our own conviction that individualism finds its fulfilment in service to the group, while group goals are of demonstrable value to individuals only if those individuals are consulted and participate in the process of developing them. The reconciliation is not easy, but possible.

Every parent knows this intuitively. Are you raising your child to become independent at the age of 18, or do you try to develop the child to become a good family member? We all know the answer to both is "yes". Parents around the world try to develop a child into a self-supporting person who will choose to become a good family member. Here again we find the essence of reconciliation. One value increases the quality of the seemingly opposing one.

Individualism versus communitarianism in international business

What are the practical issues raised by differences in degrees of individualism or communitarianism? Consider our ongoing case of MCC and the luckless Mr Johnson.

During a meeting in Milan, Mr Johnson presented ideas for the payment scheme to motivate the sales force. He became annoyed at the way these meetings were always run and decided to introduce guidelines on how all future meetings should be conducted. He did not like the Singaporean and African representatives always turning up in groups. They should, he said, confine themselves to one representative only, please. And could Mr Sin from Singapore make sure that his boss was always represented by the same person and not different people on each occasion?

These suggestions were not very popular among some of the managers. Mr Sin, Mr Nuere from Nigeria and Mr Calamier from France wanted to know the reasons for these comments. Mr Sin asked why, since different issues were on the agenda, they should not have different representatives knowledgeable on the various items. The discussion was going nowhere and, after an hour had passed, Mr Johnson suggested it be put to a vote, confident that most of his European managers would back him.

But this, too, proved controversial. Mr Calamier threw up his hands and said he was "shocked that on such a sensitive and important issue you seek to impose this decision upon a minority". He said there really should be a consensus on this even if it took another hour. Mr Sin agreed that "voting should be saved for trivial questions". Johnson looked to the German and Scandinavian representatives for support, but to his surprise they agreed that consensus should be given more of a chance. He was too frustrated to respond to the Dutch manager's suggestion that they should vote on whether to vote. Finally, the Nigerians recommended that at the very least a discussion and/or voting should be postponed until the next meeting. How else were those present supposed to solicit the views of their colleagues in their home offices? Wearily, Mr Johnson agreed. Further discussions about the reward system would have to wait too.

Representation

It should be evident from the passage above that communitarian cultures prefer plural representation. The Singaporeans, Nigerians and French seek negotiating groups, which are microcosms of the interests of their entire national subsidiaries. In the face of unexpected demands, communitarians will wish to confer with those back home. Rarely does a single Japanese go to an important negotiation. Yet to Anglo-Saxons a single representative voting on his or her private conscience on behalf of constituents is the foundation stone of parliamentary democracy. To more communitarian cultures, those at the meeting are delegates, bound by the wishes of those who sent them.

Status

Unaccompanied people in communitarian cultures are assumed to lack status. If there is no one to take notes for you or help you carry bags, you cannot be very important. If you arrive unaccompanied in Thailand, for example, they may seriously underestimate your status and power at home.

Translators

In Anglo-Saxon negotiations the translator is supposed to be neutral, like a black box through which words in one language enter and words in another language exit. The translator in more communitarian cultures will usually serve the national group, engaging them in lengthy asides and attempting to mediate misunderstandings arising from culture as well as language. Very often he or she may be the top negotiator in the group and is an interpreter rather than a translator.

Decision-making

Communitarian decision-making typically takes much longer and there are sustained efforts to win over everyone to achieve consensus. Voting down the dissenters, as often happens in English-speaking western democracies, is not acceptable. There will usually be detailed consultations with all those concerned and, because of pressures to agree collective goals, consensus will usually be achieved. If the group or home office is not consulted first, an initial "yes" can easily become a "no" later. The many minor objections raised are typically practical rather than personal or principled and the consensus may be modified in many respects. Since, however, those consulted will usually have to implement the consensus, this latter phase of implementation typically proceeds smoothly and easily. The time "wasted" (from an individualist's perspective) is saved when the new procedures operate as envisaged. The Japanese *ringi* process, where proposals circulate and are initialled by agreeing participants, is the most famous example of communitarian decision-making, but it can lead to very lengthy delays.

A Japanese company had a factory built in the south of the Netherlands. As usual, this was carried out with acute attention to detail. In the designing phase, though, it discovered that it had not considered one restriction. The legal minimum height for workshops was 4cm higher than the design. A new design, which needed extensive consultation with many people at the head office in Tokyo, took one full month per centimetre for approval.

But it is far too easy for North Americans and north-west Europeans, used to individualism, to jeer at such delays. Our own procedures can err in the opposite direction. The decision-making process in individualistic cultures is usually very short, with a "lonely individualist" making "deathless decisions" in a few fateful seconds. While this may make for quicker deliberations, "one-minute managers" and so on, it will often be discovered months later that the organisation has conspired to defeat decisions managers never liked or agreed to. Saving time in decision-making is often followed by significant delays due to implementation problems.

The individualist society, with its respect for individual opinions, will frequently ask for a vote to get all noses pointing in the same direction. The drawback to this is that within a short time they are likely to have reverted to their original orientation. The communitarian society will intuitively refrain from voting because this will not show respect to the individuals who are against the majority decision. It prefers to deliberate until consensus is reached. The final result takes longer to achieve, but will be much more stable. In individualistic societies there is frequently disparity between decision and implementation.

Individualism, communitarianism and motivation

The relationship between individual and group also plays an important role in what motivates people. Mr Johnson believed that he and MCC knew what motivated people: extra salary rewards paid to high-performing individuals. It had seemed so obvious in the meetings back in Missouri, but now he was having doubts. After the earlier discussion, could he be sure of anything?

Mr Johnson finally managed to compromise on the representation issue by allowing each national office to send up to three people, if they wished, but no more. This decision had not been voted on. Everyone had agreed. Now he could start to tackle the introduction of pay-by-performance, bonuses and merit pay for next year.

He started, as usual, with an overview of the situation in the USA. It had been three years since the system was first introduced. In general, he explained, they could detect a link between the use of this system and computer sales, although it had to be mentioned that a similar system had failed miserably in the manufacturing department. A different type of achievement-based reward system was currently being tested. No problems were anticipated with this revised system. "In summary," Johnson said, "we are strongly convinced that we need to introduce this system worldwide."

The north-west European representatives voiced their carefully considered, but positive comments. Then the Italian representative, Mr Gialli, began describing his experience with the system. In his country, the pay-for-performance experiment did much better than he had expected during the first three months. But the following three months were disastrous. Sales were dramatically lower for the salesperson who had performed the best during the previous period. "After many discussions," he continued, "I finally discovered what was happening. The salesperson who received the bonus for the previous period felt guilty in front of the others and tried extremely hard the next quarter not to earn a bonus."

The Italian manager concluded that for the next year of this experiment, the Italian market should be divided into nine regions. All sales representatives within one region should be allowed to allocate the bonus earned in their region either to individual performers or to share it equally. The blunt Dutch manager's reaction was: "I have never heard such a crazy idea."

This incident shows that there are at least two sources of motivation. People work for extrinsic money rewards and for the positive regard and support of their colleagues. In more communitarian cultures, this second source of motivation may be so strong that high performers prefer to share the fruits of their efforts with colleagues than to take extra money for themselves as individuals.

Western theories of motivation have individuals growing out of early, and hence primitive, social needs into an individually resplendent self-actualisation at the summit of the hierarchy. Needless to say, this does not achieve resonance the world over, however good a theory it may be for the USA and north-west Europe. The Japanese notion of the highest good is harmonious relationships within and with the patterns of nature; the primary orientation is to other people and to the natural world.

Differences in organisational structure

In individualistic cultures organisations (from the Greek *organon*) are essentially instruments. They have been deliberately assembled and contrived, in order to serve individual owners, employees and customers. Members of organisations enter relationships because it is in their individual interests to do so. Their ties are abstract, legal ones, regulated by contract. The organisation is a means to what its actors want for themselves. In so far as they co-operate, it is because they have particular interests at stake. Each performs a differentiated and specialised function and receives an extrinsic reward for doing so. Authority originates in an individual's skill at performing tasks, and an individual's knowledge is used to make the organisational instrument work effectively.

In communitarian cultures the organisation is not the creation or instrument of its founders so much as a social context all members share and which gives them meaning and purpose. Organisations are often likened to a large family, community or clan which develops and nurtures its members and may live longer than they do. The growth and prosperity of organisations are not considered bonanzas for individual shareholders or gravy-trains for top managers, but are valuable ends in themselves. These considerations will be discussed in depth in Chapter 11.

Reconciling individualism and communitarianism

Again, Figure 5.4 represents essentially a **vicious** circle, since one value is tied to the seemingly opposing value in such a way that they avoid each other's pathologies. And it is also a mistake to believe that individualists do not care for communities. Individualistic Americans are joiners *par excellence* and have probably formed more voluntary associations than any other culture. From Mothers Against Drunk Driving to the Michigan Militia, Americans form groups very readily. But the "voluntary association" is a give-away, because it states that in the beginning was the voluntary individual and then the group was formed from such people. In communitarian Japan, by contrast, the individual alone is not regarded as a mature state. The word for a mature individual translates as "person-among-others". In the beginning is the group: how can I as an individual serve the group better? From that competence I derive my status.

But putting the individual or the community first does not preclude a country from encompassing both values. Consider the following critical incident.

Jean Safari was investigating a serious error made by a Japanese worker at the Japanese subsidiary of a US multinational. A component had been inserted upside down and the entire batch had been pulled out of production to be reworked. The cost of this was high.

Jean asked the Japanese plant director about which employee had made the error. Had she been identified? What action was being taken against her? She was amazed when the director claimed not to know. "The whole work group has accepted responsibility," he told her. "As to the specific woman responsible, they have not told me, nor did I ask. Even the floor supervisor does not know and if he did, he would not tell me either."

But if everyone is responsible then in effect no one is, Jean argued. They are simply protecting each other's bad work.

"This is not how we see it." The plant manager was polite but firm. "I understand the woman concerned was so upset she went home. She tried to resign. Two of her co-workers had to coax her back again. The group knows she was responsible and she feels ashamed. The group also knows that she is new and that they did not help her enough, or look out for her or see that she was properly trained. This is why the whole group has apologised. I have their letter here. They are willing to apologise to you publicly."

"No, no. I don't want that", said Jean. "I want to stop it happening again..." She wondered what she should do.

Should Jean insist on knowing who the culprit was? Should the culprit be punished?

It is a fallacy to believe that because the group will not reveal who made the error the perpetrator of that error escapes without sanction. It depends whether the group supports or opposes high quality and high productivity. If the group supports management objectives, so that the community is united, those "letting the group down" will experience shame in a shame culture. There is abundant evidence that the perpetrator of this error has already experienced shame. She went home rather than face her co-workers. The issue of the extent to which other team members should have helped her learn is also something on which the team has the best information. In a Japanese context, it is best left to them.

Reconciliation has occurred. While the individualist assumption is that individuals who make a mistake should be punished for it and therefore become a better team member, communitarian logic is the reverse: through team membership we support individuals so that they become better individual workers. If a mistake is made only the immediate group needs to know this. As well as avoidance of shame, the reconciliation lies in the fact that the group has taken care of the individual's mistake and no extra punishment is required.

Test yourself

In order to measure the degree to which the individual and the group are reconciled we are asking thousands of participants to answer a series of questions. Again, two answers represent the either/or type of answer while two alternatives are reconciled answers. One starts with the individual and includes the group, while the other starts with the group and then reconciles the individual. What would be your choice?

Several managers were discussing whether close co-operation or fierce competition was the most salient mark of the successful enterprise. Below are four statements:

1 Competition is the supreme value of any successful economy or company. Attempts by major parties to co-operate usually end in collusion against one or more of them.
2 Competition is the supreme value of any successful economy or company, because this involves serving customers better than our rivals, so assuring the public interest.
3 Co-operation among stakeholders is the supreme value because this shared aim makes companies fiercely competitive towards outsiders, thereby fulfilling personal interests.
4 Co-operation among stakeholders is the supreme value. Personal rivalry and competing for self-advancement are seriously disruptive of effective operations.

Allocate "1" to the approach you prefer and "2" to your second choice. Similarly, indicate what you believe would be favoured by your closest colleagues at work.

Answer 1 affirms competitive individualism and rejects communitarian co-operation, while answer 4 is the exact oposite. Answer 2 starts by affirming competitive individualism, but by connecting it to communitarian co-operation it reconciles it into an integrity which we might call "co-opetition". Answer 3 suggests the same end result but the spiral is now anti-clockwise, from the co-operating group to the competing individual .

Figure 5.5 **Competition or co-operation?**

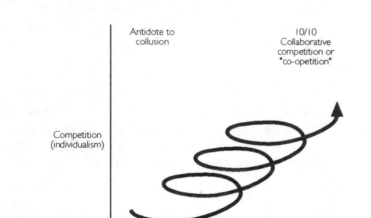

In Figure 5.5 the results of earlier competitions are co-operatively integrated, before a new phase of competition begins.

Practical tips for doing business in individualist and communitarian cultures

Recognising the differences

Individualism	Communitarianism
1 More frequent use of "I" form.	1 More frequent use of "We" form.
2 Decisions made on the spot by representatives.	2 Decisions referred back by delegate to organisation.
3 People ideally achieve alone and assume personal responsibility.	3 People ideally achieve in groups which assume joint responsibility.
4 Vacations taken in pairs, even alone.	4 Vacations in organised groups or with extended family.

Tips for doing business with:

Individualists (for communitarians)	Communitarians (for individualists)
1 Prepare for quick decisions and sudden offers not referred to HQ.	1 Show patience for time taken to consent and to consult.
2 Negotiator can commit those who sent him or her and is very reluctant to go back on an undertaking.	2 Negotiator can only agree tentatively and may withdraw an undertaking after consulting with superiors.
3 The toughest negotiations were probably already done within the organisation while preparing for the meeting. You have a tough job selling them the solution to this meeting.	3 The toughest negotiations are with the communitarians you face. You must somehow persuade them to cede to you points which the multiple interests in your company demand.
4 Conducting business alone means that this person is respected by his or her company and has its esteem.	4 Conducting business when surrounded by helpers means that this person has high status in his or her company.
5 The aim is to make a quick deal.	5 The aim is to build lasting relationships.

When managing and being managed

Individualists	Communitarians
1 Try to adjust individual needs to organisational needs.	1 Seek to integrate personality with authority within the group.
2 Introduce methods of individual incentives like pay-for-performance, individual assessment, MBO.	2 Give attention to *esprit de corps*, morale and cohesiveness.
3 Expect job turnover and mobility to be high.	3 Have low job turnover and mobility.
4 Seek out high performers, heroes and champions for special praise.	4 Extol the whole group and avoid showing favouritism.
5 Give people the freedom to take individual initiatives.	5 Hold up superordinate goals for all to meet.

References
1 Parsons, T. and Shils, E.A., *Towards a General Theory of Action*, Harvard University Press, Cambridge, Mass., 1951.
2 Hofstede, G., *Culture's Consequences*, Sage, London, 1980.
3 Tönnies, F., *Community and Society* (trans. C.P. Loomis), Harper & Row, New York, 1957.
4 Smith, A., *The Wealth of Nations*.
5 Weber, M., *The Theory of Social and Economic Organisation*, Free Press, New York, 1947.
6 Simmel, G., *The Sociology of Simmel* (trans. K.H. Wolff), Glencoe, Illinois, 1950.
7 Bell, D., *The Cultural Contradictions of Capitalism*, Basic Books, 1976.
8 Bell, D. and Nelson, B., *The Idea of Usury*, Chicago University Press, 1969.
9 Lawrence, P.R. and Lorsch, J.W., *Organisation and Environment; Managing Differentiation and Integration*, Irwin, Homewood, Illinois, 1967.
10 Hampden-Turner, C., *Charting the Corporate Mind*, Basil Blackwell, Oxford, 1991.

6

FEELINGS AND RELATIONSHIPS

In relationships between people, reason and emotion both play a role. Which of these dominates will depend upon whether we are **affective**, that is we show our emotions, in which case we probably get an emotional response in return, or whether we are emotionally **neutral** in our approach.

Affective versus neutral cultures

Members of cultures which are affectively neutral do not telegraph their feelings but keep them carefully controlled and subdued. In contrast, in cultures high on affectivity people show their feelings plainly by laughing, smiling, grimacing, scowling and gesturing; they attempt to find immediate outlets for their feelings. We should be careful not to over-interpret such differences. Neutral cultures are not necessarily cold or unfeeling, nor are they emotionally constipated or repressed. The amount of emotion we show is often the result of convention. In a culture in which feelings are controlled, irrepressible joy or grief will still signal loudly. In a culture where feelings are amplified, they will have to be signalled more loudly still in order to register at all. In cultures where everyone emotes, we may not find words or expressions adequate for our strongest feelings, since they have all been used up.

A workshop exercise under this heading asks participants how they would behave if they felt upset about something at work. Would they express their feelings openly? Figure 6.1 shows the relative positions of ten countries on the extent to which exhibiting emotion is acceptable. It is least acceptable in Ethiopia and Japan, where our database shows a score of close to 80% on the neutral orientation. There are considerable variances between European countries, with Austria the most neutral (59%) and Spain, Italy and France the least (19%, 33% and 30%). Note that Hong Kong and Singapore both score much lower than Japan or Indonesia; there is no general pattern by continent.

Typically, reason and emotion are of course combined. In expressing ourselves we try to find confirmation of our thoughts and feelings in the

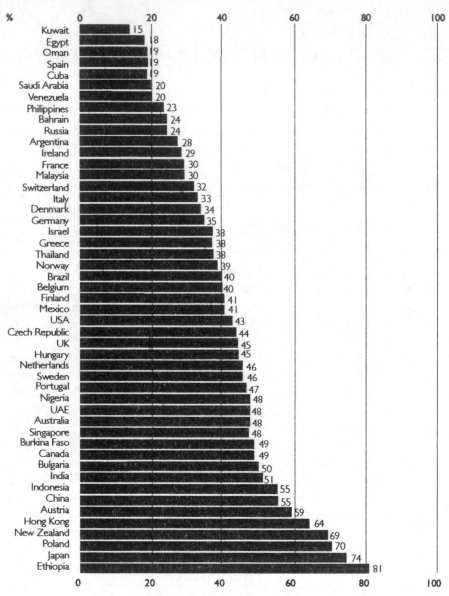

Figure 6.1 **Feeling upset at work**
Percentage of respondents who would not show emotions openly

Country	%
Kuwait	15
Egypt	18
Oman	19
Spain	19
Cuba	19
Saudi Arabia	20
Venezuela	20
Philippines	23
Bahrain	24
Russia	24
Argentina	28
Ireland	29
France	30
Malaysia	30
Switzerland	32
Italy	33
Denmark	34
Germany	35
Israel	38
Greece	38
Thailand	38
Norway	39
Brazil	40
Belgium	40
Finland	41
Mexico	41
USA	43
Czech Republic	44
UK	45
Hungary	45
Netherlands	46
Sweden	46
Portugal	47
Nigeria	48
UAE	48
Australia	48
Singapore	48
Burkina Faso	49
Canada	49
Bulgaria	50
India	51
Indonesia	55
China	55
Austria	59
Hong Kong	64
New Zealand	69
Poland	70
Japan	74
Ethiopia	81

response of our audience. When our own approach is highly emotional we are seeking a **direct** emotional response: "I have the same feelings as you on this subject." When our own approach is highly neutral we are seeking an **indirect** response. "Because I agree with your reasoning or proposition, I give you my support." On both occasions approval is being sought, but different paths are being used to this end. The indirect path gives us emotional support contingent upon the success of an effort of intellect. The direct path allows our feelings about a factual proposition to show through, thereby "joining" feelings with thoughts in a different way.

Consider a scene in which the Italian office of MCC has made a proposal to allow the sales personnel to decide as a group whether they wish to have individual incentives or to share bonus payments among the whole team, while identifying the persons responsible for winning the bonus. You will recall that this was the idea Mr Bergman, the Dutch representative, called "crazy" in Chapter 5.

Raising his voice, Mr Pauli, Gialli's colleague, asked: "What do you mean, a crazy idea? We have carefully considered the pros and cons, and consider that it would greatly benefit the buyer."

"Please, don't get over-excited," pleaded Mr Johnson. "We need to provide solid arguments and should not get side-tracked by emotional irrelevancies."

Before Bergman had a chance to explain why he thought it was a crazy idea, the two Italian colleagues left the room for a time-out. "This is what I call a typical Italian reaction," Mr Bergman remarked to his colleagues. "Before I even had a chance to give my arguments as to why I think the idea is crazy, they walk out."

The other managers were squirming uncomfortably in their chairs. They did not know what to think. Mr Johnson got up and left the room to talk to the Italians.

It is easy for British, North Americans or north-west Europeans to sympathise with Johnson or Bergman about "excitable" Italians. After all, the incentive system either works or it does not. This will not change however strongly we feel. It is a matter of trial and observation. According to this approach neutrality is a means to an end. The time to get emotional is when the incentives work or fail to work, at which point pleasure or disappointment are appropriate. After all, control of our feelings is a sign of civilisation, is it not?

Such explanations show that we can adduce good reasons for any cultural norm. The Italians were angry because they identified emotionally with their sales team and knew intuitively that working hard for each other as well as for customers was the motivation of an excellent sales person. They felt as they knew their sales force would feel about the emotional rewards for hard work. Mr Bergman's "reasonable judgment" was not relevant to Italians. Since when is the intrinsic pleasure found in work a matter of "fact" anyway? It is deeply personal and cultural. As Pascal wrote: "The heart has its reasons which reason knows not of." But he was a Frenchman.

And what about the verdict of the Prime Court in Italy in late 1996, which indicates that hubands are allowed to beat their spouses if they are in a passionate mood as long as it is done infrequently. The Italian judge did find compelling evidence that the husband had hit his wife so hard that she had to be hospitalised. But there was no "systematic and conscious brutality". The victim, Anna Mannino, was very pleased with the final verdict since she found her partner a "model husband". She had never accused her partner. The hospital did!

Degrees of affectivity in different cultures

The amount of visible "emoting" is a major difference between cultures. We may think that a Frenchman who curses us in a traffic accident is truly enraged, close to committing violence. In fact, he may simply be getting his view of the facts in first and may expect an equal stream of vituperation from us in return. He may, indeed, be further from violence as a result of this expression. There are norms about acceptable levels of vehemence and these can be much higher in some countries than in others.

Americans, for example, tend to be on the expressive side. Perhaps this is because with so many immigrants and such a large country they have had to break down social barriers again and again. The habit of using diminutives ("Chuck" instead of Charles, "Bob" instead of Robert), "smile" buttons, welcome wagons and the speed with which cordial and informal relationships are made, all testify to the need to resocialise in new neighbourhoods several times in a lifetime.

This is a very different experience from life in smaller countries like Sweden, the Netherlands, Denmark, Norway and so on. There it may be harder to avoid than to meet those of your generation with whom you grew up. Friendships tend to start early in life and last many years, so the need to be effusive with relative strangers is much less.

There is a tendency for those with norms of emotional neutrality to dismiss anger, delight or intensity in the workplace as "unprofessional". Mr Pauli at MCC has obviously "lost his cool", a judgment which assumes the desirability of a cool exterior to begin with. In fact, Pauli probably regards Bergman as emotionally dead, or as hiding his true feelings behind a mask of deceit. As we shall see in Chapter 7 when we go on to discuss how specific, as opposed to diffuse, emotions can be, there are really two issues wrapped up in the question of emotional display. Should emotion be **exhibited** in business relations? Should it be **separated** from reasoning processes lest it corrupt them?

Americans tend to exhibit **emotion, yet separate** it from "objective" and "rational" decisions. Italians and south European nations in general tend to **exhibit and not separate**. Dutch and Swedes tend **not to exhibit and to separate**. Once again, there is nothing "good" or "bad" about these differences. You can argue that emotions held in check will twist your judgments despite all efforts to be "rational". Or you can argue that pouring forth emotions makes it harder for anyone present to think straight. Similarly you can scoff at the "walls" separating reasons from emotions, or argue that because of the leakage that so often occurs, these should be thicker and stronger.

North Europeans watching a south European politician on television disapprove of waving hands and other gestures. So do the Japanese, whose saying "Only a dead fish has an open mouth" compares with the English "Empty vessels make the most noise".

Beware humour, understatement or irony

Cultures also vary on the permissible use of humour. In Britain or the USA we often start our workshops with a cartoon or anecdote which makes a joke about the main points to be covered. This is always a success. Hence one of the first workshops in Germany was launched, with some confidence, with a cartoon deriding European cultural differences. Nobody laughed; indeed, the audience was taking notes and looked more puzzled than it had done. As the week went by, however, there was a lot of laughter in the bar, and eventually even in the sessions. It was simply that it was not permissible in a professional setting, between strangers.

The British use humour a lot to release emotions dammed up behind the stiff upper lip. They also regard understatement as funny. If a Briton speaks of being "underwhelmed" by someone's presentation, or regarding it with "modified rapture", that is a way of **controlling** emotional expression, while at the same time triggering emotional release in the form of laughter. The individual thereby has it both ways. A Japanese superior will similarly rebuke an incompetent subordinate by exaggerated deference. "If you could see your way to kindly troubling yourself in a matter so minor, I would be in your debt." In affective language, this translates as "Do it or else".

Unfortunately, understatements of this kind, along with throwaway lines and jokes, are almost always lost on foreigners even if they speak the language well enough for normal discourse. Humour is language-dependent and relies on a very quick sense of the meaning of words. "She was a good cook, as cooks go, and as cooks go she went." This is only funny if you are familiar with the colloquialism "as (something) goes", meaning "compared with other (somethings)", in which case "went" takes you by surprise. Not only is it hard for foreigners to release emotion in this way, but they are unlikely to grasp that understatements are actually intended ironically. They are more likely to see the English or Japanese as being opaque, as usual. Any statement which means the opposite to what it literally states may be hard on foreign managers and should be avoided. If insiders all laugh, the foreigner feels excluded, deprived of the emotional release the rest have enjoyed.

Intercultural communication

There are a variety of problems of communication across cultural boundaries which arise from the differences between affective and neutral approaches. In our workshops we frequently ask the participants to describe the concept of intercultural communication. They list instruments – language, body language – and more general definitions like the exchange of messages and ideas. Communication is of course essentially the **exchange of information**, be it words, ideas or emotions. Information, in turn, is the **carrier of meaning**. Communication is only possible between people who to some extent share a system of meaning, so here we return to our basic definition of culture.

Verbal communication

Western society has a predominantly verbal culture. We communicate with paper, film and conversation. Two of the best-selling computer programmes in the western world, wordprocessing and graphics, have been developed to support verbal communication. We become nervous and uneasy once we stop talking. But we have very different styles of discussion. For the Anglo-Saxons, when A stops, B starts. It is not polite to interrupt. The even more verbal Latins integrate slightly more than this; B will frequently interrupt A and vice versa to show how interested each is in what the other is saying.

The pattern of silent communication shown in Figure 6.2 for oriental languages frightens the westerner. The moment of silence is interpreted as a failure to communicate. But this is a misunderstanding. Let us reverse the roles; how can the westerner communicate clearly if the other person is not given time to finish his or her sentence, or to digest what the other has been saying? It is a sign of respect for the other person if you take time to process the information without talking yourself.

Figure 6.2 **Styles of verbal communication**

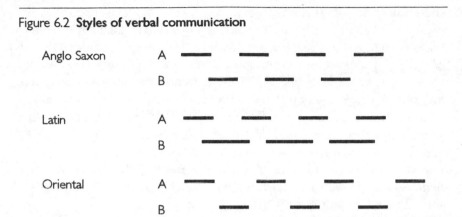

Tone of voice. Another cross-cultural problem arises from tone of voice. Figure 6.3 shows typical patterns for Anglo-Saxon, Latin and oriental languages. For some neutral societies, ups and downs in speech suggest that the speaker is not serious. But in most Latin societies this "exaggerated" way of communicating shows that you have your heart in the matter. Oriental societies tend to have a much more monotonous style; self-controlled, it shows respect. Frequently, the higher the position a person holds, the lower and flatter their voice.

Figure 6.3 **Tone of voice**

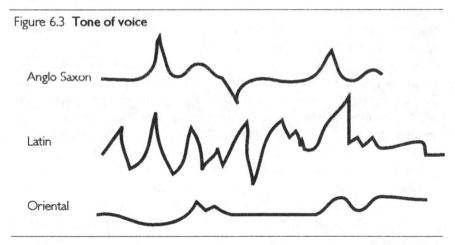

A British manager posted to Nigeria found that it was very effective to raise his voice for important issues. His Nigerian subordinates saw this unexpected explosion by a normally self-controlled manager as a sign of extra concern. After success in Nigeria he was posted to Malaysia. Shouting there was a sign of loss of face; his colleagues did not take him seriously and he was transferred.

The spoken word. The most obvious verbal process is the spoken word. Regardless of rhythm, pace or humour, this needs to be taken into consideration. The English-speaking nations have the enormous advantage of more than 300m speakers who understand their language. However, as we all know, even the English and Americans are separated by a common language which is used quite differently in different contexts and which has some serious differences in the meanings of individual words. English speakers also face an enormous disadvantage, which is that it is very difficult ever to speak another language; its nationals will only allow you so much accent before switching to English themselves. To express yourself in another language is a necessary, if not a sufficient, condition for understanding another culture.

Non-verbal communication

Research has shown that at least 75% of all communication is non-verbal. This figure is the minimum for the most verbal cultures of all. In western societies **eye-contact** is crucial to confirm interest. However, the amount differs sharply from society to society. An Italian visiting professor at Wharton arrived on campus and was surprised to be greeted by a number of students. His expressive Italian nature drove him eventually to catch one of them and ask him if he knew who he was. The student said he was afraid he did not. "So why did you greet me?" "Because it seemed like you knew me, sir." The professor realised that in the USA eye-contact between strangers is only supposed to last for a split second.

Leonel Brug, a colleague at CIBS, was brought up in both Curaçao and Surinam. As a boy he would try to avoid eye-contact, whereupon his Curaçao grandmother would slap him in the face (in some cultures body-talk is very effective) and say, "Look me in the face". Respecting an elder involves eye-contact. Leonel learned fast, and when in Surinam looked his other grandmother straight in the face to show respect. She slapped him too; respectful kids in Surinam do not make eye-contact.

Touching other people, the **space** it is normal to keep between you, and assumptions about **privacy** are all further manifestations of affective or neutral cultures. Never help an Arab lady out of a bus; it might cost you your contract.

Reconciling neutral and affective cultures

Overly neutral or affective (expressive) cultures have problems in doing business with each other. The neutral person is easily accused of being ice-cold with no heart; the affective person is seen as out of control and inconsistent. When such cultures meet the first essential is to recognise the differences, and to refrain from making any judgments based on emotions, or the lack of them.

The power of reconciliation can be shown if we see what happens when seemingly opposing values are disconnected. Emotions that are expressed without any "neutral" brake easily verge on the uncontrolled "neurotic". An overly neutral person may become an iceman who dies of a heart attack because of unexpressed emotions.

The traditional wooden rollercoaster ride has been a major attraction of fun-fairs for nearly 100 years. In the last decade promoters have tried to give even greater thrills with "white knuckle rides". The engineering of such rides requires the design engineer to provide a series of accelerations and twists to excite with just enough respite to recover before the next thrill. Western joyriders scream and wave their arms to participate in the spirit of the experience.

Supported by modern electronics and safety features, this is now big business and specialist manufacturers from the USA and Europe have sought to export their offerings. One Californian company installed several of its rides in Japan. In spite of a well-proven design, Japanese riders continued to receive head injuries. Observation revealed that the Japanese riders were more likely to keep their heads low or forward in a semi-bowed posture, thereby striking their heads on the bar designed to hold them in place, rather than taking a more upright, arm-waving position. Expensive modifications were required that prevented head injuries – to the point where safety legislation in Japan requires design solutions to take regard of their relative neutrality. Their neutrality did not, of course, mean that they were not experiencing the thrill! It is just that they were trying to control it by lowering their heads.

Test yourself
Consider the following question:

> In a meeting you feel very insulted because your business counterpart tells you that your proposal is insane. What is your response?

> 1 I will not show that they have hurt/insulted me, because that would be seen as a sign of weakness and would make me more vulnerable in the future.
> 2 I will not show that I am hurt because that would spoil our relationship. This will allow me later to tell the counterpart

how much I was hurt by their comment so they might learn from it. I rather show my emotions when they have more chance to improve our business relationship.

3 I will show clearly that I am insulted so that my counterpart gets the message. I believe the clarity of my message will allow me to be able to control even greater emotional upset in the future.

4 I will show clearly that I am insulted so that my counterpart gets the message. If business partners cannot behave themselves properly they have to bear the consequences.

Indicate with "I" the approach you prefer and with "2" your second choice. Similarly, indicate with "I" the approach you believe would be favoured by your closest colleagues at work, and "2" the approach you believe would be their second choice.

Obviously, answer "1" indicates that you prefer to be neutral and reject affectivity in response. Answer "4" clearly reflects a preference for emotional outbursts regardless of their consequences for the relationship. Answer "2" supports the neutral point of departure in order to show emotions more effectively in the future. Answer "3" takes an expressive point of departure in order to stabilise future emotional interactions.

Practical tips for doing business in neutral and affective cultures

Recognising the differences

Neutral	Affective
1 Do not reveal what they are thinking or feeling.	1 Reveal thoughts and feelings verbally and non-verbally.
2 May (accidentally) reveal tension in face and posture.	2 Transparency and expressiveness release tensions.
3 Emotions often dammed up will occasionally explode.	3 Emotions flow easily, effusively, vehemently and without inhibition.
4 Cool and self-possessed conduct is admired.	4 Heated, vital, animated expressions admired.
5 Physical contact, gesturing or strong facial expressions often taboo.	5 Touching, gesturing and strong facial expressions common.
6 Statements often read out in monotone.	6 Statements declaimed fluently and dramatically.

Tips for doing business with:

Neutrals (for affectives)	Affectives (for neutrals)
1 Ask for time-outs from meetings and negotiations where you can patch each other up and rest between games of poker with the Impassive Ones.	1 Do not be put off your stride when they create scenes and get histrionic; take time-outs for sober reflection and hard assessments.
2 Put as much as you can on paper beforehand.	2 When they are expressing goodwill, respond warmly.
3 Their lack of emotional tone does not mean they are disinterested or bored, only that they do not like to show their hand.	3 Their enthusiasm, readiness to agree or vehement disagreement does not mean that they have made up their minds.
4 The entire negotiation is typically focused on the object or proposition being discussed, not so much on you as persons.	4 The entire negotiation is typically focused on you as persons, not so much on the object or proposition being discussed.

When managing and being managed

Neutrals	Affectives
1 Avoid warm, expressive or enthusiastic behaviours. These are interpreted as lack of control over your feelings and inconsistent with high status.	1 Avoid detached, ambiguous and cool demeanour. This will be interpreted as negative evaluation, as disdain, dislike and social distance. You are excluding them from "the family".
2 If you prepare extensively beforehand, you will find it easier to "stick to the point", that is, the neutral topics being discussed.	2 If you discover whose work, energy and enthusiasm has been invested in which projects, you are more likely to appreciate tenacious positions.
3 Look for small cues that the person is pleased or angry and amplify their importance.	3 Tolerate great "surfeits" of emotionality without getting intimidated or coerced and moderate their importance.

7

HOW FAR WE GET INVOLVED

Closely related to whether we show emotions in dealing with other people is the degree to which we engage others in **specific** areas of life and single levels of personality, or **diffusely** in multiple areas of our lives and at several levels of personality at the same time.

Specific versus diffuse cultures

In specific-oriented cultures a manager **segregates out** the task relationship she or he has with a subordinate and insulates this from other dealings. Say a manager supervises the sale of integrated circuits. Were he to meet one of his sales reps in the bar, on the golf course, on vacation or in the local DIY superstore, almost none of his authority would diffuse itself into these relationships. Indeed, he might defer to the sales rep as a more skilled DIY practitioner, or ask advice on improving his golf game. Each area in which the two encounter each other is considered apart from the other, a **specific** case.

However, in some countries every life space and every level of personality tends to permeate all others. *Monsieur le directeur* is a formidable authority wherever you encounter him. If he runs the company it is generally expected that his opinions on *haute cuisine* are better than those of his subordinates. His taste in clothes and value as a citizen are all permeated by his directorship and he probably expects to be deferred to by those who know him, in the street, the club or a shop. Of course reputation always leaks to some extent into other areas of life. This extent is what we measure for specificity (small) versus diffuseness (large).

Kurt Lewin,[1] the German-American psychologist, represented the personality as a series of concentric circles with "life spaces" or "personality levels" between. The most personal and private spaces are near the centre. The most shared and public spaces are at the outer peripheries. As a German-Jewish refugee in the USA, Lewin was able to contrast U-type (American) life spaces with G-type (German) life spaces. These are illustrated overleaf.

Figure 7.1 **Lewin's circles** (author's adaptation)

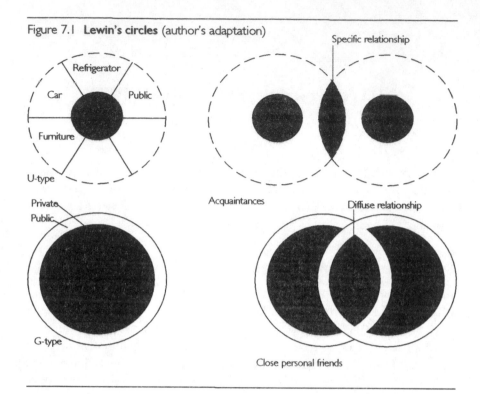

Lewin's circles show Americans, in the U-type circle, as having much more public than private space, segregated into many specific sections. The American citizen can have a standing and reputation at work, in the bowling club, at the Parent–Teachers' Association, at the Oddfellows Hall, among fellow computer hackers and in the local chapter of the Veterans of Foreign Wars. Colleagues who enter any of these spaces are not necessarily close or life-time buddies. They may not feel free to call on you if the subject is not computers or bowling. One reason why the American personality is so friendly and accessible (illustrated by the dotted lines) is that being admitted into one public layer is not a very big commitment. You "know" the other for limited purposes only.

Contrast this with the G-type circle. Here access to life spaces is guarded by a thick line. It is harder to enter and you need the other's permission. The public space is relatively small. The private spaces are large and **diffuse**, which means that once a friend is admitted, this lets him or her into all, or nearly all, your private spaces. Moreover, your standing and reputation crosses over these spaces. Herr Doktor Muller is Herr Doktor Muller at his university, at the butcher's and the garage; his wife is also Frau Doktor

Muller in the market, at the local school and wherever she goes. She is not simply joined diffusely to her husband but to his job and title. In the USA, in contrast, the British author has been introduced at a reception following a graduation ceremony as Dr Hampden-Turner, but at a party for much the same people a few hours later as Charles Hampden-Turner. He have also been introduced as "I want you all to meet my very good friend Charles... (what's your surname?)". In the USA a title is a **specific** label for a **specific** job in a **specific** place.

For all these reasons Germans may be thought of by Americans as remote and hard to get to know. Americans may be thought of by Germans as cheerful, garrulous, yet superficial, who let you into a very small corner of their public life and regard you as peripheral.

Borders and barriers between "life spaces" have physical dimensions as well. The Dutch author remembers arriving as a student at the Wharton School in Philadelphia, Pennsylvania. Bill, a new American friend, rushed to help him move in. In gratitude for his hard work on the hot summer day I asked him to stay for a while and have a beer. I went to wash up and came back to get him a beer out of the refrigerator. I did not need to, he had already opened the refrigerator and was helping himself. For him, a refrigerator was my public space into which I had invited him. To me and most of my Dutch compatriots, it was definitely private space. A few days later I was struck by a similar event. I was inquiring about transportation across town when Denise, a fellow student, tossed me her car keys and said to call her when I was finished with my errand. I could not believe it. To me, a car was certainly private space. Have you ever tried to borrow a German acquaintance's Mercedes?

In the USA, where people are relatively mobile, furniture, cars and so on can be semi-public. People moving will hold "garage sales", exhibiting very personal items on tables in a yard for all not only to see, but to purchase. They may be as open with intimate personal experiences. It is not rare to be regaled at a drinks party with confessions of sexual incompatibility from a complete stranger. You even suspect he has forgotten your name by the time his adventure climaxes. An American cartoon by Jules Feiffer[2] has the anti-hero Bernard Mergendeiler explain to his audience:

"I met this **marvellous** girl. I've told all my friends and colleagues at work. I go up to strangers in the street and tell them about her. I've told nearly **everyone** – except her. Why give her the advantage?"

Clearly this character's public spaces overwhelm his private one. He confesses in the first to avoid communication in the second.

The situation in France or Germany is quite different. You have only to note the high hedges and shuttered windows to appreciate French concern for large private spaces. If you are invited to dinner in a French home, that invitation extends to the rooms in which that hospitality occurs. If you start wandering around the house you may offend. If your hostess goes into her study to find a book you are discussing, and you follow her, that may be considered a trespass into her private domain.

The concentric circles are not simply in the mind, but refer to spaces in which we live.

The concepts of the specific and the diffuse help us to make sense of the dispute being described in the MCC head office, which involved Mr Johnson (American), Mr Bergman (Dutch) and Messrs Gialli and Pauli (Italian). Both Mr Johnson and Mr Bergman, while not in agreement on permissible levels of emotional expression (Mr Johnson being more affective), **are** in agreement on the separation of reason from emotion. Americans and Dutch both believe that there are specific times, places and spaces for being reasonable and specific times, places and spaces for being affective. To their perplexity and dismay the Italians have "thrown a tantrum" in the middle of a meeting, on serious, professional issues.

Let us continue the story.

As the representative from head office, Mr Johnson felt very responsible for the developments at the meeting. The Italians' behaviour seemed strange to him. Mr Bergman just wanted to discuss an important aspect of the consistency of the reward system and they did not even give him a chance to explain his position. Moreover the Italians had refused to put any solid arguments on the table themselves.

When Johnson entered Mr Gialli's room he said: "Paolo, what's the problem? You shouldn't take this too seriously. It's just a business discussion."

"Just a business discussion?" Gialli asked with unconcealed rage. "This has nothing to do with a business discussion. It is typical for that Dutchman to attack us. We have our own ways of being effective, and then he calls us crazy."

"I didn't hear that," Johnson said. "He simply said that he found your group bonus idea crazy. I know Bergman and he didn't intend that to refer to you."

"If that's so," answered Gialli, "why is he behaving so rudely?"

Johnson realised how deeply his Italian colleagues had been offended. He went back to Bergman, took him aside and told him about his conversation with Gialli. "Offended!" said Bergman. "Let them have the self-control to respond to professional arguments. I don't understand why they are so hot-headed anyway. They know we have done extensive research on this. Let them listen first. You have to remember that these Latins never want to be bothered with facts."

The Italian reaction is of course quite understandable if we grasp that their feelings about group bonuses as opposed to individual bonuses, their sympathy with their sales force and customers and the proposal they put forward are **one diffuse whole**. To call "the idea" crazy is to call **them** crazy and to question their ability to represent the cultural views of fellow Italians. It offends them deeply. Their ideas are not separated from themselves. If they "thought of it" and if it represents "Italian thinking" then the proposition is an extension of their personal honour.

One problem with the overlap between U-types and G-types is that the U-type sees as impersonal something the G-type sees as highly personal. Italian views on the effectiveness of group bonuses are tied to their diffuse sense of private space. It is not "just a business discussion" taking place in a realm apart from their private selves, but a discussion touching on what it means to be a feeling, thinking Italian. Pleasure and pain, acceptance and rejection ramify more widely in the diffuse system. You cannot criticise Italians as "generators of a crazy idea" without profoundly affecting their whole system. When Americans "let in" a German, French or Italian colleague into one compartment of their public space and show their customary openness and friendliness, that person may assume that they have

Figure 7.2 **The danger zone: the specific–diffuse encounter**

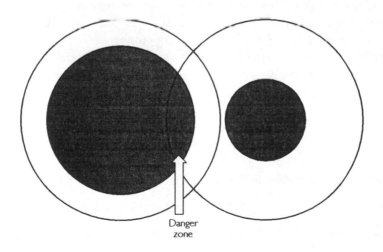

Danger
zone

been admitted to diffuse private space. They may expect the American to show equivalent friendship in all life spaces and be offended if he or she comes to their town without contacting them. They may also be offended by criticism-as-a-professional, which they take to be attack-by-a-close-friend. Or they may be offended when admiration-as-between-electronic-engineers goes no deeper than that.

Losing face

Specific cultures, with their small areas of privacy clearly separated from public life, have considerable freedom for direct speech. "Do not take this personally" is a frequent observation. In relationships with diffuse people this approach can be an insult. American and Dutch managers find it particularly easy to insult their opposite diffuse partners (see Mr Johnson's problems with the Italians, above). This is because they do not understand the principle of losing face, which is what happens when something is made public which people perceive as being private. The importance of avoiding loss of face is why in diffuse cultures so much more time is taken to get to the point; it is necessary to avoid private confrontation because it is impossible for participants not to take things personally. I try to avoid asking a Dutch audience for criticism after one of my workshops; the experience is much the same as being machine-gunned. Afterwards, however, they tend to ask the corpse for the next date it will be available. In contrast English and French managers will make a few mild suggestions in a context of positive congratulation, never to be heard from again.

At an international university at which I was teaching a Ghanaian student wrote a paper for me which I was unable to grade at more than four out of ten, a fail. All scores were posted on a noticeboard. The student said that this would be a public insult to him, impossible for me as a respected professor to perpetrate, although he agreed with the mark. What I should do was to mark the paper "I" (incomplete) for the board, while feeding the actual grade into the system.

National differences

National differences are sharp under the headings of specificity and diffuseness. The range is illustrated well by responses to the following situation.

> A boss asks a subordinate to help him paint his house. The subordinate, who does not feel like doing it, discusses the situation with a colleague.

A The colleague argues: "You don't have to paint if you don't feel like it. He is your boss at work. Outside he has little authority."
B The subordinate argues: "Despite the fact that I don't feel like it, I will paint it. He is my boss and you can't ignore that outside work either."

In specific societies, where work and private life are sharply separated, managers are not at all inclined to assist. As one Dutch respondent observed: "House painting is not in my collective labour agreement." Figure 7.3 shows the proportion of managers that would not paint the house, around 80% or higher in the UK, the USA, Switzerland and most of northern Europe. 71% of Japanese would not either, but in the diffuse Asian societies of China and Nepal and African societies of Nigeria and Burkina Faso the majority would. (Surprised by the Japanese score, we re-interviewed some Japanese respondents. They replied that it most probably had to do with the fact that the Japanese never paint houses, which illustrates the relativity of empirical data.) The range of differences is not so steeply graded as when we looked at the basic cultural divides of Chapters 3 and 4, but it is nevertheless clearly a source of deep potential incomprehension.

Negotiating the specific–diffuse cultural divide

Doing business with a culture more diffuse than our own feels very time-consuming. Some nations refuse to do business in a mental subdivision called "commerce" or "work" which is kept apart from the rest of life. In diffuse cultures, everything is connected to everything. Your business partner may wish to know where you went to school, who your friends are, what you think of life, politics, art, literature and music. This is not "a waste of time" because such preferences reveal character and form friendships. They also make deception nearly impossible. As with the example in Chapter 1 of the Swedish company which beat an American company with a technically superior product for a contract with an Argentinian customer, the upfront investment in building relationships in such cultures is as important, if not more so, than the deal. The Swedes invested a whole week in the selling trip, the first five days of which were not related to the business at all. They just shared the diffuse life spaces of their hosts, talking about common interests. Only **after** a "private space" relationship had been established were the Argentinians willing to talk business. And that had to include several life spaces, not just one. In contrast, the Americans invested only two days in the trip, knowing they had a superior product and presentation, and were turned down.

Figure 7.3 **Paint the house**

Percentage of respondents who would not help the boss

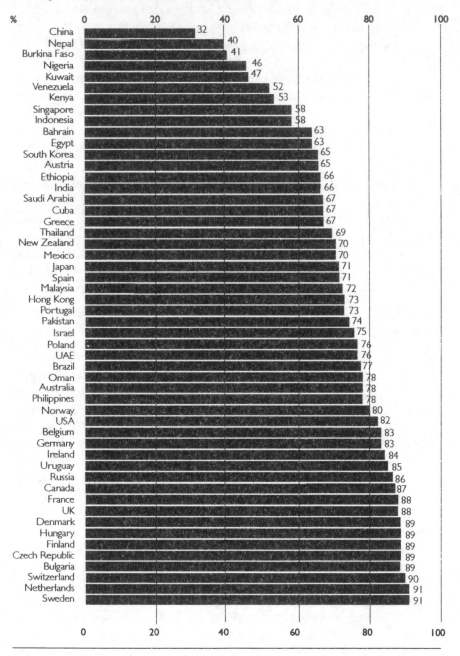

It is really a question of priority. Do you start with the specific and neutral proposition and later get to know those interested in that proposition? Or do you start with people you can trust because you have invited them into multiple life spaces and then move on to business? Both approaches make good sense to those living in that culture, but each plays havoc with the other. The American team found themselves continually interrupted by "personal" questions and "social distractions" and when the corporate jet arrived on schedule to take them home, they had not adequately covered the business agenda. The Argentinians, to the Americans, seemed unable or unwilling to stick to the point. The Argentinians, for their part, found the Americans too direct, impersonal and pushy. They were surprised by the Americans' apparent belief that you could use logic to force someone to agree with you.

In other words, specificity and diffuseness are about strategies for getting to know other people.

The diagram on the left of Figure 7.4 shows the typically diffuse strategy common in Japan, Mexico, France and much of southern Europe and Asia. Here you "circle around" the stranger, getting to know him diffusely, and come down to the specifics of the business only later when relationships of trust have been established. On the right you get "straight to the point", to the neutral, "objective" aspects of the business deal, and if the other remains interested then you "circle around" getting to know them in order to facilitate the deal.

Both approaches claim to save time. In the diffuse approach you do not get trapped in an eight-year relationship with a dishonest partner because you detect any unsavoury aspects early on. In the specific approach you do not waste time wining and dining a person who is not fully committed to the specifics of the deal.

Specific and diffuse cultures are sometimes called **low** and **high context**. Context has to do with how much you have to know before effective

Figure 7.4 **Circling round or getting straight to the point**

Diffuse, high context
(from general to
specific)

Specific, low context
(from specific to
general)

communication can occur; how much shared knowledge is taken for granted by those in conversation with each other; how much reference there is to tacit common ground. Cultures with high context like Japan and France believe that strangers must be "filled in" before business can be properly discussed. Cultures with low context like the USA or the Netherlands believe that each stranger should share in rule-making, and the fewer initial structures there are the better. Low-context cultures tend to be adaptable and flexible. High-context cultures are rich and subtle, but carry a lot of "baggage" and may never really be comfortable for foreigners who are not fully assimilated. There is growing evidence, for example, that westerners working for Japanese companies are never wholly "inside". It is similarly hard to feel fully accepted within the richness of French culture with its thousands of diffuse connections.

There is a tendency for specific cultures to look at objects, specifics and things before considering how these are related. The general tendency for diffuse cultures is to look at relationships and connections before considering all the separate pieces. The configuration is circular.

The effect of specific–diffuse orientation on business

That Americans choose MBO (management-by-objectives) and pay-for-performance as favourite devices to motivate employees testifies in part to their specific orientation. In MBO you first agree on the "objectives", that is, the specifics. Supervisor A agrees with subordinate B that B will work towards agreed objectives in the coming quarter and that evaluation of his or her work will take as a benchmark the objectives agreed to. Good objectives satisfactorily achieved will make for a productive relationship between A and B. What could be fairer or more logical? Why would the whole world not agree to do this?

This system does not appeal to diffuse cultures because they approach the issue from the opposite direction. It is **the relationship between A and B that increases or reduces output, not the other way round**. Objectives or specifics may be out of date by the time evaluation comes around. B may not have performed as promised yet done something more valuable in altered circumstances. Only strong and lasting relationships can handle unexpected changes of this kind. Contracts and small print face backwards in such cultures.

Japanese corporate cultures, for example, use terms unfamiliar to westerners which are clearly aimed at putting the diffuse before the specific. They speak of "acceptance time", the time necessary to discuss proposed changes before these are implemented. They speak of *nemawashi*, literally binding the

Figure 7.5 **The specific–diffuse circle**

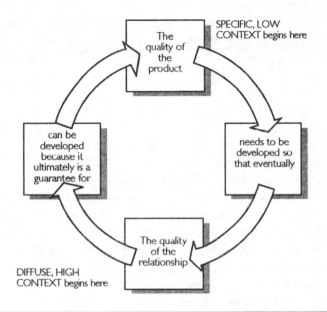

roots of shrubs and trees before transplanting them. This refers to extensive consultations before implementing changes. All these constitute "the circling around before coming to the point" which we saw in Figure 7.4.

Pay-for-performance is not very popular in diffuse cultures because it arbitrarily severs relationships. It says "you are solely responsible for what you sold this month" when, in fact, other sales people may have helped you and your superiors may have inspired you or instructed you to act in more effective ways. To claim most or all of the rewards for yourself denies the importance of relationships, including feelings of affection and respect for superiors and peers with whom you have diffuse contacts and shared private life spaces.

Norms like "do not mix business with pleasure" and "don't let's talk shop" testify to the desire in some cultures to keep specific life spaces separate from each other. Arguably it is harder to coerce people or subordinate them if their lives are honeycombed with separate compartments. In this situation only one area of somebody's life can be dominated and they can call on the resources they have in other areas. Diffuse cultures have "all their eggs in one basket". Again, we are talking about **relative** separation, not absolute. There are always "Chinese walls", at least, between life spaces in most cultures.

Diffuse cultures tend to have lower turnover and employee mobility because of the importance of "loyalty" and the multiplicity of human bonds. They tend not to "headhunt" or lure away employees from other companies with high (specific) salaries. Takeovers are rarer in diffuse cultures because of the disruption caused to relationships and because shareholders (often banks) have longer-term relationships and cross-holdings in each other's companies and are less motivated by the price of shares.

Pitfalls of evaluation and assessment

Specific cultures find it much easier to criticise people without devastating the whole life space of the target of that criticism. There are at least two tragic corporate cases where criticism during performance evaluations by western superiors led to their murder by outraged targets.

In one case a Dutch doctor whose job was to evaluate a Chinese subordinate in the company clinic had a "frank discussion" of the latter's shortcomings. In his view these could easily be remedied by the company's training courses. Yet to the Chinese doctor who had worked closely with the Dutch doctor, and whom he regarded as a "father figure", the criticism was a savage indictment, a total rejection and a betrayal of mutual confidence. The next morning he knifed his critic to death. It is easy to imagine the Dutch ghost protesting that he had never said his Chinese colleague was not a great fellow; it was only his medicine he was worried about.

In a second case a British manager who fired an employee in Central Africa was later poisoned, with the seeming connivance of the other African employees. The fired man had a large number of hungry children and had stolen meat from the company cafeteria. In a diffuse culture "stealing" is not easily separable from domestic circumstances and the western habit of separating an "office crime" from a "problem at home" is not accepted.

We must be careful, however, not to regard diffuse cultures as "primitive". Japanese corporations give bigger salaries to workers with larger families, help in the search for housing and often provide recreation facilities, vacations and consumer products at favourable prices. Another pair of questions we use to test for cultural diffuseness is the following.

> **A** Some people think a company is usually responsible for the housing of its employees. Therefore, a company has to assist an employee in finding housing.
> **B** Other people think the responsibility for housing should be carried by the employee alone. It is so much to the good if the company helps.

Figure 7.6 shows the percentage of managers who do not think that housing is a company's responsibility. Only 45% of Japanese managers

Figure 7.6 **Should the company provide housing?**
Percentage of respondents who disagree

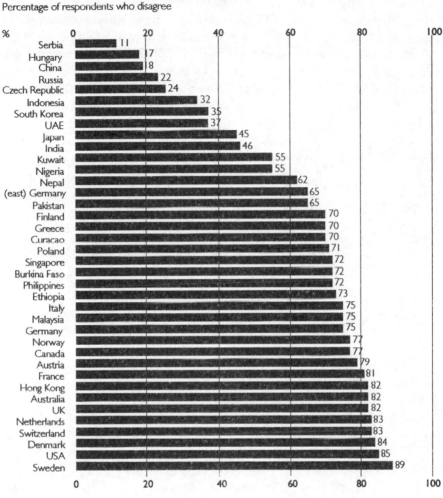

think that it is not, as opposed to 85% of Americans. The great majority of all north European managers do not expect company help, but in most Asian countries the majority do. The exception is Singapore, where western principles have become much more widespread. It is also interesting to note the impact of Communist regimes on the various European countries which appear at the top of the chart.

Japanese consumers may reject western imported goods because their value is specific; Japanese corporations produce goods with benefits diffused through their society. So we buy more than a Honda motor scooter, we "buy" economic and social development for our society, a highly diffuse concept.

The mix of emotion and involvement

There are of course various combinations of levels of emotion or affectivity (high to low, or neutral) with its "reach" or scope (diffusing several life spaces or remaining specific). A business partner can be emotional and expressive yet not be involved **with you**. He may be cool and neutral, yet deeply involved in your private spaces. He can be expressive and involved, or neutral and uninvolved. Four combinations are described by Talcot Parsons,[3] which as Figure 7.7 shows yield four different sorts of primary response.

Figure 7.7 **The emotional quadrant**

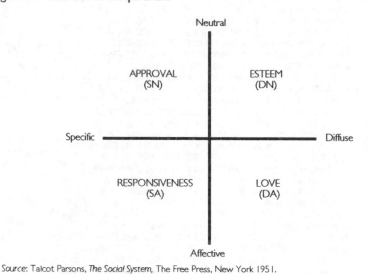

Neutral

APPROVAL
(SN)

ESTEEM
(DN)

Specific ——————————————————— Diffuse

RESPONSIVENESS
(SA)

LOVE
(DA)

Affective

Source: Talcot Parsons, *The Social System*, The Free Press, New York 1951.

In diffuse–affective (DA) interactions the expected relational reward is **love**, a strongly expressed pleasure diffusing many life spaces. In diffuse–neutral (DN) interactions the expected reward is **esteem**, a less strongly expressed admiration also spread over many life spaces. In specific–affective (SA) interactions the expected reward is **responsiveness**, a strongly expressed pleasure specific to a certain occasion or performance. In specific–neutral (SN) interactions the expected reward is **approval**, a job, task, or occasion-specific expression of positive, yet neutral approbation. Of course these four quadrants might also contain negative evaluations, **hate** (DA), **disappointment** (DN), **rejection** (SA) and **criticism** (SN). It is important to remember that love and responsiveness have their mirrors in hate and rejection, while more neutral cultures do not risk such extreme mood swings.

We have tried to measure the relative national preferences for love, esteem, enjoyment and approval by using the following question, which is taken from some earlier work by L.R. Dean.[4]

Which of the following four types of people do you prefer to have around you? Review these descriptions carefully, then circle the one that most closely relates to your preference and the one that represents your second preference.

A People who completely accept you the way you are and feel responsible for your personal problems and welfare (combines diffuse and affective: love).

B People who do their work, attend to their affairs and leave you free to do the same (specific and neutral: approval).

C People who try to improve themselves and have definite ideals and aims in life (diffuse and neutral: esteem).

D People who are friendly, lively and enjoy getting together to talk or socialise (specific and affective: enjoyment).

Figure 7.8 shows how a number of nationalities score in this exercise. We see that a typical American approach is quite close to the mean both for emotion and in balance between the specific and the diffuse. Eastern and western Germans are very similar in emotional levels, but eastern Germans are appreciably more specific, if nothing like as specific as the Poles or the Japanese. Once again there are no very clear rules by continent, although if we try to picture the most important regional cultural differences, we get the following division.

American (West Coast) enthusiasms tend to be for specific issues and causes and belong as it were in separate boxes, that is, saving the redwoods, rebirthing, mamotechnology, virtual reality and so on. DA cultures spill over between life spaces. Dishonour to one member of a family disgraces the family and must be avenged. You may not be able to work in the same company as a person with whom your uncle has a feud going back ten years.

On one occasion a Dutch and a Belgian manager disagreed on a fiscal issue in politics. The Dutch manager let the disagreement stand, in a separate compartment as he saw it, and tried to get on with other business. But for the Belgian their disagreement coloured everything. The Dutch man-

Figure 7.8 **Who do you prefer around you?**
(answers to questions A–D)

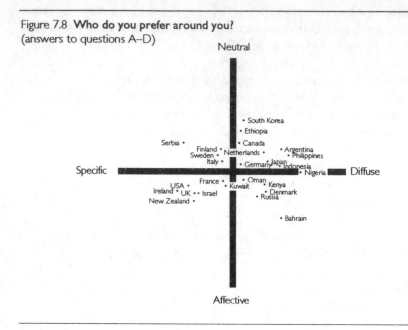

Figure 7.9 **Regional cultural differences**

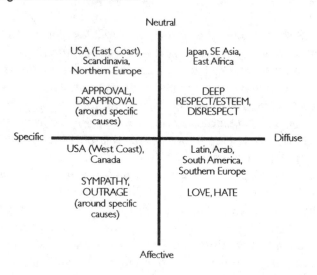

ager could not be a trusted partner if his views on the fiscal issue were so mistaken. The Dutchman's desire to move on to other business was a slight to the Belgian's feeling of profound disturbance in their relationship.

Their business dealings were broken off.

North Europeans, especially Scandinavians, are somewhat less specific than Americans, but are more disapproving of overt emotion. Like the Japanese, however, they sanction alcohol to loosen inhibitions. The lack of explicit emotion does not mean that people do not feel for each other. It means that a "soft pedal" is used to communicate emotions, but these small signs can, of course, speak volumes to the recipient who understands how to read them.

Reconciling specific–diffuse cultures

This is perhaps the area in which balance is most crucial, from both a personal and a corporate point of view. The specific extreme can lead to disruption, the diffuse extreme to a lack of perspective; a collision between them results in paralysis. It is the interplay of the two approaches which is the most fruitful, recognising that privacy is necessary, but that complete separation of private life leads to alienation and superficiality; that business is business, but stable and deep relationships mean strong affiliations.

The need for interplay is shown by the following case.

It was in the late 1980s and early 1990s that merger mania hit the airline industry. John Perrish of BA was sitting at his desk wondering what to do in the latest discussions on the alliance with US Air. As a marketing manager he was worried that the results of passenger studies would jeopardise the long-term development of an airline serving the global passenger. The studies revealed that American passengers were increasingly less willing to pay high ticket prices. Competition between American airlines was a price rather than a quality issue.

In Europe business-class travel was still characterised by high prices and competition was aimed at leg room, quality of meals and flexibility of changing routes. It seemed that the service was seen in dramatically different ways by American passengers and Europeans. The globalisation that would result from the alliance would force both partners to rethink what a true global client expects.

Peter Butcher, John's counterpart at US Air, could not resist making cynical comparisons and often said: "John, you might say that we in the USA tend to serve our passengers as a 'piece of meat' that needs to travel from NY to LA, in Europe people are willing to include their stomach for an extra $300 during a one hour flight." Indeed, at BA passengers are served a hot breakfast on a flight from London to Amsterdam that is no longer than 40 minutes. John's reply was as biting: "I remember I once had a first-class flight from Detroit to

Chicago of just over an hour. It took off at 6.30am and around 7, long after our seatbelts were loosened, I wondered when breakfast would be served. I couldn't smell anything. I asked the flight attendant when I could expect a breakfast. I took her by surprise with that question. Two minutes later she came back with a big smile asking: 'Sir, we have pretzels or potato chips, which do you prefer?' I said that a cup of coffee would do."

When clients' expectations are so diverse around the world, how would you advise John and Peter to approach their global marketing campaign?

It is obvious that American passengers and the airlines serving them share a perception of a very specific relationship. You are a person who needs to go from A to B in a safe, reliable and inexpensive way. Period. In Europe and Asia the involvement is perceived as going beyond safety and reliability. When flying with Singapore Airlines, for example, we can see a mutual need to involve the whole person. This diffuse relationship is expressed by excellent service, food and a general attitude of **service**. In much of the USA and on some airlines in Europe neither client nor airline feels the need to get involved beyond a safe and fast trip for as low a price as possible. All fine, it is up to the client to decide.

However, in the case of BA and US Air it was not as simple. To serve a global client we need to decide what level of integration is necessary. KLM and NorthWest Airlines, for example, have decided to integrate their schedules and parts of their financial and booking systems. But KLM's service is still quite different from that on NorthWest Airlines.

What do you do when the alliance goes beyond the technicalities and includes the service on board? A compromise is not desirable, because not many passengers like hot pretzels or lukewarm breakfasts. SAS tried by the introduction of the business class to leave the choice to the passenger. But what about serving the global customer? The challenging question becomes: how could the excellence of our specific services increase the quality of the holistic approach to the passenger? The reconciling graph could be as shown in Figure 7.10.

Test yourself

Consider the following question:

> A group of managers and financial analysts were arguing about whether profitability or ongoing stakeholder relationships, most especially between company and customers, formed the best way of monitoring organisational effectiveness. The following positions were advanced:

Figure 7.10 **Moments of truth**

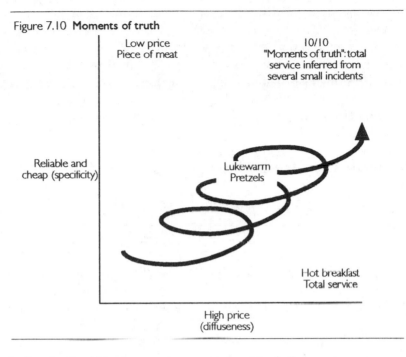

I Feedback within close customer relationships is the most timely advice about corporate effectiveness. Its value is its inclusivity. Profits measure what is taken out of a relationship, not what is staked or contributed.

2 Feedback within close customer relationships is the most timely advice about corporate effectiveness. Because customers generate the funds used to pay profits, the quality of these relationships anticipates profitability.

3 Profitability or shareholder value is the prime criterion of corporate effectiveness, because it distils in one precise and unambiguous measure the vitality and value of all activities by other stakeholders.

4 Profitability or shareholder value is the prime criterion of corporate effectiveness, because it proclaims in one precise and unambiguous measure that labour works for capital and business exists to enrich individual owners.

Indicate with "1" the approach you prefer and with "2" your second choice. Similarly, indicate with "1" the approach you believe would be favoured by your closest colleagues at work, and with "2" the approach you believe would be their second choice.

This question reveals quite clearly four alternative approaches to the criteria which need to be used to define organisational effectiveness. If you think an organisation is primarily a money-making machine you would opt for answer 4. Answer 1 rejects specificity, while answer 2 is a reconciliation starting from a diffuse point of departure. Answer 3 reconciles the diffuse responsibility starting from a specific standpoint of profitability or shareholder value.

Practical tips for doing business in specific and diffuse cultures

Recognising the differences

Specificity	Diffuseness
1 Direct, to the point, purposeful in relating.	1 Indirect, circuitous, seemingly "aimless" forms of relating.
2 Precise, blunt, definitive and transparent.	2 Evasive, tactful, ambiguous, even opaque.
3 Principles and consistent moral stands independent of the person being addressed.	3 Highly situational morality depending upon the person and context encountered.

Tips for doing business with:

Specific-oriented (for diffuse individuals)	Diffuse-oriented (for specific individuals)
1 Study the objectives, principles and numerical targets of the specific organisation with which you are dealing.	1 Study the history, background and future vision of the diffuse organisation with which you expect to do business.
2 Be quick, to the point and efficient.	2 Take time and remember there are many roads to Rome.
3 Structure the meeting with time, intervals and agendas.	3 Let the meeting flow, occasionally nudging its process.
4 Do not use titles or acknowledge skills that are irrelevant to the issue being discussed.	4 Respect a person's title, age, background connections, whatever issue is being discussed.

When managing and being managed

Specific-oriented	Diffuse-oriented
1 Management is the realisation of objectives and standards with rewards attached.	1 Management is a continuously improving process by which quality improves.
2 Private and business agendas are kept separate from each other.	2 Private and business issues interpenetrate.
3 Conflicts of interest are frowned upon.	3 Consider an employee's whole situation before you judge him or her.
4 Clear, precise and detailed instructions are seen as assuring better compliance, or allowing employees to dissent in clear terms.	4 Ambiguous and vague instructions are seen as allowing subtle and responsive interpretations through which employees can exercise personal judgment.
5 Begin reports with an executive summary.	5 End reports with a concluding overview.

References
1 Lewin, K., "Some Social-Psychological Differences between the US and Germany" in Lewin, K., ed., *Principles of Topological Psychology*, 1936.
2 Feiffer, J., *Hold Me*, Knopf, New York, 1968.
3 Parsons, T. and Shils, E.A., *Towards a General Theory of Action*, Harvard University Press, Cambridge, Mass., 1951, pages 128–33.
4 Dean, L.R., "The Pattern Variables: Some Empirical Operations", *American Sociological Review*, No. 26, 1961, pages 80–90.

8

HOW WE ACCORD STATUS

All societies give certain of their members higher status than others, signalling that unusual attention should be focused upon such persons and their activities. While some societies accord status to people on the basis of their achievements, others ascribe it to them by virtue of age, class, gender, education, and so on. The first kind of status is called **achieved** status and the second **ascribed** status. While achieved status refers to **doing**, ascribed status refers to **being**.

When we look at other people we are partly influenced by their track record (top Eastern Division salesman for five consecutive years). We may also be influenced by their:

- age (a more experienced salesperson);
- gender (very masculine and aggressive);
- social connections (friends in the highest places);
- education (top scholar at the Ecole Polytechnique); or
- profession (electronics is the future).

While there are ascriptions that are not logically connected with business effectiveness, such as masculine gender, white skin or noble birth, there are some ascriptions which do make good sense in predicting business performance: age and experience, education and professional qualifications. Education and professional qualifications, moreover, are related to an individual's earlier schooling and training and are therefore not unconnected with achievement. A culture may ascribe higher status to its better educated employees in the belief that scholarly success will lead to corporate success. This is a generalised expectation and may show up as a "fast-track" or "management-trainee" programme that points a recruit to the top of the organisation.

With the issue of status in mind, let us get back to the trials of Mr Johnson, who we may recall is struggling with a walk-out by Italian managers. Mr Gialli and Mr Pauli left the room furious when their suggested modification to the pay-for-performance plan was called "a crazy idea" by Mr

Bergman from the Netherlands. In order to save the situation Johnson has turned to shuttle diplomacy. Like a youthful Henry Kissinger (Johnson is only 35), he finds himself moving between the two parties to settle the dispute. He rapidly begins to feel less like Kissinger and more like Don Quixote.

The Italian managers were far from assuaged. One even referred unpleasantly to "the American cult of youth: mere boys who think they know everything". So when the Spanish HR manager, Mr Munoz, offered to mediate, Johnson readily agreed. It occurred to him that Spanish culture might be closer to Italian culture, apart from the fact that Munoz was some 20 years his senior, so could hardly be accused of inexperience.

While hopeful that Munoz might succeed, Johnson was astonished to see him bring the Italians back into the conference room in minutes. Munoz was not, in Johnson's view, the most professional of HR managers, but he was clearly expert at mending fences. It was at once apparent, however, that Munoz was now backing the Italians' call for modifications to the pay-for-performance plan. The problem as he saw it, and the Italians agreed, was that under the current plan winning salespeople were going to earn more than their bosses. Subordinates, they believed, should not be allowed to undermine their superiors in this way. Mr Munoz explained that back in Spain his salesforce would probably simply refuse to embarrass a boss like this; or perhaps one or two, lacking in loyalty to the organisation, might, in which case they would humiliate their boss into resignation. Furthermore, since the sales manager was largely responsible for the above-average performance of his team, was it not odd, to say the least, that the company would be rewarding everyone except the leader? The meeting broke for lunch, for which Johnson had little appetite.

As we can see, different societies confer status on individuals in different ways. Mr Munoz carried more clout with the Italians for the same reason that Johnson had less; they respected age and experience much more than the specific achievements that had made Johnson a fast-tracker in the company. Many Anglo-Saxons, including Mr Johnson, believe that ascribing status for reasons other than achievement is quite archaic and inappropriate to business. But is achievement orientation really a necessary feature of economic success?

Status-by-achievement and economic development

Most of the literature on achievement orientation sees it as part of "modernisation", the key to economic and business success. The theory goes that once you start rewarding business achievement, the process is self-perpetuating. People work hard to assure themselves of the esteem of their culture and you get *The Achieving Society*, as David McClelland, the Harvard professor, defined his own culture in the late 1950s.[1] Only nations setting out upon an empirical investigation of "what works best", and conferring status on those who apply it in business, can expect to conduct their economies successfully. This is the essence of Protestantism: the pursuit of justification through works which long ago gave achievers a religious sanction – and capitalism its moving spirit.

According to this view, societies which ascribe status are economically backward, because the reasons they have for conferring status do not facilitate commercial success. Catholic countries ascribing status to more passive ways of life, Hinduism associating practical achievements with delusion and Buddhism teaching detachment from earthly concerns are all forms of ascribed status which are thought to impede economic development. Ascription has been seen as a feature of countries either late to develop, or still underdeveloped. In fact ascribing status has been considered "dangerous for your economic health".

To measure the extent of achieving versus ascribing orientations in different cultures, we used the following statements, inviting participants to mark them on a five-point scale (1 = strongly agree, 5 = strongly disagree).

> **A** The most important thing in life is to think and act in the ways that best suit the way you really are, even if you do not get things done.
> **B** The respect a person gets is highly dependent on their family background.

Figures 8.1 and 8.2 show the percentage of participants who disagree with each of these statements. The countries in Figure 8.1 where only a minority disagree with "getting things done" are broadly speaking ascriptive cultures; very broadly speaking, because there are in fact less than ten societies – English-speaking and Scandinavian countries – where there is a majority in favour of getting things done even at the expense of personal freedom to live as you feel you should. The USA is clearly a culture in which status is mainly achieved, as shown by Figure 8.2; 87% of Americans disagree that status depends mainly on family background. A number of societies

Figure 8.1 **Acting as suits you even if nothing is achieved**
Percentage of respondents who disagree

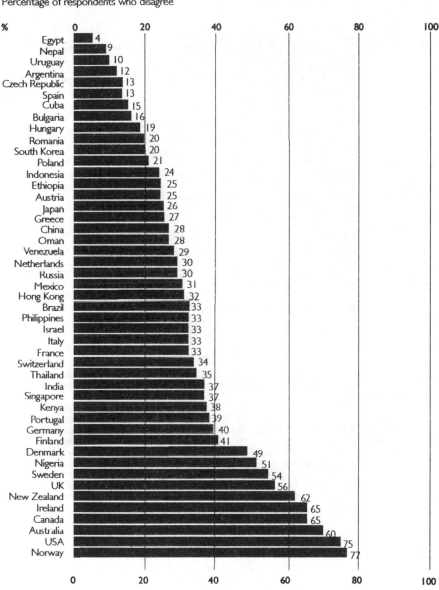

Country	%
Egypt	4
Nepal	9
Uruguay	10
Argentina	12
Czech Republic	13
Spain	13
Cuba	15
Bulgaria	16
Hungary	19
Romania	20
South Korea	20
Poland	21
Indonesia	24
Ethiopia	25
Austria	25
Japan	26
Greece	27
China	28
Oman	28
Venezuela	29
Netherlands	30
Russia	30
Mexico	31
Hong Kong	32
Brazil	33
Philippines	33
Israel	33
Italy	33
France	33
Switzerland	34
Thailand	35
India	37
Singapore	37
Kenya	38
Portugal	39
Germany	40
Finland	41
Denmark	49
Nigeria	51
Sweden	54
UK	56
New Zealand	62
Ireland	65
Canada	65
Australia	60
USA	75
Norway	77

which are ascriptive in the first figure (the Czech Republic, for example) do in fact show majorities against the proposition that status is largely dependent on family; aspects of ascription vary greatly from country to country.

Both figures show that there is a correlation between Protestantism

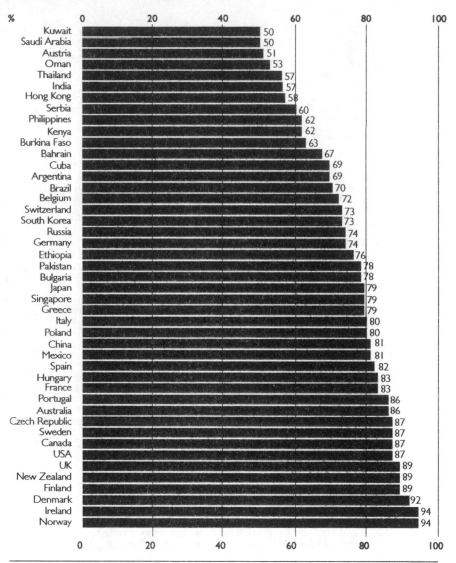

Figure 8.2 **Respect depends on family background**
Percentage of respondents who disagree

Country	%
Kuwait	50
Saudi Arabia	50
Austria	51
Oman	53
Thailand	57
India	57
Hong Kong	58
Serbia	60
Philippines	62
Kenya	62
Burkina Faso	63
Bahrain	67
Cuba	69
Argentina	69
Brazil	70
Belgium	72
Switzerland	73
South Korea	73
Russia	74
Germany	74
Ethiopia	76
Pakistan	78
Bulgaria	78
Japan	79
Singapore	79
Greece	79
Italy	80
Poland	80
China	81
Mexico	81
Spain	82
Hungary	83
France	83
Portugal	86
Australia	86
Czech Republic	87
Sweden	87
Canada	87
USA	87
UK	89
New Zealand	89
Finland	89
Denmark	92
Ireland	94
Norway	94

and achievement orientation, with Catholic, Buddhist and Hindu cultures scoring considerably more ascriptively. There is, incidentally, no correlation between support for achievement or ascription and the age, sex or education of respondents across our database as a whole, although there is for these factors in some societies.

A second glance at the scores shows that there are growing difficulties with the thesis that an achievement orientation is the key to economic success. In the first place, Protestant cultures are no longer growing faster than Catholic or Buddhist ones. Catholic Belgium, for example, has a slightly higher GDP per head than the more Protestant Netherlands. Catholic France and Italy have been growing faster than the UK or parts of Protestant Scandinavia. Japan, South Korea, Taiwan, Singapore and Hong Kong are influenced by Buddhism and Confucianism. It is certainly not evident that Japan's habit of promoting by seniority has weighed its corporations down beneath piles of dead wood. In short, there is no evidence that either orientation belongs to a "higher" level of development, as modernisation theorists used to claim.

What appears to be happening is that some very successful business cultures are ascribing status to persons, technologies or industries which they anticipate will be important to their future as an economy, with the result that these persons and sectors receive special encouragement. In other words, ascribing **works with** achieving by generating social and economic momentum towards visualised goals.

Ascription and performance

Andrew, a British manager and trained geologist, had been working for a French oil company for 20 years and was still confused by one aspect of his colleagues' behaviour. He found that his fellow French geologists would simply not tolerate outside criticism of their profession. Initially he would get puzzled looks and frowns if he admitted he did not know the answer to some technical question in front of lay persons. Once when he said he would have to "look something up", his French colleagues were overtly annoyed with him. He was confused because in his view geologists are frequently asked questions for which they do not have answers right at hand, or for which there is no answer. But his French fellows would chide him for admitting this publicly. They believed he was letting his profession down.

This experience is supported by research undertaken at INSEAD business school in France by André Laurent.[2] He found that French and Italian managers were much more emphatic about "knowing all the answers" than managers from many other cultures.

Notice, though, the effect that ascription has on performance. The French geologists are determined to live up to their ascribed status which, in turn, can lead to higher performance. Hence, it can be a self-fulfilling prophecy: through living up to the status ascribed to them, they "deserve" the status that was given to them before they actually earn it. In practice, then, achieving and ascribing status can be finely interwoven.

The European Union is a very good example of an ascribed self-fulfilling prophecy; its importance and power in the world was proclaimed before it had achieved anything.

The interweaving of ascribing and achieving orientations is a feature of the world's leading economies, Japan and Germany. Both cultures tend to confine achieving **as individuals** to the school days of their economic actors. Thereafter, managers are supposed to co-operate. Achievement becomes less a task for individuals jostling each other for advantage than for whole groups, led by those who excelled earlier and individually.

We must bear these distinctions in mind when we examine the data presented earlier. Ascribing and achieving can be exclusive of each other, but are not necessarily so. Your achieving can drive your ascribing, as when you "land winners". Or ascribing can drive achieving, as when key industries are first targeted and then won by "national champions".

The belief that electronic equipment made by Olivetti, Bosch, Siemens or Alcatel is more important to the EC than enhanced expertise in distributing hamburgers or bottling colas is not entirely mistaken. You can ascribe greater importance to supposedly "key" industries on the basis of bad judgment or of good judgment. It is at least arguable that an economy needs to master electronics if it seeks to maintain competitiveness in manufacturing since machines are increasingly monitored, controlled and re-tooled electronically. You have a choice, then, of ascribing status to electronics **before** the achievements of manufacturing lapse, or **afterwards**. A culture that insists on waiting for dire results before changing course may handicap itself. Intelligent anticipation requires ascribing importance to certain projects, just as joint ventures, strategic alliances and partnerships require us to value a relationship **before** it proves successful.

Achievement- and ascription-oriented cultures' negotiations

It can be extremely irritating to managers from achieving cultures when an ascriptive team of negotiators has some *éminence grise* hovering in the background to whom they have to submit any proposals or changes. It is not even clear what this person does. He (usually male) will not say what he wants, but simply expects deference not just from you but from his own team, which is forever watching him for faint signs of assent or dissent. It is, of course, equally upsetting for ascriptive cultures when the "achieving team" wheels on its aggressive young men and women who spout knowledge as if it were a kind of ammunition before which the team opposite is expected to surrender. It is rather like having to play a game with a toddler and a toy gun; there is a lot of noise coming from someone who is of no known authority or status.

Indeed, sending whiz-kids to deal with people 10–20 years their senior often insults the ascriptive culture. The reaction may be: "Do these people think that they have reached our own level of experience in half the time? That a 30-year-old American is good enough to negotiate with a 50-year-old Greek or Italian?" Achievement cultures must understand that some ascriptive cultures, the Japanese especially, spend very heavily on training and in-house education to ensure that older people actually are wiser for the years they have spent in the corporation and for the sheer numbers of subordinates briefing them. It insults an ascriptive culture to do anything which prevents the self-fulfilling nature of its beliefs. Older people are held to be important **so that** they will be nourished and sustained by others' respect. A stranger is expected to facilitate this scheme, not challenge it.

Consider a Japanese–Dutch negotiating session. When Dutch experts in finance, marketing and human resources meet their Japanese opposite numbers, the Dutch approach is to try to clarify facts and determine who holds the decision-making power. To the Dutch, the Japanese will appear evasive and secretive, not revealing anything. For the Japanese, these are not "facts" so much as mutual understandings between their leaders and themselves, which the Dutch seem to be prying into. This may come across as disrespectful. Anyway, it is for the leader of the negotiating team to say what these relationships are if he or she chooses to.

At a conference on a Japanese–Dutch joint venture held in Rotterdam, a Japanese participant fell ill. A member of the Dutch delegation approached Mr Yoshi, another Japanese delegate with fluent English and outstanding technical knowledge, and asked if he would replace the sick man in a particular forum. Mr Yoshi demurred and the Dutchman was annoyed at the lack of a straight response. Several minutes later the leader of the Japanese delegation, Mr Kaminaki, announced that Mr Yoshi would replace the sick man because Mr Kaminaki was appointing him to the task. It was made very clear whose decision that had been.

The translator's role

In this and other negotiations it often becomes clear that the translator from an ascriptive culture behaves "unprofessionally" according to the standards of achieving cultures. According to British, German, North American, Scandinavian and Dutch values, the translator is an achiever like any other participant and the height of his or her achievement should be to give an accurate, unbiased account of what was said in one language to those speaking the other language. The translator is supposed to be neutral, a black box serving the interests of modern language comprehension, not the interests of either party who may seek to distort meanings for their own ends.

In other cultures, however, the translator is doing something else. A Japanese translator, for example, will often take a minute or more to "translate" an English sentence 15 seconds long. And there is often extensive colloquy between the translator and the team he or she serves about what the opposite team just said. The translator on the Japanese side is an interpreter, not simply of language but of gesture, meaning and context. His role is to support his own team and possibly even to protect them from confrontational conduct by the western negotiators. He may protect superiors from rudeness and advise the team how to counter opposition tactics. The "translator" is very much on the ascribing team's side, and if the achievement-oriented team seeks flawless, if literal, translation they should bring their own. This may not actually improve relationships because Asian teams are quite used to speaking among themselves in the belief that foreigners do not understand. If you bring someone fluent in their tongue, they will have to withdraw in order to confer. Your "contribution" to mutual understanding may not be appreciated.

The role of titles

The use of and mention of titles with business cards and formal introductions can be complex. Both authors carry three kinds of cards to introduce themselves. In the Middle East and southern Europe formal titles received for formal education are diffused through several different contexts to elevate my status. In Britain, however, presenting myself as "doctor" may suggest a rather too academic bent for a business consultant. It may not be considered relevant for a consultant to have a PhD, and if attention is drawn to it, the status claimed is not necessarily legitimate. Achievement in a university may even disqualify a person from likely achievement in a corporation.

We might expect a similar situation in the USA, another achievement-oriented, yet specific society. However, the "inflation" of qualifications in the USA makes it legitimate to draw attention to higher degrees from good universities, provided it is relevant to the task at hand. Typically the speciality is mentioned: MBA, Sociology and so on.

In diffuse cultures it is important to **tie in** your status with your organisation. Indeed your achievement as an individual will be discounted compared with the status your organisation ascribes to you. It is therefore important to say not just that you are chief, but what you are chief of: marketing, finance, human resources and so on. Many a deal has been lost because the representative was not seen to have high status back home. Ascriptive cultures must be assured that your organisation has great respect for you and that you are at or near the top.

Relationship with mother company

In the value system of individualist, achievement-oriented cultures, the specific "word" of the representative pledges the company to any commitment made. The individual has delegated authority to use personal judgment. In ascriptive cultures, the individual, unless head of the organisation, almost never has the personal discretion to commit the company without extensive consultations. An individual from an ascriptive culture may not really believe that the achieving representative has this authority either. Hence agreements are tentative and subject to back-home ratification. It is partly for this reason that your title and power "back home" is important to the ascriptive negotiator. How can you deliver your company if you are not high in its status hierarchy? If you send an impetuous, though clever youth, you cannot be very serious. It is important to send senior people if you are visiting an ascriptive culture, even if they are less knowledgeable about the product. It could also be important to ask for senior persons in the ascriptive culture to attend in person and meet their opposite numbers. The closer you get to the top, the more likely it is that promises made in negotiations will be kept.

Signs of ascriptive status are carefully ordered

We are now beginning to see why pay-for-performance and bonuses to high achievers whatever their rank can be upsetting to ascriptive cultures. The superior is **by definition** responsible for increased performance, so that relative status is unaffected by higher group sales. If rewards are to be increased, this must be done proportionately to ascribed status, not given to the person closest to the sale. If the leader does something to reduce his own status, **all his subordinates are downgraded as a consequence**.

A British general manager upon arrival in Thailand refused to take his predecessor's car. The Thai finance manager asked the new GM what type of Mercedes he would like, then. The GM asked for a Suzuki or a Mini, anything that could be handled easily in the congested traffic in Bangkok.

Three weeks later the GM called the finance manager and asked about prospects for the delivery of his car. The Thai lost his reserve for a moment and exclaimed: "We can get you a new Mercedes by tomorrow, but Suzukis take much, much longer." The GM asked him to see what he could do to speed up the process. After four weeks the GM asked to see the purchase order for the car. The purchasing department replied that, because it would take so long to get a small car, they had decided to order a Mercedes.

The GM's patience had run out. At the first management meeting he brought the issue up and asked for an explanation. Somewhat shyly, the predominantly Thai management team explained that they could hardly come to work on bicycles.

In this case the status of each member was interdependent. Had the British GM ordered an even more expensive car all the other managers might have moved up a notch. In ascriptive societies you "are" your status. It is as natural to you as your birth or formal education (rebirth) through which your innate powers were made manifest. Ascribed status simply "is" and requires no rational justification, although such justifications may exist. For example, a preference for males, for greater age or social connections is not usually justified or defended by the culture ascribing importance to older men from "good" families. That does not mean it is irrational or without competitive advantage, however, it simply means that justifications are not offered and not expected. It has always been so, and if this means a major effort to educate staff as they age, that is all the better, but it is **not** the basis for preferring older people in the first place.

Achievement-oriented organisations justify their hierarchies by claiming that senior persons have "achieved more" for the organisation; their authority, justified by skill and knowledge, benefits the organisation. Ascription-oriented organisations justify their hierarchies by "power-to-get-things-done". This may consist of power **over** people and be coercive, or power **through** people and be participative. There is high variation within ascriptive cultures and participative power has well-known advantages. Whatever form power takes, the ascription of status to persons is intended to be exercised as power and that power is supposed to enhance the effectiveness of the organisation. The sources of ascribed status may be multiple and trying to alter it by promotion-on-the-grounds-of-achievement can be hazardous.

An achievement-oriented Swedish manager was managing a project in Pakistan. A vacancy needed to be filled and after careful assessment the Swedish manager chose one of his two most promising Pakistani employees for promotion. Both candidates were highly educated, with PhDs in mechanical engineering, and in Pakistan both were known authorities in their field. Although both had excellent performance records, Mr Kahn was selected on the basis of some recent achievements.

Mr Saran, the candidate not chosen, was very upset by the turn of events. He went to his Swedish boss for an explanation. However, even an explanation based on the specific needs of the business did not calm him. How could this loss of face be allowed?

The Swedish manager tried to make the engineer understand that only one of the two could be promoted because there was only one vacancy. One of them was going to be hurt, even though they were both valued employees. He made no progress. The reason, as he eventually learned, was the fact that Mr Saran received his PhD two years before Mr Khan from the same American university. Saran was expected to have more status than his colleague because of this. His family would never understand. What was this western way of treating ascribed status so lightly? Should not more than just the achievements of the past months be considered?

It is important to see how different the logics of achievement and ascription are and not consider either as worthless. In achieving countries the actor is evaluated by how well he or she performed the allocated function. Relationships are functionally specific; I relate to you as, say, a sales manager. The justification of my role lies in the sales records. Another person in that role must be expected to be compared with me and I with that person. Success is universally defined as increased sales. My relationship to manufacturing, R&D, planning and so on is instrumental. I either sell what they have developed, manufactured and planned, or I do not. I **am** my functional role.

In ascribing cultures, status is attributed to those who "naturally" evoke admiration from others, that is, older people, males, highly qualified persons and/or persons skilled in a technology or project deemed to be of national importance. To show respect for status is to assist the person so distinguished to fulfil the expectations the society has of him or her. The status is generally independent of task or specific function. The individual is particular and not easily compared with others. His or her performance is partly determined by the loyalty and affection shown by subordinates and which they, in turn, display. He or she **is** the organisation in the sense of personifying it and wielding its power.

Achievement-oriented corporations in western countries often send young, promising managers on challenging assignments to faraway countries without realising that the local culture will not accept their youthfulness and/or gender however well they achieve. A young (aged 34) talented and female marketing manager had worked for an American company in both the USA and Britain. She was so successful in her second year there that she was named the most promising female manager in Britain. This vote of confidence influenced her decision to accept an offer to transfer as director of marketing to her company's operation in Ankara, Turkey. She knew she had always been able to win the support and trust of her subordinates and colleagues.

The first few weeks in Ankara were as usual in a new job, getting to know the local business, the staff and how to get things done. Luckily, she knew one of the marketing managers, Guz Akil, who had been her marketing assistant in London. They had worked very well together.

Working as hard as she could over the first few months, she found her authority gradually slipping away. The most experienced Turk, Hasan (aged 63), informally but consciously took over more and more of her authority, getting things done where her own efforts were frustrated, although his marketing knowledge was only a fraction of her own. She had to watch him exercise influence which most often led to unsatisfactory results. Through Guz she learned that head office complied with this arrangement, communicating more and more through Hasan, not her. She also heard that ten years earlier an American male manager the same age as her had been withdrawn for his inability to command local managers effectively. He was now working very effectively indeed for a competitor back in the USA.

When presenting this case in a workshop in San Francisco, pointing out the dangers of a universalist system for personnel planning, one female manager expressed concern. "You should not linger on this issue. You are advising us to discriminate on the basis of gender and age, or allow our overseas subsidiaries to do so. In this country you could get sued for that."

Indeed cultural preferences often have the force of law as well as custom. Refusal to send young women managers to Turkey because they are young and female is probably illegal, yet to send them is to confront them with difficulties which they may not have the capacity to surmount, through no fault of their own. The more they achieve, the more they seem to subvert the ascription process. A better tactic can be to make a young female an assistant or adviser to indigenous managers. She will make up for any deficits in knowledge they have, while using local seniority to get things done. Such a posting could be paid and evaluated in the same way as being chief in an achievement-oriented culture, perhaps with a bonus for culture-shock. You cannot replace Turkish with American cultural norms if you seek to be effective in Turkey. This will not be effective in the long run, and in the short run can be very expensive.

Towards reconciliation

Despite far greater emphasis on ascription or achievement in certain cultures, they do in my view develop together. Those who "start" with ascribing usually ascribe not just status but future success or achievement and thereby help to bring it about. Those who "start" with achievement usually start to ascribe importance and priority to the persons and projects which have been successful. Hence all societies ascribe and all achieve after a fashion. It is once again a question of where a cycle starts.

It was in 1985 that Belly Electronics (BE) started to manufacture in South Korea. The fast changing prices in consumer electronics had forced the San Francisco-based company to decentralise its production facilities. After some quite serious starting losses BE began to recover and late in 1989 it could report some promising profits. Early in 1991 margins came under pressure because of Thai and Vietnamese competition. BE decided to reengineer its business processes following its major competitors in the region.

For the first time BE flew in experienced US managers from the Bay area. Their approach was consistent and had made them managers of the year in BE for similar turnaround projects in California and Massachusetts. On the basis of a continuous improvement programme Korean managers were put under pressure to "get their act together". Something said by the first US manager is still remembered in Seoul: "Ladies and gentlemen, we are on a burning platform. Figures tell us there is not much time left. Competitors in the region are doing much better than us; in fact comparative research shows that in terms of quality our benchmark companies in California and Thailand are outperforming us by 35% on quality and 42% on quantity per worker. I therefore give you six months to get the numbers up and then to become a profit-generating company. Let us show that we are a worthwhile company in BE by achievements and not just promises."

After very disappointing results a second US manager was flown in, but his similar approach made no difference. Interviews with the key Korean players were not helpful. Loss after loss was defended by: "We are trying, but it is not easy in Korea. Fierce competition explains a lot. But we need to stop turnover of personnel so we can trust each other more."

Jerome Don was asked to come to the rescue of still loss-making BE-Korea. He was known for turning companies around with great skill in both South America and Asia. He started by telling Korean managers that his predecessors were quite right in their approach: "We are on a burning platform, but I ask you to help us to save this facility because it is so important to BE. I'll give you three years to get your act together and I'll help you whenever you need me."

Within six months BE-Korea was in profit. Quality went up and morale resulted in 60% lower staff turnover. Mr Don did not know exactly what happened, but he had done the same in South America and now in Asia.

Why would Jerome Don be successful in Korea, while his predecessors had not been?

Figure 8.3 **Reconciling achievement and ascription**

ACHIEVEMENT

We need to reward what our people achieve based on skill, but ...

We do not want to be hindered in our achievement by not challenging the status quo, so ...

Respect what people are so we can better take advantage of what they do

We want to avoid the instability that comes from only valuing most recent performance, so we must ...

Respect who our people are based on their experience, although ...

ASCRIPTION

The initial actions by the American managers were counter-productive. In the great American tradition the turnaround managers started at the top of Figure 8.3 and focused on the reward which people could get for their achievements. The Koreans became even more nervous than they had been before the intervention, because basic trust seemed to be lacking. They were afraid to be judged on their past performance.

Jerome Don gave his Korean colleagues three years to get their act together. By doing so he intuitively ascribed status to the Korean organisation. This gave the Koreans the trust they needed because they were feeling that they were respected for who they were based on their years at BE. This made them work even harder. From ascribed status comes achievement.

Test yourself

Consider the following problem:

> There are different grounds for according status to employees, based on what people have succeeded in doing or on what qualities are attributed to them by the social system.
> Consider the statements opposite:

1   Status should lie in the permanent attributes of
    employees, i.e. their education, seniority, age, position and the
    level of responsibility ascribed. Status should not change
    according to occasion or just because of recent successes. It
    reflects intrinsic worth, not the latest forays.
2   Status should lie in the permanent attributes of employees, i.e.
    their education, seniority, age, position and the level of
    responsibility ascribed. Such status tends to be self-fulfilling,
    with achievement and leadership resulting from what the
    corporation values in you and expects of you.
3   Status is a matter of what the employee has actually achieved,
    his or her track record. Yet over time this deserved reputation
    becomes a permanent attribute, allowing success to be
    renewed and enabling even more achievement to occur.
4   Achievement or success is the only legitimate source of status
    in business. The more recent the achievement, the better and
    more relevant it is to current challenges. Achievement gets its
    significance from the humble nature of the individual's birth
    and background, and from beating the odds.

Indicate with "1" the approach you believe would be favoured by
your closest colleagues at work, and with "2" the approach which
you believe would be their second choice.

If you have chosen 2 or 3 you have expressed a belief in reconciling
achieved and ascribed status. Answer 2 affirms socially ascribed status
which leads to achievement and success (the Korean case was based on a
similar principle). Answer 3 affirms achieved status that is believed to lead
to social ascription. In both cases the integrity lies in the self-fulfilling
sense of self-worth. Answers 1 and 4 respectively reject achieved and
ascribed status.

Practical tips for doing business in ascription- and achievement-oriented cultures

Recognising the differences

Achievement-oriented	Ascription-oriented
1 Use of titles only when relevant to the competence you bring to the task.	1 Extensive use of titles, especially when these clarify your status in the organisation.
2 Respect for superior in hierarchy is based on how effectively his or her job is performed and how adequate their knowledge.	2 Respect for superior in hierarchy is seen as a measure of your commitment to the organisation and its mission.
3 Most senior managers are of varying age and gender and have shown proficiency in specific jobs.	3 Most senior managers are male, middle-aged and qualified by their background.

Tips for doing business with:

Achievement-oriented (for ascriptives)	Ascription-oriented (for achievers)
1 Make sure your negotiation team has enough data, technical advisers and knowledgeable people to convince the other company that the project, jointly pursued, will work.	1 Make sure your negotiation team has enough older, senior and formal position-holders to impress the other company that you consider this negotiation important.
2 Respect the knowledge and information of your counterparts even if you suspect they are short of influence back home.	2 Respect the status and influence of your counterparts, even if you suspect they are short of knowledge. Do **not** show them up.
3 Use the title that reflects how competent you are as an individual.	3 Use the title that reflects your degree of influence in your organisation.
4 Do not underestimate the need of your counterparts to do better or do more than is expected.	4 Do not underestimate the need of your counterparts to make their ascriptions come true.

When managing and being managed

Achievement-oriented	Ascription-oriented
1 Respect for a manager is based on knowledge and skills.	1 Respect for a manager is based on seniority.
2 MBO and pay-for-performance are affective tools.	2 MBO and pay-for-performance are less effective than direct rewards from the manager.
3 Decisions are challenged on technical and functional grounds.	3 Decisions are only challenged by people with higher authority.

References
1 McClelland, D., *The Achieving Society*, Van Nostrand, New York, 1950.
2 Laurent, A., *op.cit.*, see footnote 1, page 180.

9

HOW WE MANAGE TIME

If only because managers need to co-ordinate their business activities, they require some kind of shared expectations about time. Just as different cultures have different assumptions about how people relate to one another, so they approach time differently. This chapter is about the relative importance cultures give to the past, present and future. Does an achievement-oriented culture believe that the future must be better than the past or present, since it is there that aspirations are realised? Does a relationship-oriented culture, on the other hand, see the future as threatening, likely to loosen current bonds of affection? How we think of time has its own consequences. Especially important is whether our view of time is **sequential**, a series of passing events, or whether it is **synchronic**, with past, present and future all interrelated so that ideas about the future and memories of the past both shape present action.

The concept of time

Primitive societies may order themselves by simple notions of "before" and "after" moons, seasons, sunrises and sunsets. For educated societies the concept of time is increasingly complex. Running through all our ideas of time are two contrasting notions: time as a line of discrete events, minutes, hours, days, months, years, each passing in a never-ending succession, and time as a circle, revolving so that the minutes of the hour repeat, as do the hours of the day, the days of the week and so on.

In the Greek myth the Sphinx, a monster with the face of a woman, the body of a lion and the wings of a bird, asked all wayfarers on the road to Thebes: "What creature is it that walks on four legs in the morning, two legs at noonday and three legs in the evening?" Those unable to answer she ate. Oedipus, however, answered "man" and the Sphinx committed suicide. He had grasped that this riddle was a metaphor for time. Four legs was a child crawling, two legs the adult and three legs an old person leaning on a stick. By thinking in a longer sequence about time, the riddle was solved. He had also understood that within the riddle time orientations had been compressed or synchronised, and that language allows us to do this.

Anthropologists have long insisted that how a culture thinks of time and manages it is a clue to the meanings its members find in life and the supposed nature of human existence. Kluckhohn and Strodtbeck[1] identified three types of culture: present-oriented, which is relatively timeless, traditionless and ignores the future; past-oriented, mainly concerned to maintain and restore traditions in the present; and future-oriented, envisaging a more desirable future and setting out to realise it. It is chiefly people that fall into the latter category who experience economic or social development.

Time is increasingly viewed as a factor that organisations must manage. There are time-and-motion studies, time-to-market, just-in-time, along with ideas that products age, or mature, and have a life cycle similar to that of human beings. Uniquely in the animal kingdom, man is aware of time and tries to control it. Man thinks almost universally in categories of past, present and future, but does not give the same importance to each. Our conception of time is strongly affected by culture because time is an idea rather than an object. How we think of time is interwoven with how we plan, strategise and co-ordinate our activities with others. It is an important dimension of how we organise experience and activities.

When we create man-made instruments to measure time we shape our experience of it. We can differentiate between duration and succession and make fine distinctions within the compass of astronomical time, the time taken for the earth to revolve around the sun. We can think of time as fixed in this way by the motion of the earth, or we can think of time as experienced subjectively; on a jet aircraft, the position of the plane is sometimes shown on a map of the earth. We appear to be crawling very, very slowly towards our destination.

The experience of time means that we can consider a past event now (out of sequence as it were), or envisage a future event. In this way past, present and future are all compressed. We can consider what competitive move to make today, based on past experience and with expectations of the future. This is an interpretative use of time.

Time has meaning not just to individuals but to whole groups or cultures. Emile Durkheim, the French sociologist, saw it as a social construct enabling members of a culture to co-ordinate their activities.[2] This has important implications in a business context. The time agreed for a meeting may be approximate or precise. The time allocated to complete a task may be vitally important or merely a guide. There may be an expectation of mutual accommodation as to the exact time when a machine and its microprocessor are ready to be assembled, or there may be a penalty clause of thousands of dollars a day imposed by one party upon another. Intervals between inspections may be indicators of a manager's level of responsibility. Is he or she left for three months or three years to get on with the job? Organisations may look ahead a long way, or get obsessed by the monthly reporting period.

Orientations to past, present and future

Saint Augustine pointed out in his *Declarations* that time as a subjective phenomenon can vary considerably from time in abstract conception. In its abstract form we cannot know the future because it is not yet here, and the past is also unknowable. We may have memories, partial and selective, but the past has gone. The only thing that exists is the present, which is our sole access to past or future. Augustine wrote: "The present has, therefore, three dimensions ... the present of past things, the present of present things and the present of future things."

The idea that at any given moment the present is the only real thing, with the past and future ceasing to be or yet to come, must be qualified by the fact that we think **about** past and future in the present. However imperfect our ideas about past or future, they influence our thinking powerfully. These subjective times are ever-present in our judgment and our decision-making. Although our lives may be consciously oriented to the future success of the enterprise, past experiences have deeply affected our perceptions of that future, as does our present mood. There is a potentially productive tension between the three, along with the ever-pressing question as to whether the future can benefit from past and present experiences (although companies, it is often remarked, have no memory). All three time zones unite in our actions. It is as true to say that our expectations of the future determine our present, as to say our present action determines the future; as true to say that our present experience determines our view of the past, as to say that the past has made us what we are today. This is not juggling with terms but describing how we think. We can make ourselves miserable in the present if a long expected payment is delayed to the future. We can discover in the present a fact that makes what we did in the past far more justifiable. In fact, an important part of creativity is to assemble past and present activities, plus conjectures about the future, in new combinations.

Different individuals and different cultures may be more or less attracted to past, present or future orientations. Some live entirely in the present, or try to. "History is bunk", as Henry Ford put it, and inquiry into things past is best forgotten. Some dream of a world that never was and seek to create it from their own imaginings and yearnings, or they may seek the return of a golden age, a Napoleonic Legend reborn, a New Frontier similar in its challenges to the Wild West. They believe the future is coming **to** them, as a destiny, or that they alone must define it. Others live in a nostalgic past to which everything attempted in the present must appeal.

Sequentially and synchronically organised activities

We have seen that there are at least two images which can be extracted from the concept of time. Time can be legitimately conceived of as a line of sequential events passing us at regular intervals. It can also be conceived of as cyclical and repetitive, compressing past, present and future by what these have in common: seasons and rhythms. At one extreme, then, we have the person who conceives of time as a dotted line with regular spacings. Events are organised by the number of intervals before or after their occurrence. Everything has its time and place as far as the sequential thinker is concerned. Any change or turbulence in this sequence will make the sequential person more uncertain. Try jumping a queue in Britain. You will find that orderly sequence has very stern defenders. Everyone must wait their turn; first come, first served. It is part of "good form". In London I once saw a long queue of people waiting for a bus when it started pouring with rain. They all stood stolidly getting soaked, even though cover was close by, lest they lose their sequential order. They preferred to do things right rather than do the right thing. In the Netherlands you could be the queen but if you are in a butcher's shop with number 46 and you step up for service when number 12 is called, you are still in deep trouble. Nor does it matter if you have an emergency; order is order.

Going from A to B in a straight line with minimal effort and maximum effect is known as efficiency. It has a major influence on the conduct of business in north-western Europe and North America. The flaw in this thinking is that "straight lines" may not always be the best way of doing something; it is blind to the effectiveness of shared activities and cross-connections.

In a butcher's shop in Italy I once saw the butcher unwrap salami at the request of one customer and then shout "who else for salami?". The sequential idea is not entirely absent. People still pay in turn when they are finished, but if a customer has all she wants, she might as well pay and leave earlier than someone wanting additional cuts. The method serves more people in less time.

At a butcher's shop in Amsterdam or London, the butcher calls a number, unwraps, cuts and rewraps each item the customer wants, and then calls the next number. Once one of us ventured the suggestion, "While you have the salami out, cut a pound for me too." Customers and staff went into shock. The system may be inefficient, but they were not about to let some wise guy change it.

The synchronic method, however, requires that people track various activities in parallel, rather like a juggler with six balls in the air with each being caught and thrown in rhythm. It is not easy for cultures which are not used to it. Edward T. Hall, the American anthropologist,[3] described what we call synchronic as **polychronic**, putting emphasis on the number of activities run in parallel. There is a final, established goal but numerous and possibly interchangeable stepping stones to reach it. A person can "skip between stones" on the way to the final target.

In contrast, the sequential person has a "critical path" worked out in advance with times for the completion of each stage. They hate to be thrown off this schedule or agenda by unanticipated events. In *The Silent Language* Hall revealed that Japanese negotiators would make their major bids for a concession **after** their American partners were confirmed on their return flights from Tokyo. Rather than risk their schedules, Americans would often concede to the Japanese demands.

Synchronic or polychronic styles are extraordinary for those unused to them. The Dutch author once purchased an airline ticket from a woman at a ticket counter in Argentina, who, while making out the ticket (correctly), was talking on the telephone to a friend and admiring her coworker's baby. People who do more than one thing at a time can, without meaning to, insult those who are used to doing only one thing.

Likewise, people who do only one thing at a time can, without meaning to, insult those who are used to doing several things. A South Korean manager explained his shock and disappointment upon returning to the Netherlands to see his boss.

> "He was on the phone when I entered his office and as I came in he raised his left hand slightly at me. Then he rudely continued his conversation as if I were not even in the room with him. Only after he had finished his conversation five minutes later did he get up and greet me with an enthusiastic, but insincere, 'Kim, happy to see you'. I just could not believe it."

To a synchronic person, not being greeted spontaneously and immediately, even while still talking on the telephone, is a slight. The whole notion of "sequencing" your emotions and postponing them until other matters are out of the way suggests insincerity. You show how you value people by "giving them time" even if they show up unexpectedly.

Sequential people tend to schedule very tightly, with thin divisions between time slots. It is rude to be even a few minutes late because the whole day's schedule of events is affected. "I'm running late ..." the scheduler will complain, as if he were himself a train or airline. Time is viewed as a commodity to be used up and lateness deprives the other of precious minutes in a world where "time is money".

Synchronic cultures are less insistent upon punctuality, defined as a person arriving at the agreed moment of passing time increments. It is not that the passage of time is unimportant, but that several other cultural values vie with punctuality. It is often necessary to "give time" to people with whom you have a particular relation (see the discussion of universalism versus particularism in Chapter 4). It may be required that you show affective pleasure on meeting a friend or relation unexpectedly (see the discussion of the affective versus the neutral approach in Chapter 6). Your schedule is not an excuse for passing them by. Your mother, fiancée or friend could be seriously offended. Raymond Carroll, the French anthropologist,[4] tells of an American girl who left a note for her French lover. Could he let her know if he wanted to see her this evening, as if not she would like to make other plans? The Frenchman was offended. Her schedule should not get in the way of their spontaneously affective and particular relationship. People prominent in a hierarchy must also be "given time" if encountered (see status by achievement versus status by ascription in Chapter 8). For all such reasons, meeting times may be approximate in synchronic cultures. The range is from 15 minutes in Latin Europe to part or all of a day in the Middle East and Africa. Given the fact that most of those with appointments to meet are running other activities in parallel, any waiting involved is not onerous and late arrival may often even be a convenience, allowing some time for unplanned activities.

Even the preparation of food is affected by time orientations. In sequential, punctual cultures, exactly the right quantity of food will usually be prepared, and in such a way that it might spoil or get cold if the guests are not on time. In synchronic cultures, there is usually more than enough food in case more guests drop by unexpectedly, and it is either not the kind that spoils or else is cooked as wanted.

Measuring cultural differences in relation to time

The methodology used to measure approaches to time in this book comes from Tom Cottle, who created the "Circle Test".[5] The question asked was as follows.

Think of the past, present and future as being in the shape of circles. Please draw three circles on the space available, representing past, present and future. Arrange these circles in any way you want that best shows how you feel about the relationship of the past, present and future. You may use different size circles. When you have finished, label each circle to show which one is the past, which one the present and which one the future.

Cottle ended up with four possible configurations. First, he found absence of zone relatedness. Figure 9.1 shows that on our measurements this is a typically Russian approach to time; there is no connection between past, present or future, though in their view the future is much more important than the present and more important than the past. The second Cottle configuration was temporal integration, the third a partial overlap of zones and the fourth zones touching but not overlapping, hence not "sharing" regions of time between them. Figure 9.1 shows that this last approach is characteristic of the Belgians, who see a very small overlap between present and past but the present and future as just touching. In this they are not dissimilar to the British, who have a rather stronger link with the past but see it as relatively unimportant, whereas the Belgians view all three aspects of time as equally important. Both are quite different from the French, for whom all three aspects overlap considerably; they share this view with the Malaysians. The Germans think the present and the future are very strongly interrelated. What the figure does not show is that half the Japanese see the three circles as concentric.

Time horizon

The circles test measured how different cultures assign different meanings to past, present and future. We have used another test developed by Cottle to see whether people share a short-term or a long-term time horizon.[6] The Duration Inventory inquires into the manner in which people perceive the boundaries separating time zones as well as the extension of these zones. We have paraphrased the Inventory in order to make it shorter, since we are concerned with only one of the 58 items in the questionnaire.

The question is as follows:

Consider the relative significance of the past, present and future. You will be asked to indicate your relative time horizons for the past, present and future by giving a number:

Figure 9.1 Past, present and future

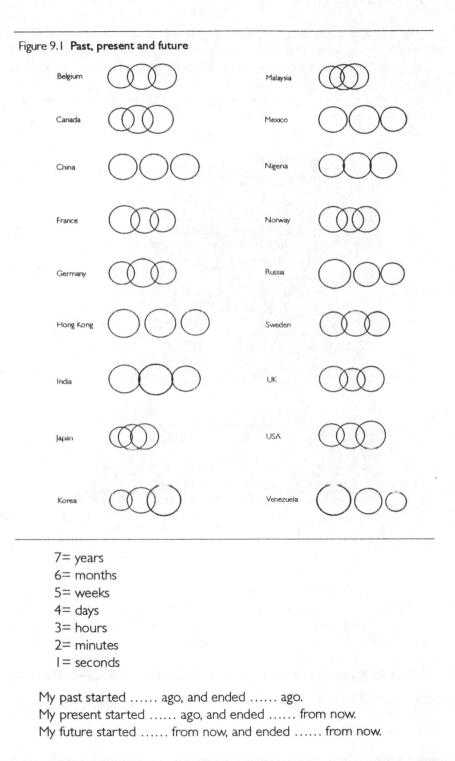

7= years
6= months
5= weeks
4= days
3= hours
2= minutes
1 = seconds

My past started ...... ago, and ended ...... ago.
My present started ...... ago, and ended ...... from now.
My future started ...... from now, and ended ...... from now.

We have taken the average of each of the six scores and calculated an average score per country, for which very significant differences can be found (see Figure 9.2). The longest horizon is found in Hong Kong and the shortest in the Philippines.

Figure 9.2 **Long- versus short-termism: time horizon**
7 = years, 1 = seconds

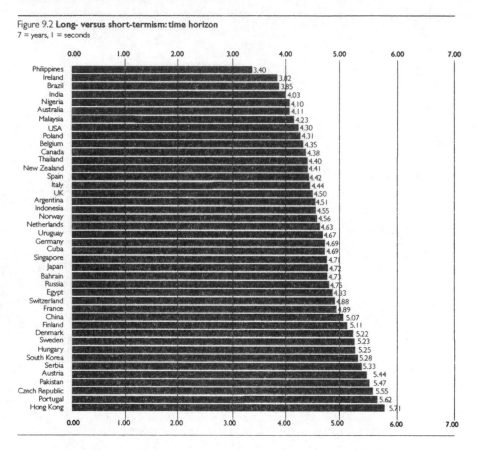

	Score
Philippines	3.40
Ireland	3.82
Brazil	3.85
India	4.03
Nigeria	4.10
Australia	4.11
Malaysia	4.23
USA	4.30
Poland	4.31
Belgium	4.35
Canada	4.38
Thailand	4.40
New Zealand	4.41
Spain	4.42
Italy	4.44
UK	4.50
Argentina	4.51
Indonesia	4.55
Norway	4.56
Netherlands	4.63
Uruguay	4.67
Germany	4.69
Cuba	4.69
Singapore	4.71
Japan	4.72
Bahrain	4.73
Russia	4.75
Egypt	4.83
Switzerland	4.88
France	4.89
China	5.07
Finland	5.11
Denmark	5.22
Sweden	5.23
Hungary	5.25
South Korea	5.28
Serbia	5.33
Austria	5.44
Pakistan	5.47
Czech Republic	5.55
Portugal	5.62
Hong Kong	5.71

Our time horizon significantly affects how we do business. It is obvious that the relatively long-term vision of the Japanese contrasts with the "quarterly thinking" of the Americans. This was shown in a striking way when the Japanese were trying to buy the operations of Yosemite National Park in California. The first thing they submitted was a 250-year business plan. Imagine the reactions of the Californian authorities: "Gee, that is 1000 quarterly reports."

The long Swedish horizon is explained by their long winters. There are only a few months in which you have to plan for the whole year.

However, there are some striking differences between long-term past orientation, the perceived extension of the present and a long-term view of the future. A selection of scores are presented in Figure 9.3 and 9.4.

The duration questionnaire also allowed us to check the overlap between time zones, i.e. the degree of synchronicity. Correlations found are high and significant compared to the overlap of the circles discussed earlier.

Figure 9.3 **Average time horizon: past**
7 = years, I = seconds

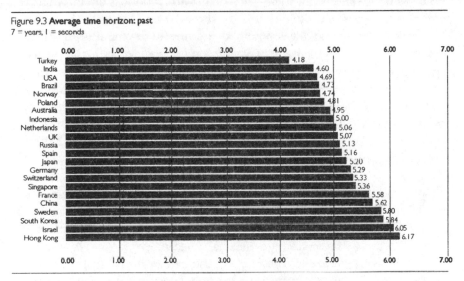

Figure 9.4 **Average time horizon: future**
7 = years, I = seconds

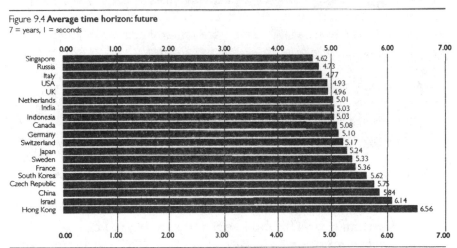

Time orientations and management

Business organisations are structured in accordance with how they conceive of time. Corporations have whole departments given over to planning, to scanning the environment for new trends, to getting production out faster, to shortening the time-to-market, that is, the time interval between a customer demanding a product and that product being designed, manufactured and delivered. Strategies, goals and objectives are all future-oriented. Joint ventures and partnerships are agreements about how the future should jointly be engaged. "Motivation" is about what we can give to a person now so that he or she will work better in the future. Progress, learning and development all assume an augmentation of powers over time, as does the habit of paying senior people more for the experience supposedly accumulated over time. When orientations to time differ within corporations spanning different cultures confusion can occur. Let us return to the sorrows of young Mr Johnson of MCC. A good lunch makes even the most fundamental intercultural misunderstandings seem like ripples on a lake. Johnson had asked that the group reconvene at 2.00pm precisely because they had a tight agenda for the afternoon.

At 1.50pm most participants returned to the meeting room. At 2.05pm Johnson started pacing restlessly up and down. Munoz and Gialli were still down the hall making telephone calls. They came in at 2.20pm. Johnson said, "Now, gentlemen, can we finally start the meeting." The Singaporean and African representatives looked puzzled. They thought the meeting had already started.

The first point on the agenda was the time intervals determining bonuses and merits. All except the American, Dutch and other north-west European representatives complained that these were far too frequent. To Johnson and his Dutch and Scandinavian colleagues the frequency was obviously right. "Rewards must closely follow the behaviour they are intended to reinforce, otherwise you lose the connection." The manager from Singapore said:

> "Possibly, but this go-for-the-quick-buck philosophy has been losing us customers. They don't like the pressure we put on at the end of the quarter. They want our representatives to serve them, not to have private agendas. We need to keep our customers long-term, not push them into buying so that one salesperson can beat a rival."

The American view of the future is that the **individual** can direct it by personal achievement and inner-directed effort. This is why Johnson, backed by Dutch and Scandinavian managers, is keen to give pay-for-performance at regular intervals. Yet because the individual achiever cannot do very much about the **distant** future – there are simply too many events that could occur – the USA's idea of the future is short-term, something controllable from the present. Hence the accusation of "going for the quick buck" and the great importance given to the next quarterly figures.

If the future is to be better it is by steadily increasing increments of sales and profits. There is no excuse, ever, for not doing better now, since success now causes greater successes in the future.

It is interesting to compare the French respondents with the Americans. In French culture the past looms far larger and is used as a context in which to understand the present. Past, present and future overlap synchronically so that the past informs the present, and both inform the future. The Dutch author was once visiting the futuristic La Défense in Paris. As my French colleague was delayed, I picked up a brochure at the reception desk. It was about the company's achievements during the 1980s. I read it with interest and, as my colleague was further delayed, I asked the receptionist for a more recent one. She handed me the same brochure I had just read. She said it had been printed only two months ago and was the most recent available. Future opportunities for this company were very apparently connected to the success of the past.

Human relations and orientations to time

Different orientations are also reflected in the quality of human bonds within an organisation, and between the corporation and its partners. Any lasting relationship combines past, present and future with ties of affection and memory. The relationship is its own justification and is enjoyed as a form of durable companionship extending both far back and far forward. Cultures which think synchronically about time are more we-oriented (communitarian) and usually more particularist in valuing people known to be special.

The cultures concerned with sequential time tend to see relationships as more instrumental. The separation between time intervals seems also to separate means from ends, so that higher pay is the means towards still higher performance and my customer's purchase is the means by which I will receive a higher bonus. The relationship is not entered into for its own sake but in order to enhance the income of each party and the profit of the organisation. The future looms large because present activity is but a means for realising it. The important result is in the (near-term) future. Gratification is postponed because it will soon be greater.

Whether relationships unmediated by calculation of future gain are not closer and more amenable to dialogue is of course a very interesting question. Given the sheer complexity of modern business and the mounting volume of information that must be communicated, the durable, synchronic relationship in which the past, present and future of the partners are bound together in co-evolution may be becoming a more effective way to manage. Certainly the idea that synchronic cultures are somehow "primitive" because their schedules are looser is not borne out. Sequential cultures where human resources are seen as a variation on physical plant, equipment and cash are more likely to have we-them relationships or, to quote Martin Buber, I-it.[7]

Time orientation and authority

In nations in which the past looms large and where time orientations overlap, status is more likely to be legitimised by ascription based on durable characteristics such as age, class, gender, ethnicity and professional qualification. Past qualifications, for example at *les grandes écoles*, explain present eminence and promising futures, all of which are closely connected and synchronised.

On the other hand when a person's career in Hollywood is "only as good as the last performance" the future is a sequence of episodes of relative success and failure. People will unburden themselves of relationships and dependencies not useful in the next stage of their career, just as the original American immigrants cut off their roots. The authority of the individual will depend upon the latest achievement; those on the up today may be gone tomorrow. Yet the authority of the individual can easily be challenged and assessed. What did they do in the most recent time interval? We find a reflection of this in the project-group organisation pioneered by NASA and popular in North America and north-western Europe. Different parts of the organisation are identified by and rewarded according to the fortunes in the future of the project being undertaken. Successes grow incrementally; failures are pruned back. Within the group those contributing most to the project are also rewarded accordingly.

Policies of promotion and assessment

Sequential or synchronic cultures, and those concerned more with the past or with the future, may also assess and promote differently. In sequential cultures the supervisor asks how the employee has performed over the previous interval. The more that employee can be held responsible for a rise or fall in fortune the better, and the supervisors will be tempted to minimise their own roles, or that of their relationship with the employee, since this does not help the employee to see his or her own recent achievement separated out as an increment of gain or loss. In more synchronic organisations, on the other hand, the employee may be favourably assessed and promoted for the positive relationship established with the supervisors, who see that relationship developing over time and accumulating knowledge and mutuality. The supervisors gladly acknowledge their role in making the subordinate's career, as in the master–apprentice system in Germany.

Managing change in a past-oriented culture

The English author was recently in Ethiopia with a Dutch manager who was terribly frustrated by his unsuccessful efforts to organise a Management of Change seminar with Ethiopian managers. They all kept harking back to a distant and wealthy era in Ethiopian civilisation and would not incorporate any developmental principles that were not based in this past. After a discussion with Ethiopian colleagues, we decided to study some Ethiopian history books, looking at them from the perspective of modern management. What had Ethiopia done right in that period to make its cities and trade so flourishing? The company also had a rich history within Ethiopia and these records too were studied. The Dutch manager posed the challenge anew. The future was now seen as a way of recreating some of the greatest glories of the past; suddenly, the Management of Change seminar had captured everyone's enthusiastic support.

This is not a remote case applicable only to Ethiopia. All change includes continuity, that is, staying the same **in some** respects so as to preserve your identity. Many cultures decline to change at the behest of western consultants unless the ways in which they will preserve their identity are made clear to them. Synchronic cultures carry their pasts through the present into the future and will refuse to consider changing unless convinced that their heritage is safe.

A large American telecommunications company introduced a technically superior product on the world market. It planned to focus specifically on increasing sales in Latin America, where it had not been very successful previously. The only serious competitor was a French company which had an inferior product, but whose after-sales support was reputedly superior.

The Americans went to great pains to prepare their first presentation in Mexico. "Judgment day" would begin with a video presentation of the company and its growth potential in the medium–long term. After this the vice-president of the group would personally give a presentation to the Mexican minister of communications. Also meticulously planned was the two-hour lunch. Knowing Mexican culture, they believed this was where the battle would be fought. The afternoon session was reserved for questions and answers. The company jet would then be ready to leave Mexico City in the last departure "slot". It was tight, efficient and appreciated; right?

Wrong; the Mexican team threw off the schedule right away by arriving one hour late. Then, just as the Americans were introducing the agenda for the day, the minister was called out of the room for an urgent phone call. He returned a while later to find that the meeting had gone on without him. The Mexicans were upset that the presentation had proceeded, that the after-sales service contract was separate from the sales contract and that the presentation focused only on the first two years after installation rather than the longer-term future together.

The French, on the other hand, prepared a loosely structured agenda. They determined some of the main goals to be attained by the end of the two-week visit. The timing, the where and the how were dependent on factors beyond their control, so they left them open. A long presentation on the historical background of the French state-owned company was prepared for the minister and his team. It had done business with Mexico's telephone system as early as 1930 and wanted to re-establish an historic partnership. As far as the French were concerned, the after-sales service, which extended indefinitely, was part of the contract. It was the French who received the order for a product known in the industry to be technologically less sophisticated.

What had gone wrong for the Americans? The main mistake was creating a tight, sequential agenda which was almost inevitably thrown off by Mexican officials who had deliberately built slack into their procedures and pursued agendas which were multiple and (to the Americans) distracting. The belief that the technologically superior product **should** win the contract is part of the original cultural bias in which each episode within a sequence is separated out. The Mexicans were only interested in the product as part of an on-going relationship, an issue which the synchronic French were also careful to stress. Similarly the Americans separated the after-sales service contract from the rest, presumably because it occurred at a later period. French and Mexican culture sees these time intervals as joined.

The French emphasis on the historic renewal of French-Mexican bonds was also effective with a culture that identifies with Spain and has deep European roots. American sequencing strikes synchronic cultures as aggressive, impatient and seeking to use customers as stepping-stones to personal advantage. If the relationship is genuinely to last, what is the hurry? Because the Mexicans did not agree that technological perfection was the key issue, they did not want to be on the receiving end of a detailed presentation timed to end just before the American departure. They wanted to experience a relationship they could partly control. In synchronic time, the demeanour of the American corporation during the presentation presaged its conduct in the future and the Mexicans did not like it.

However, the biggest advantage the French had was their willingness to spend two weeks dedicated to an agreement and leave it up to their hosts to use those two weeks in a flexible programme aimed at synchronising mutual efforts, rather than trying to agree a schedule in advance. For the French and Mexicans, what was important was **that** they get to the end,

not the particular path or sequence by which that end was reached. Similarly, the details of the equipment were less important to the Mexicans than the responsiveness of the supplier, since they could not know what problems might surface in the future. All they could really ask for, given this concern, was someone willing to alter a schedule to their convenience, and that the French showed they could do.

Moreover, the Americans had a narrower definition of how the negotiation should end. There should come a deadline when the Mexicans would say "yes". For the French, and synchronic cultures generally, there is no real "end"; the partnership continues. Instead of the **efficiency** of getting from A to B in the shortest possible time, there is the **effectiveness** of developing closer relationships long-term. The Americans also made one more serious mistake. Anticipating that the Mexicans would be late returning from lunch, as they had been several times, the Americans caucused for half an hour among themselves. This failed to show respect for the buyer. You "give them time" by waiting for them to join you. You do not use that time yourself in a way that makes you unavailable should they enter the room. A "readiness to synchronise" must be shown, as opposed to a mere delay in the sequence.

Planned sequences or planned convergence?

In sequentially organised cultures planning consists largely of forecasts, that is, of extending existing trend lines into the future and seeing this as "more of the same". Strategies consist of choosing desirable goals and then discovering by analysis the most logical and efficient means of attaining them. It is commonly believed that present and future are causally linked so that rewards now produce future achievements, which produce greater achievements, which produce greater rewards. Deadlines are important because they signal the end of one link in a causal chain and the beginning of the next and keep you "on schedule".

Planning varies considerably between sequential and synchronic cultures. In sequential planning it is vital to get all the means or stages right and completed on time. "In Britain," an Italian female researcher told me, "everything needs to be planned from start to finish. When the environment changes, everything needs to be recalculated from the start." For the more synchronic Italians the goals are what is most important, and the more paths you can devise to their realisation, the better you fare against unforeseen events that block one path or another.

The 1990 Mundialito (Football World Cup) in Italy was an interesting example of Italian organisation. The challenge was to complete the championships by a certain date on which the finals would be staged. To the dismay of the British and other north-west Europeans, the Italians would periodically rejig the entire programme to bring about this result. To the surprise of these other cultures, though, the Italians were able to pull it off. The 1992 Olympic games in Spain had many similarities with Italian planning. In Atlanta in 1996 it seemed that the sequential Americans had much more trouble in adapting to non-expected circumstances.

There is accumulating evidence that sequential planning processes work less well in turbulent environments. They are too brittle, too easily upset by unforeseen events. The fact that they tend to concentrate on the near future testifies to the vulnerability of long sequences. Synchronic plans tend to converge or "home in" upon predetermined targets, taking into consideration fusions and lateral connections **between** trends that sequential planning often overlooks.

A most interesting example of a shift by a major corporation to a synchronic style of planning was the adoption by the Shell International Petroleum Corporation of **scenario planning**. In this exercise, scenarios for three alternative futures are written as if the writer was a contemporary commentator explaining how business had reached that point. In other words, past, present and future are synchronised within the imagination, and three developments are traced from the past through the present into diverging futures and are written up as stories or narratives. For example, a scenario for 2003:

> "In retrospect it was inevitable that California would be the launching pad for the electric car. So polluted had the Los Angeles area grown, that the world's strictest emission standards, originating in the 1980s, led to partly electric cars in 1995 and the fully electric car eight years later. Slowly the pall began to lift. The final breakthrough was the '1,000 mile electric' with batteries that were rechargeable overnight. Was this, at last, the end of the internal combustion engine?"[8]

In this type of planning we see sequential and synchronic thinking combined. It proves possible to re-establish forecasts within the scenarios, so that each "synchronic scene" has a different sequence of events.

Once again we find that differences in cultural orientation are not truly alternatives but are capable of being used in conjunction. The wise crosscultural manager perceives **all** the ways preferred by different cultures. In scenario planning, sequencing and synchronising work together.

Reconciling the sequential and the synchronic

It is frequently suggested that synchronic people are difficult to do business with because they tend to ignore deadlines and are imprecise in appointments. Take the following example.

Jan Kuipers, a Dutch manager of a wholesale distributor of Italian *haute couture*, was getting very worried about late delivery times to his Dutch clients. The short Dutch summer did not allow delivery of high-priced goods a week late, which was the average delay from the Italian group. Kuipers had tried many ways of solving the problem but with no result. He tried to order early, but the Italians were not impressed. He tried to have them sign a contract so that they would take back the clothes unconditionally. Kuipers was now fighting the Italian transport firm because the fashion partner denied any responsibility. What would you advise him to do to solve the late delivery problem?

The Italian designers in Milan were giving a signal by delivering late. It meant that they had no respect for the relationship. Italians are able to deliver on time, but they prefer to follow the subjective time of the relationship than the objective time of the clock. While sequential Germans and Americans would follow the clock, Italians are very much concerned about delivering in time for you. Jan Kuipers went to Milan and befriended the head of logistics. He discovered that in the Italians' view the contract intended to ensure on-time delivery was a reason for delivering even later. The problem never recurred.

Test yourself

Consider the following problem:

> Some managers are arguing about the best ways of improving cycle time and getting products to market when they are needed. There were four possible views:
>
> 1 It is crucial to speed up operations and shorten time to market. Time is money. Enemies of tighter schedules and faster deliveries are too much talking and relating to each other.
> 2 It is crucial to speed up operations and shorten time to market. The faster jobs are done the sooner you can "pass the baton" to colleagues/customers in the relay race.
> 3 Just-in-time synchronisation of processes and with customers is the key to shorter cycle times. The more processes overlap and run simultaneously the more time saved.

4 Just-in-time synchronisation of processes and with customers is the key to shorter cycle times. Doing things faster results in exhaustion and rushed work.

Indicate with "1" the approach you believe would be favored by your closest colleagues at work, and with "2" the approach you believe would be their second choice.

Answers 1 and 4 show approval of respectively high-speed sequences and just-in-time synchronicity, but reject the opposite orientation. Answer 2 approves of high-speed sequences and connects it to synchronic processes. Answer 3 approves of just-in-time synchronicity connected to high-speed sequences.

Practical tips for doing business in past-, present- and future-oriented cultures

Recognising the differences

Past	Present	Future
1 Talk about history, origin of family, business and nation.	1 Activities and enjoyments of the moment are most important (not *mañana*).	1 Much talk of prospects, potentials, aspirations, future achievements.
2 Motivated to recreate a golden age.	2 Plans not objected to, but rarely executed.	2 Planning and strategising done enthusiastically.
3 Show respect for ancestors, predecessors and older people.	3 Show intense interest in present relationships, "here and now".	3 Show great interest in the youthful and in future potentials.
4 Everything viewed in the context of tradition or history.	4 Everything viewed in terms of its contemporary impact and style.	4 Present and past used, even exploited, for future advantage.

Tips for doing business

Past- and present-oriented	Future-oriented
1 Emphasise the history, tradition and rich cultural heritage of those you deal with as evidence of their great potential.	1 Emphasise the freedom, opportunity and limitless scope for that company and its people in the future.
2 Discover whether internal relationships will sanction the kind of changes you seek to encourage.	2 Discover what core competence or continuity the company intends to carry with it into the envisaged future.
3 Agree future meetings in principle but do not fix deadlines for completion.	3 Agree specific deadlines and do not expect work to be complete unless you do.
4 Do your homework on the history, traditions and past glories of the company; consider what re-enactments you might propose.	4 Do your homework on the future, the prospects and the technological potentials of the company; consider mounting a sizeable challenge.

Recognising time orientation

Sequential	Synchronic
1 Only do one activity at a time.	1 Do more than one activity at a time.
2 Time is seizable and measurable.	2 Appointments are approximate and subject to "giving time" to significant others.
3 Keep appointments strictly; schedule in advance and do not run late.	3 Schedules are generally subordinate to relationships.
4 Relationships are generally subordinate to schedule.	4 Strong preference for following where relationships lead.
5 Strong preference for following initial plans.	

When managing and being managed

Sequential	Synchronic
1 Employees feel rewarded and fulfilled by achieving planned future goals as in MBO.	1 Employees feel rewarded and fulfilled by achieving improved relationships with supervisors/customers.
2 Employees' most recent performance is the major issue, along with whether their commitments for the future can be relied upon.	2 Employees' whole history with the company and future potential is the context in which their current performance is viewed.
3 Plan the career of an employee jointly with him/her, stressing landmarks to be reached by certain times.	3 Discuss with employee his/her final aspirations in the context of the company; in what ways are these realisable?
4 The corporate ideal is the straight line and the most direct, efficient and rapid route to your objectives.	4 The corporate ideal is the interacting circle in which past experience, present opportunities and future possibilities cross-fertilise.

References
1 Kluckhohn, F. and Strodtbeck, F.L., *Variations in Value Orientations*, Greenwood Press, Westport, Conn., 1960.
2 Durkheim, E., *De la division du travail social*, 7th edition, 1960.
3 Hall, E.T., *The Silent Language*, Anchor Press, Doubleday, New York, 1959.
4 Carroll, R., *Cultural Misunderstandings; the French-American Experience*, University of Chicago Press, 1987.
5 Cottle, T., "The Circles Test; an investigation of perception of temporal relatedness and dominance", *Journal of Projective Technique and Personality Assessments*, No. 31, 1967, pages 58–71.
6 Cottle, T.J. and Howard, P., "Time perception by Indian adolescents", *Perceptual and Motor Skills*, No. 28, 1969, pages 599–612.
7 Buber, M. (Kauffman, W., ed.), *I and Thou*, Scribners' Books, New York, 1970.
8 Shell International, Group Planning Department, London (personal communication).

10

HOW WE RELATE TO NATURE

The last dimension of culture we shall consider in this book concerns the role people assign to their natural environment. This, like the other dimensions, is at the centre of human existence. Man has from the beginning been besieged by natural elements: wind, floods, fire, cold, earthquakes, famine, pests and predators. Survival itself has meant acting **against** and **with** the environment in ways to render it both less threatening and more sustaining. Constant action was originally an inescapable necessity.

Man's economic development can be viewed as a gradual strengthening of his devices to keep nature at bay. In the course of human existence there has been a shift from a preponderant fear that nature would overwhelm human existence to the opposite fear that human existence may overwhelm and degrade nature, so that, for example, a genetic storehouse of incredible richness in the Amazon rain forest may be bulldozed to oblivion before we have even discovered it.

Controlling nature, or letting it take its course

Societies which conduct business have developed two major orientations towards nature. They either believe that they can and should **control** nature by imposing their will upon it, as in the ancient biblical injunction "multiply and subdue the earth"; or they believe that man is part of nature and must **go along** with its laws, directions and forces. The first of these orientations we shall describe as **inner-directed**. This kind of culture tends to identify with mechanisms; that is, the organisation is conceived of as a machine that obeys the will of its operators. The second, or **outer-directed**, tends to see an organisation as itself a product of nature, owing its development to the nutrients in its environment and to a favourable ecological balance.

The American psychologist, J.B. Rotter, working in the 1960s, developed a scale designed to measure whether people had an **internal locus of control**, typical of more successful Americans, or an **external locus**

of control, typical of relatively less successful Americans, disadvantaged by their circumstances or shaped by the competitive efforts of their rivals.[1] The questions he devised we used to assess our 30,000 managers' relationship with natural events, and the answers suggest that there are some very significant differences here between geographical areas. These questions all take the form of alternatives; managers were asked to select the statement they believed most reflected reality. The first of these pairs is as follows.

A It is worthwhile trying to control important natural forces, like the weather.

B Nature should take its course and we just have to accept it the way it comes and do the best we can.

Figure 10.1 shows the percentage of respondents who chose A, that is, the inner directors. No country produces a totally internalised reaction to this statement; the highest score is only 68%, but we see considerable variations between countries and, again, no marked pattern by continent. Only 19% of Japanese believe it is worth trying to control the weather, and as few as 22% of Chinese; only 21% of Swedes but 36% of the British. The British, Germans and Americans are above the middle of the range, but by no means among the top scorers. If the alternatives are made to appear more personally related, however, we get a different result. Figure 10.2 shows the percentage of respondents who chose A when asked to choose between the following.

A What happens to me is my own doing.

B Sometimes I feel that I do not have enough control over the directions my life is taking.

On this basis a number of countries appear almost completely internalised; in the USA, for instance, 82% of managers believe they control their own destinies, as do 76% of the French. Most European countries score high, in fact, though not the Russians, on whom 45 years of Communism may have had some effect. Similarly the Chinese now rank much lower than the Japanese, although in Japan as in Singapore managers are far less likely to believe in internal control than they are in North America or Europe.

Control and success

The extremes of possible relationships between man and nature are perhaps best instanced by contrasting the ancient Greeks with twentieth-

Figure 10.1 **Controlling nature**
Percentage of respondents who believe it is worth trying

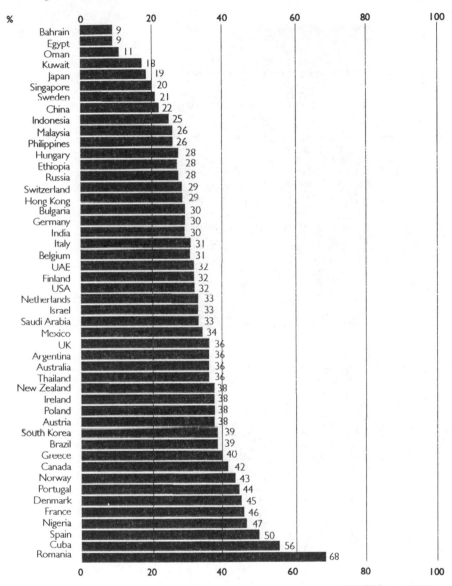

Country	%
Bahrain	9
Egypt	9
Oman	11
Kuwait	18
Japan	19
Singapore	20
Sweden	21
China	22
Indonesia	25
Malaysia	26
Philippines	26
Hungary	28
Ethiopia	28
Russia	28
Switzerland	29
Hong Kong	29
Bulgaria	30
Germany	30
India	30
Italy	31
Belgium	31
UAE	32
Finland	32
USA	32
Netherlands	33
Israel	33
Saudi Arabia	33
Mexico	34
UK	36
Argentina	36
Australia	36
Thailand	36
New Zealand	38
Ireland	38
Poland	38
Austria	38
South Korea	39
Brazil	39
Greece	40
Canada	42
Norway	43
Portugal	44
Denmark	45
France	46
Nigeria	47
Spain	50
Cuba	56
Romania	68

century Americans. For the Greeks the world was ruled by natural god-like forces: beauty (Aphrodite), truth (Apollo), justice (Athena), passion (Diony-sus). These forces would contend for human allegiance and were often in conflict, leading to tragedy. Virtue was to achieve *harmonia*, harmony

Figure 10.2 **The captains of their fate**
Percentage of respondents who believe what happens to them is their own doing

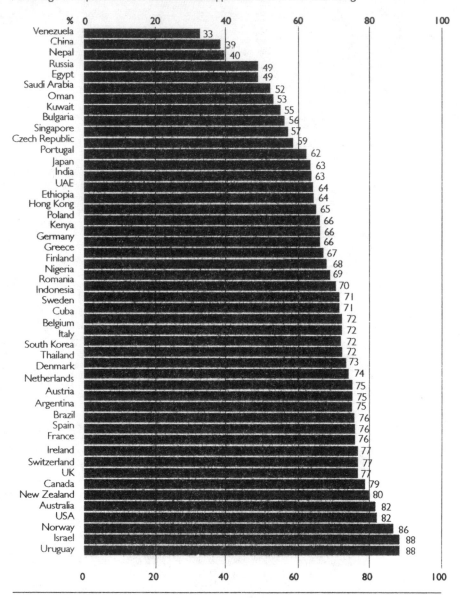

among the natural forces acting through you. Those who wanted their own will to triumph, like Oedipus or Jason, were frequently confounded in a struggle with their fates. The post-Industrial Revolution society, on the other hand, has made heroes of entrepreneurs, whose struggles to tame nature are not expected to end in tragedy. This is especially the American view, shaped by the experience of discovering a new continent of immense size and small indigenous population and turning a wilderness into a new nation. Success is identified with control over outside circumstances.

However, internal versus external loci of control do not necessarily distinguish the successful from the less successful in non-American cultures. There are ways of adapting to external influences which can prove economically effective. To accept direction from customers, market forces or new technologies **can be more advantageous than opposing these with your own preferences**. The "obvious" advantages (to Americans) of being inner-directed may not be obvious at all to managers in Japan or Singapore, and will be at least less obvious in Italy, Sweden or the Netherlands, for example. Outer-directed need not mean God-directed or fate-directed; it may mean directed by the knowledge revolution or by the looming pollution crisis, or by a joint venture partner. The ideal is to fit yourself advantageously to an external force.

In the original American concept of internal and external sources of control, the implication is that the outer-directed person is offering an excuse for failure rather than a new wisdom. In other nations it is not seen as personal weakness to acknowledge the strength of external forces or the arbitrariness of events.

In outer-directed behaviour the reference point for actors lies outside themselves. A good example is the history of the Sony Walkman, already described in Chapter 1. In an interview in 1982, Akio Morita of Sony explained that he conceived of the notion of the Walkman while he was searching for a way to enjoy music without disturbing others. This is in sharp contrast to the normal motivation for using a Walkman in northwest Europe and North America, where most users do not want to be disturbed by other people.

The preponderant inner-directedness of North America and parts of western Europe may help to explain why we have to go out of our way to teach "customer orientation" and "scanning the business environment". To outer-directed cultures, like Japan and Singapore, this comes so naturally that they do not need to teach it. It is also noteworthy that outer-directedness does **not** preclude rivalry or competition but rather can help to give it form and style. To be directed by a customer or by the force of an opponent, as in Indo (Japanese wrestling) and Judo, is not to lack combativeness but to use another's powers in a more effective combination or harmony (*wa*). The word *do* in Judo, Indo, Kendo and Bushido means "way of". You follow the way of the sword (Kendo) or the warrior (Bushido), their practices and disciplines, until they become part of your nature. You may, as a result, be a more formidable competitor, not less. Like a surf-rider you respond to the waves and keep your balance where others lose theirs.

In contrast to many eastern sports, in which the opponent's force is harnessed to your own, western sports like American football or baseball idealise the zero-sum game, the clash of opposites, the rivalry of inner-directed wills, one-on-one. Only "if you can't beat 'em" should you "join 'em". Even negotiations are "won" or "lost" depending on how much of what you originally wanted was gained, while compromise reduces the moral stature of all concerned.

Our western contention that Asians "steal our ideas" is also shaped by our proprietary notions about what comes from **inside** of us and is therefore "ours". Asians may regard western technologies as part of the environment, like fruit on a tree, which wise people pick and incorporate into themselves. Moreover concepts such as *kaizen*, refinement, have very high cultural prestige. To take something from the external environment and then refine or improve it is not "copying" but celebrating that environment, letting the finest forces shape your character. Even when the forces are violent and humiliating, such as devastation, surrender and occupation by Americans, the Japanese prove masters at adapting to external circumstances and emerging on top. As they like to say, "a crisis is an opportunity".

Inner-directed mechanism: the Renaissance ideal
The West is heavily influenced by Copernican and Newtonian views of the universe as a vast perpetual motion machine which God wound up and left for His faithful to discover. To discover the laws of this universe, laws of time and motion, was to worship its creator. To understand the laws of the mechanism it was necessary to predict and control the operation of nature's machinery, that is, to internalise natural law and then show that nature obeyed you. Against this background to be inner-directed has become proof of scientific veracity. We hypothesise and deduce, and the principle is correct if the predicted result follows. Enlightened man is the master mechanic, the driver with his hand on the throttle.

While the early physicists left the description of man to religious authorities, this division of labour broke down in the seventeenth and eighteenth centuries. Man, too, became a machine, using reason to drive a somewhat reluctant body to obey rational dictates. According to Jacques Ellul the earlier belief in magic was now replaced by **technique**, applied not simply to external nature but to man's head and body. "Technique," writes Ellul, "is the translation into action of man's concern to master things by means of reason, to account for what is subconscious, make quantitative what is qualitative, make clear and precise the outlines of nature, take hold of chaos, and order it."[2]

After the Renaissance, then, nature became objectified so that manipulation could be more easily demonstrated over passive entities. Quantification and measurement became central to science, including social science.

The modern view of nature: the cybernetic cosmology

While for the Greeks nature was a living organism and for the Renaissance it was a machine potentially controllable by human reason, in modern system-dynamics or cybernetics both these views are transcended into a more inclusive concept of a living system which both nurtures the individual and can be developed by individuals dependent upon that system.[3] There is a shift from trying to seize control **over** nature to identifying with its ecological self-regulation and natural balance. The manager **intervenes** but is not the **cause** of what occurs; the systems of organisations and markets have their own momentum which we can influence but not drive. As the world fills up with economic actors and forces, we are simultaneously more influenced by external forces, yet more determined to create our own space among these.

Figure 10.3 summarises these changing views.

Figure 10.3 **Changing views of nature**

Era	Kind of nature	Productive functions	Philosophies	Focus of control
Primitive	organic nature	arts: to form	natural; natural world	external control
Renaissance	mechanistic nature	techniques: to transform	mechanical; technical world	internal control
Modern	cybernetic nature	applied sciences: to develop	scientific; social world	reconciliation of internal and external control

How important is a culture's orientation to nature?

Orientations to nature have much to do with how we conduct our day-to-day lives and manage businesses. Cultures may seek to master nature, accept and be subjugated by it, or live in the most effective harmony with it. Nature is both controllable by man and liable to show sudden reversals of relative strength, becoming man's master, not slave. Neither situation is very stable nor very desirable, since a subjugated nature may fail to sustain man on earth.

A relationship closely analogous to man and nature is that of organisation and markets. A product may succeed not simply because we will it to, or because the special features designed into it delight customers. It may succeed for reasons **other than those which come from inside of us**, reasons which have to do with the way **other** people in the environment think rather than we ourselves. Are we then willing to take direction from customers, where this is not our original direction? Are we willing to change our minds when it becomes clear that customers' preferences are different from our own?

One powerful logic of outer-directedness is the theory of evolution. According to evolutionary biologists, it is the environment which decides which creatures fit and which do not, so by extension markets decide, not managers. The business world does not see the survival of the fittest, driven by mechanisms determined to outfight each other, but the survival of those best able to form a nurturant relationship with external niches and conditions. It may be for this reason that some outer-directed cultures are among the world's better economic performers. While the belief that the environment is all-powerful in deciding the future can lead to fatalism or resignation, the belief that we are all responsible can lead to scapegoating, blaming-the-victim and a lack of compassion for those who have suffered misfortune.

An important aspect of inner-directedness is the notion of business **strategy**, that is a plan designed in advance to wrest competitive advantage from other corporations. The metaphor comes from the military sphere and it is clear that either the organisation prevails in its strategic intention or it is beaten by its environment. The seeming lack of interest in strategy per se by the Japanese and similar outer-directed cultures has been noted, and the whole "militaristic" concept of strategy criticised, by Henry Mintzberg. Mintzberg points out that, in any organisation, those interfacing with customers have **already devised strategies for coping with day-to-day problems**.[4] The job of top management, therefore, is to take these emergent strategies and give recognition, status and formal sanction to those which have proved most valuable. This is an outer-directed process for adopting strategies **already initiated** at the organisation's grassroots and is a further example of the need to let the environment shape **you**.

Managing between different orientations to nature

Paradoxically, western and inner-directed managers trying to impose uniform procedures and methods on foreign and outer-directed cultures often "succeed" better than they expect, just because at least some of those cultures are accustomed to being heavily influenced from external sources and taking their cue from the environment. But it is a mistake to assume that **accepting** guidance from outside is the same as internalising it or using it successfully. Some outer-directed cultures do not like to debate or confront, but this does not mean that the directive is appropriate to their culture. The source of authority is seen as "natural" and will quickly be dissipated if the manager behaves in "unnatural" ways, for example by imposing his or her will for its own sake rather than because of a natural endowment of wisdom to sustain and nurture the organism. Other-directed cultures often regard nature as **benign**. If, therefore, you behave in ways interpreted as hostile, your "natural powers" will be forfeit.

At a Gabon subsidiary of a French oil company, the Dutch author discovered that a change management programme initiated by headquarters was failing miserably. The French managers, when interviewed, could not really explain what was going on. The Gabonese seemed to agree completely with the drafted mission statement. They even accepted the operational steps that had been discussed and planned at length. But when the plan had to be put into action, nothing happened. The employees behaved precisely as before. After careful inquiry it turned out that the Gabonese did indeed endorse the change but did not believe that it was for them as individuals to direct its implementation. The signal had to come from their French superiors who alone had the natural authority to command action. When no command came, no action was taken. The idea that self-directed change would emerge from reasoned principles was **not** culturally shared.

It was the same with the pay-for-performance programme initiated by MCC. Such a programme assumes that each employee can behave in ways that increase the sales of computers, that he or she can personally induce greater effort and hence greater sales. This assumption was questioned by an Asian manager.

Mr Djawa from Indonesia raised two objections to Mr Johnson.

> "Pay-for-performance does not work in our sales territories. It leads to customers being overloaded with products they never wanted and do not need. Furthermore, when things are not going well for our people, it is a mistake to hurry them or blame them. There are good times and bad times. Paying them for performance does not change inevitable trends."

This did not impress Johnson and his western colleagues. "We want to develop something at HQ that will motivate everyone. Are you saying that link-ing reward to success has no influence at all? Surely you must agree there is some connection." Mr Djawa said:

> "It certainly has effects, but these tend to be swamped by economic booms and busts. Moreover the customer needs to be assisted and protected from these fluctuations. It is not wise to push customers into buying more than they should. We need to ride out bad times together, and then take joint advantage of good times."

Many of Mr Djawa's eastern and Latin colleagues concurred. Mr Johnson was exasperated. "Why don't some of you suggest a method that **does** work?"

Here the Indonesians, seeing themselves as relatively more controlled by external forces, seek to join with customers and each other to "ride out the inevitable waves". They can be motivated, but in directions consistent with their culture, and that is to make skilful adjustments to the ups and downs which they experience as "natural" and not caused by their own greater or lesser determination to prosper. They seem to regard the turbulence of their environment as a sufficient challenge to the members of their organisation, without needing to attribute blame to those caught in a downturn, or reward those caught in an upturn. To do either would sap group morale by adding to the arbitrariness of events and tempt sales personnel to put their own advantage ahead of the customers'.

In contrast, the mechanistic view of man sees the salesperson cutting through the waves like a ship heading for its own planned destination and not being diverted from its path by poor weather. The test of the good engineer or MBA is to do things right the first time and have their judgment vindicated by results. The good company promises "to put you in the driver's seat". Ideal mechanisms obey the will of their operators and enable them to overcome natural obstacles to achieve personal goals.

Is modern management a battle between private agendas?

One problem with the inner-directed person seeking mastery over nature is that **everyone else** may come to stand for "nature". We all want power, but can only achieve it if others are viewed as means to our ends. By definition we cannot **all** direct the environment from within ourselves, since we ourselves constitute great parts of that environment. The invitation to others to "participate" is largely vitiated if, in fact, you are trying to steer them towards a conclusion you arrived at before the discussion began. Yet the relentlessly inner-directed manager has no other option. He or she is obliged to define social relationships objectively, as if moving pieces on a chess board. This is what Chris Argyris calls "Model I behaviour", behaviour designed to motivate the employee into doing what the manager formulated earlier.[5] Mr Johnson, too, uses motivation in this sense, a method of persuading salespeople to sell more in any or all circumstances and regardless of what they say or want, or what their cultures believe in.

The HAY method of evaluation of personnel is similarly inner-directed in identifying managers with their function. In this system it is not the employee that is being evaluated, but the efficiency with which he or she completes a task assumed to be directed from within their supervisor, within their organisation. It is this that gives authority its reason and legitimacy. Suppose the company exists to turn natural raw materials into products. It requires these functions to be fulfilled by a division of labour. It hires people who agree to fill these functions. They are directed by a chief executive officer who personifies the organisation's inner-directed purpose. Persons trying to fulfil these functions are then paid according to the complexity and difficulty of the function and how well they have discharged it and how they used their own (inner-directed) judgment. This is all logical, neat and obvious, yet it treats physical and social environments as if they were objects and is not the way large parts of the world economy think. It is also blind to some of the most obvious social facts, that during a conversation both parties may change their minds and transform their joint thought processes into something new and better.

Reconciling internal and external control

We all make mistakes in life. Some three weeks ago the Dutch author asked his wife if he could borrow her car – a Mitsubishi Space Wagon – to pick up some loudspeakers in town. I was driving and had to stop for a pedestrian crossing. Just after coming to a stop I heard a noise indicating that I had been hit by a car from behind. I stepped out and saw that the length of our impressive Japanese car had diminished by at least 20%. Psychologically I thought the whole back of the car had disappeared in the crash. Pulling away from my car was a Volvo 200 series, better known as "the tank". Not a scratch could I observe on this vehicle even when I examined it closely. The driver emerged with one hand covering a severe cut on his head. He apologised almost routinely: "There is not much left of your car, sir," he said, "but are you OK?" I was fine, because I had hardly felt the collision.

The externally controlled Japanese evidently apply martial arts to safety. Japanese cars are designed to take the energy out of their opponent to their advantage. The Volvo and BMWs of this world seem to operate like an American football player. If I am stronger than you I'll win and be safe. The end result, however, was that the driver of the Japanese car did not feel the collision while the Volvo driver took it all.

The newest safety designs are built to reconcile flexibility and strength. The similarity with the Dutch poldering system is striking. Dikes are built to stop the water with great strength. If the pressure becomes too great doors are opened to relieve the pressure. In turn the next diking system takes the second overflow.

And doesn't your organisation struggle to achieve a balance between technology push and market pull? Intuitively we know that if we push the technology to its extreme we might end up in the ultimate niche market, best defined as that part of the market with no clients. But what if we just follow what clients desire? We might not deliver fast enough and be at their mercy. The most effective organisations are those which are better at connecting the push of the technology to the pull of the market. Isn't it curious that the Americans are superior in both marketing techniques and in developing innovative products? But the Japanese wiped out the US consumer electronics industry. The Japanese seem to be very good at connecting what has been developed elsewhere. They also apply martial arts to essential economic laws.

Figure 10.4 shows that too much inner directedness can lead to the lack of a market. Conversely an overly developed customer focus risks leaving the organisation at the mercy of market forces. Inner and outer directedness have to be reconciled.

Test yourself

Several senior strategists were discussing whether strategy should be devised at the top of the corporation and "cascaded down" to be implemented locally, or emerge from the grassroots and successful interfaces with customers. The following views were expressed:

1   No one dealing with customers is without a strategy of sorts. Our task is to find out which of these strategies work, which don't and why. Devising our own strategy in the abstract and imposing it downwards only spreads confusion.
2   No one dealing with customers is without a strategy of sorts. Our task is to find out which of these strategies work and then create a master strategy from proven successful initiatives by commending and combining the best.

Figure 10.4 **Reconciling internal and external control**

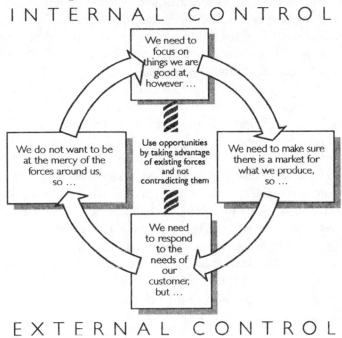

INTERNAL CONTROL

We need to focus on things we are good at, however …

We do not want to be at the mercy of the forces around us, so …

Use opportunities by taking advantage of existing forces and not contradicting them

We need to make sure there is a market for what we produce, so …

We need to respond to the needs of our customer, but …

EXTERNAL CONTROL

3 To be a leader is to be the chief devisor of strategy. Using all the experience, information and intelligence we can mobilise, we devise an innovative strategy and cascade it down to be vigorously implemented.

4 To be a leader is to be the chief devisor of strategy. Using all the experience, information and intelligence we can mobilise, we create a broad thrust, leaving it to subordinates to fit these to customer needs.

Indicate with "1" the approach you believe would be favoured by your closest colleagues at work, and with "2" the approach you believe would be their second choice.

Answer 1 affirms an outer-directed strategy and rejects inner direction, while answer 3 represents the opposite. Answer 2 affirms a connection between an outer-directed strategy and an inner-directed strategy, while answer 4 affirms the opposite connection.

SUMMARY

Cultures vary in their approaches to the given environment, between belief that it can be controlled by the individual and belief that the individual must respond to external circumstances. We should not, however, make the error of assuming that inner-direction and outer-direction are exclusive options. All cultures necessarily take **some** notice of what is inside or outside. To fail to do so would lead inner-directed cultures into a headlong rush to disaster, while outer-directed cultures would try to please everyone and dissipate their energies by over-compliance.

Inner-directed managers are never happier than when they have won over other people to their own way of thinking. This is the ideal they strive for, but it is one which may be deemed aggressive and uncouth in outer-directed cultures. Leaders in these stress how much they have learnt from their mistakes and from other's objections or criticisms. One reason staff suggestions enrich several Asian organisations and participation is so high is because listening rather than declaiming is seen as the more admirable trait. Such cultures do not clash openly. To negate what someone else is saying is to ride roughshod over nature. The alternative is to take the proposal on board and alter its import subsequently if it remains unpopular.

The word "feedback" is an interesting one in western management jargon. It recognises the need to correct periodically an ongoing thrust or function. But **rarely is feedback considered as important as that original direction**. Indeed feedback is the means by which the original direction is **maintained**.

To participate fully in an outer-directed culture, inner-directed managers must accept that feedback can alter the whole direction of the organisation. They must listen to the customer and aim to fill their need as opposed to win their allegiance.

Major change can come from both outside and inside. Once again we see that culture is about where a circle "starts" or where a manager conceives of change originating. To conceive of the organisation as an open system operating within a larger system allows both inner-directed and outer-directed orientations to develop.

Practical tips for doing business in internal- and external-oriented cultures

Recognising the differences

Internal control	External control
1 Often dominating attitude bordering on aggressiveness towards environment.	1 Often flexible attitude, willing to compromise and keep the peace.
2 Conflict and resistance means that you have convictions.	2 Harmony and responsiveness, that is, sensibility.
3 Focus is on self, function, own group and own organisation.	3 Focus is on "other", that is customer, partner, colleague.
4 Discomfort when environment seems "out of control" or changeable.	4 Comfort with waves, shifts, cycles if these are "natural".

Tips for doing business with:

Internally controlled (for externals)	Externally controlled (for internals)
1 Playing "hard ball" is legitimate to test the resilience of an opponent.	1 Softness, persistence, politeness and long, long patience will get rewards.
2 It is most important to "win your objective".	2 It is most important to "maintain your relationship".
3 Win some, lose some.	3 Win together, lose apart.

When managing and being managed

Internally controlled	Externally controlled
1 Get agreement on and ownership of clear objectives.	1 Achieve congruence among various people's goals.
2 Make sure that tangible goals are clearly linked to tangible rewards.	2 Try to reinforce the current directions and facilitate the work of employees.
3 Discuss disagreements and conflicts openly; these show that everyone is determined.	3 Give people time and opportunities to work quietly through conflicts; these are distressing.
4 Management-by-objectives works if everyone is genuinely committed to directing themselves towards shared objectives and if these persist.	4 Management-by-environments works if everyone is genuinely committed to adapting themselves to fit external demands as these shift.

References

1 Rotter, J.B., *Generalised Expectations for Internal versus External Control of Reinforcement*, Psychological Monograph 609, 1966, pages 1–28. (Some items have been designed by CIBS.)

2 Ellul, J., *The Technological Society*, Vintage, New York, 1964.

3 Moscovici, S., *Essai sur l'histoire humaine de la nature*, Flammarion, Paris, 1977.

4 Mintzberg, H., *The Structure of Organisations*, Prentice-Hall, Englewood Cliffs, New Jersey, 1979.

5 Argyris, C., *Strategy Change and Defensive Routines*, Pitman, London, 1985.

11
NATIONAL CULTURES AND CORPORATE CULTURE

When people set up an organisation they will typically borrow from models or ideals that are familiar to them. The organisation, as we explored in Chapter 2, is a subjective construct and its employees will give meaning to their environment based on their own particular cultural programming. The organisation is like something else they have experienced. It may be deemed to resemble a family, or an impersonal system designed to achieve targets. It may be likened to a vessel which is travelling somewhere, or a missile homing in on customers and strategic objectives. Cultural preferences operating across the dimensions described in the previous chapters influence the models people give to organisations and the meanings they attribute to them.

This chapter explores four types of corporate culture and shows how differences between national cultures help determine the type of corporate culture "chosen". Employees have a shared perception of the organisation, and what they believe has real consequences for the corporate culture that develops.

Different corporate cultures

Organisational culture is shaped not only by technologies and markets, but by the cultural preferences of leaders and employees. Some international companies have European, Asian, American or Middle Eastern subsidiaries which would be unrecognisable as the same company save for their logo and reporting procedures. Often these are fundamentally different in the logic of their structure and the meanings they bring to shared activity.

Three aspects of organisational structure are especially important in determining corporate culture.

1 The general relationship between employees and their organisation.
2 The vertical or hierarchical system of authority defining superiors and subordinates.
3 The general views of employees about the organisation's destiny, purpose and goals and their places in this.

Thus far we have distinguished cultures along single dimensions; universalism–particularism, for example, and individualism–communitarianism. In looking at organisations we need to think in two dimensions, generating four quadrants. The dimensions we use to distinguish different corporate cultures are **equality-hierarchy** and **orientation to the person-orientation to the task**.

This enables us to define four types of corporate culture, which vary considerably in how they think and learn, how they change and how they motivate, reward and resolve conflicts. This is a valuable way to analyse organisations, but it does have the risk of caricaturisation. We tend to believe or wish that all foreigners will fit the stereotypes we have of them. Hence in our very recognition of "types" there is a temptation to oversimplify what is really quite complex.

The four types can be described as follows.

1 The family
2 The Eiffel Tower
3 The guided missile
4 The incubator

These four metaphors illustrate the relationship of employees to their notion of the organisation. Figure 11.1 summarises the images these organisations project.

Each of these types of corporate culture are "ideal types". In practice the types are mixed or overlaid with one culture dominating. This separation, though, is useful for exploring the basis of each type in terms of how employees learn, change, resolve conflicts, reward, motivate and so on. Why, for example, do norms and procedures which seem to work so well in one culture lose their effectiveness in another?

The family culture

I use the metaphor of family for the culture which is at the same time **personal**, with close face-to-face relationships, but also **hierarchical**, in the sense that the "father" of a family has experience and authority greatly exceeding those of his "children", especially where these are young. The result is a **power-oriented** corporate culture in which the leader is regarded as a caring father who knows better than his subordinates what should be done and what is good for them. Rather than being threatening, this type of power is essentially intimate and (hopefully) benign. The work of the corporation in this type of culture is usually carried forward in an

Figure 11.1 **Corporate images**

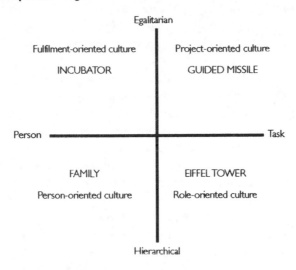

atmosphere that in many respects mimics the home.

The Japanese recreate within the corporation aspects of the traditional family. The major business virtue is *amae*, a kind of love between persons of differing rank, with indulgence shown to the younger and respect reciprocated to the elder. The idea is always to do **more** than a contract or agreement obliges you to. The idealised relationship is *sempai-kokai*, that between an older and younger brother. Promotion by age means that the older person will typically be in charge. The relationship to the corporation is long-term and devoted.

A large part of the reason for working, performing well and resolving conflict in this corporate culture is the pleasure derived from such relationships. To please your superior (or elder brother) is a reward in itself. While this affection may or may not be visible to outsiders (the Japanese, for example, are very restrained emotionally) it is nevertheless **there**, whether subdued in a Japanese-style, or conveyed unmistakably by voice, face and bodily gesture, Italian-style. The leader of the family-style culture weaves the pattern, sets the tone, models the appropriate posture for the corporation and expects subordinates to be "on the same wavelength", knowing intuitively what is required; conversely, the leader may empathise with the subordinates.

At its best the power-oriented family culture exercises power **through** its members acting with one accord. Power is not necessarily **over** them, although it may be. The main sanction is loss of affection and place in the family. Pressure is moral and social rather than financial or legal. Many corporations with family-style cultures are from nations which industrialised late: Greece, Italy, Japan, Singapore, South Korea, Spain. Where the transition from feudalism to industrialism was rapid, many feudal traditions remain.

Family-style corporate cultures tend to be **high context** (see Chapter 7), a term which refers to the sheer amount of information and cultural content **taken for granted** by members. The more in-jokes there are, the more family stories, traditions, customs and associations, the higher the context and the harder it is for outsiders to feel that they belong or to know how to behave appropriately. Such cultures exclude strangers without necessarily wishing to do so and communicate in codes which only members understand.

Relationships tend to be **diffuse** (see Chapter 7). The "father" or "elder brother" is influential in **all** situations, whether they have knowledge of the problem or not, whether an event occurs at work, in the canteen or on the way home, and even if someone else present is better qualified. The general happiness and welfare of all employees is regarded as the concern of the family-type corporation, which worries about their housing, the size of their families and whether their wages are sufficient for them to live well. The corporation may assist in these areas.

Power and differential status are seen as "natural", a characteristic of the leaders themselves and not related to the tasks they succeed or fail in doing, any more than a parent ceases to be a parent by neglecting certain duties. Above the power of the leader may be that of the state, the political system, the society or God. Power is **political** in the sense of being broadly ordained by authorities, rather than originating in roles to be filled or tasks to be performed. This does not mean that those in power are unskilled or cannot do their jobs; it means that for such an organisation to perform well the requisite knowledge and skills must be brought **to** the power centres, thereby justifying the existing structure. Take the following testimony by a British manager.

"In Italy I was introduced to my counterpart, the head of applications engineering. I asked him about his organisation, his department and the kind of work they were engaged in. Within minutes he had given me a dozen names and his personal estimate of their political influence, their proximity to power and their tastes, preferences and opinions. He said almost nothing about either their knowledge, their skills or their performance. As far as I could tell, they had no specific functions, or if they had my informant was ignorant of them. I was amazed. There seemed to be no conception of the tasks that had to be done or their challenge and complexity."

It did not occur to the British manager that this "family model" is capable of processing complexity without necessarily seeing itself as a functional instrument to this end. The authority in the family model is unchallengeable in the sense that it is not seen to depend on tasks performed but on status ascribed. A major issue becomes that of getting the top people to notice, comprehend and act. If older people have more authority, then they must be briefed thoroughly and supported loyally in order to fulfil the status attributed to them. The **culture works to justify its own initial suppositions**.

In our own research, we tested to what extent managers from different cultures saw their leaders "as a kind of father" or to what extent they thought the leader "got the job done". The results are shown in Figure 11.2, where we see one of the widest ranges of national variances of response, and a marked grouping of Asian countries towards the top of the chart. Another question asked of managers in the process of this research was to think of the company they work for in terms of a triangle, and to pick the one on the diagram (Figure 11.3) which best represents it. The steepest triangle scores five points and so on down to one.

The scores of nations where the leader is seen as a father (Figure 11.2) correlate closely with the steepness of the triangles in Figure 11.3. The familial cultures of Turkey, Venezuela and several Asian countries have the steepest hierarchies; the image combines attachment to subordination with relative permanence of employment. Nearly all of these are also to be found in the top third of Figure 11.2.

Family cultures at their least effective drain the energies and loyalties of subordinates to buoy up the leader, who literally floats on seas of adoration. Leaders get their sense of power and confidence **from** their followers, their charisma fuelled by credulity and by seemingly childlike faith. Yet skilful leaders of such cultures can also catalyse and multiply energies and appeal to the deepest feelings and aspirations of their subordinates. They avoid the depersonalisation of management by objectives; management by subjectives works better. They resemble the leaders of movements aiming to emancipate, reform, reclaim and enlighten both their members and society, like the American civil rights movement; such movements also are essentially family-type structures, resocialising members in new forms of conduct.

Family cultures have difficulty with project group organisation or matrix-type authority structures, since here authority is divided. Your function has one boss and your project another, so how can you give undi-

Figure 11.2 What makes a good manager?

Percentage of respondents opting to be left alone to get the job done

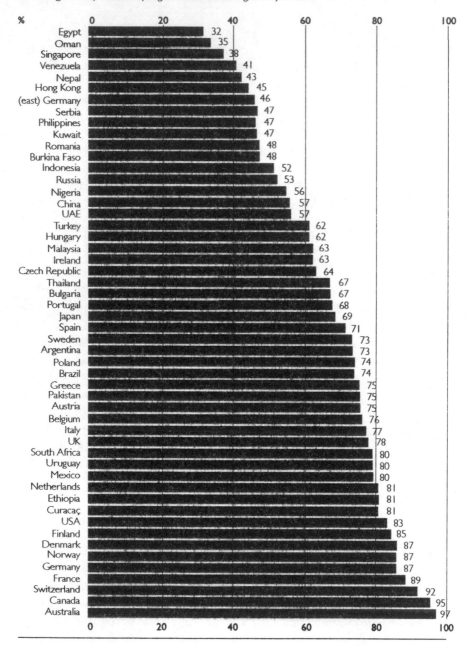

Figure 11.3 **Company triangles**

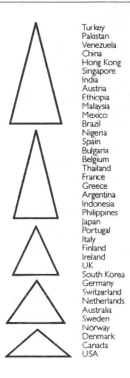

Turkey
Pakistan
Venezuela
China
Hong Kong
Singapore
India
Austria
Ethiopia
Malaysia
Mexico
Brazil
Nigeria
Spain
Bulgaria
Belgium
Thailand
France
Greece
Argentina
Indonesia
Philippines
Japan
Portugal
Italy
Finland
Ireland
UK
South Korea
Germany
Switzerland
Netherlands
Australia
Sweden
Norway
Denmark
Canada
USA

vided loyalty to either? Another problem is that the claims of **genuine** families may intrude. If someone is your brother or cousin they are **already** related to your family back home and should therefore find it easier to relate closely to you at work. It follows that, where a role or project culture might see nepotism as corruption and a conflict of interest, a family culture could see it as reinforcing its current norms. A person connected to your family at home **and** at work has one more reason not to cheat you. Families tend to be strong where universalism is weak.

A Dutch delegation was shocked and surprised when the Brazilian owner of a large manufacturing company introduced his relatively junior accountant as the key co-ordinator of a $15m joint venture. The Dutch were puzzled as to why a recently qualified accountant had been given such weighty responsibilities, including the receipt of their own money. The Brazilians pointed out that this young man was the best possible choice among 1,200 employees since he was the nephew of the owner. Who could be more trustworthy than that? Instead of complaining, the Dutch should consider themselves lucky that he was available.

The eldest child

Quite often employees in family cultures will behave like "the eldest child" left in charge of the family while their parents are out, but relinquishing that authority as soon as a "parent" returns. The American manager of a plant in Miami, Florida, found this relationship with his Venezuelan second-in-command. The plant processed and packaged PVC. The process required high standards of quality control. The product had to be mixed in exactly the correct proportions or it was dangerous. Irregularity in mixing and blending had to be reported immediately it occurred and the line concerned closed down at once, or unsaleable product would accumulate. A decision to shut down was an expert one requiring detailed knowledge. Even a delay of minutes was extremely costly. It was better on the whole to shut down prematurely than to shut down too late.

The Venezuelan deputy knew very well when the product was satisfactory and when it was not. When his manager was away from the plant and he was in charge, he brought any line whose quality was failing to an immediate halt. His judgment was both fast and accurate. When the manager was there, however, he would look for him, report what was happening and get a decision. In the time it took to do that, considerable product was wasted. However many times he was told to act on his own, that his judgment was respected and that his decision would be upheld, he always reverted to his original practice.

This was a simple case of a clash between the task orientation assumed by the American and the family orientation of the Venezuelan. The American had delegated the job of controlling the quality of PVC production. As he saw it this was now his deputy's responsibility, whether he himself was in his office or away. It was required by the necessity of the process. But for the deputy, his authority grew when he was left in charge and shrank the moment his "parent" returned. Decisions should be taken by the most authoritative person **present**. He would no more usurp the authority of his parents once they returned home than would any child left temporarily in charge.

Some well-known research by Inzerilli and Laurent,[1] an Italian and a French researcher, showed the much higher appeal among Italian, French and Japanese managers of the "manager who knows everything". This was on the basis of posing the question: "Is it important for a manager to have at hand precise answers to most of the questions raised by subordinates?" We all know that in the complexity of modern conditions it is becoming harder for managers to know even part of what their subordinates know as a group. Yet the supposition that your manager **does** know everything may require you to discuss everything with him, thus encouraging the upward movement of information to the apex of the organisation, a process that contributes to learning. We must beware, therefore, of dismissing the family metaphor as primitive, pretentious or feudal. Its intimacies can process complex information effectively, and wanting your "father" to know a great deal may have more desirable results than neither expecting nor wanting your boss to know very much. A visionary leader who mobilises his or her employees around superordinate goals needs their trust, their faith and their knowledge. The family model can often supply all three.

The results of the question posed in Chapter 7 on whether a company is responsible for providing housing (see Figure 7.6) also show those nations in which the family is a natural model. In these cultures there is almost no boundary for the organisation's responsibilities to the people in its employ. These even extend to where and how they are housed. Japanese employers make it their business as to whether you are married, how many children you have and accordingly how much more you need to be paid. The company may help you find housing, help get your children into schools, offer you consumer products at reduced prices, make recreational facilities available and even encourage you to take vacations with work colleagues. The belief is that the **more the company does for your family the more your family will wish its breadwinner to do for the company**.

Thinking, learning and change

The family corporate culture is more interested in intuitive than in rational knowledge, more concerned with the development of people than with their deployment or utilisation. Personal knowledge of another is rated above empirical knowledge about him or her. Knowing is less hypothetical and deductive, more by trial and error. Conversations are preferred to research questionnaires and insights to objective data. **Who** is doing something is more important than **what** is being done. If you invite the Japanese to a meeting they will want to know who will be there before specific details about the agenda.

Change in the power-oriented family model is essentially political, getting key actors to modify policies. Among favourite devices are new visions, charismatic appeals, inspiring goals and directions, and more authentic relationships with significant people. Bottom-up change is unlikely unless it is insurgent and seriously challenges the leaders, in which case major concessions may be made.

Training, mentoring, coaching and apprenticeship are important sources of personal education but these occur at the behest of the family and do not in themselves challenge authority but rather perpetuate it. Family-style cultures can respond quickly to changing environments that affect their power. Their political antennae are often sharp.

A Dutch manager delegated to initiate change in the French subsidiary of a Dutch group described to us how impressed he was at the precision and intelligence of the French managers' response to his proposals. He returned three months later to find that nothing had happened. He had failed to realise that it was also necessary to change the management team; the strategic proposals had simply been a front behind which the family continued to operate as before.

Motivating, rewarding and resolving conflict

Because family members enjoy their relationships they may be motivated more by praise and appreciation than by money. Pay-for-performance rarely sits well with them, or any motivation that threatens family bonds. They tend to "socialise risk" among their members and can operate in uncertain environments quite well. Their major weakness occurs when intra-family conflicts block necessary change.

Resolving conflict often depends on the skill of a leader. Criticisms are seldom voiced publicly; if they are the family is in turmoil. Negative feedback is indirect and sometimes confined to special "licensed" occasions. (In Japan you can criticise your boss while drinking his booze.) Care is taken to avoid loss of face by prominent family members since these are points of coherence for the whole group. The family model gives low priority to **efficiency** (doing things right) but high priority to **effectiveness** (doing the right things).

The Eiffel Tower culture

In the western world a bureaucratic division of labour with various roles and functions is prescribed in advance. These allocations are co-ordinated at the top by a hierarchy. If each role is acted out as envisaged by the system then tasks will be completed as planned. One supervisor can oversee the completion of several tasks; one manager can oversee the job of several supervisors; and so on up the hierarchy.

We have chosen the Eiffel Tower in Paris to symbolise this cultural type because it is steep, symmetrical, narrow at the top and broad at the base, stable, rigid and robust. Like the formal bureaucracy for which it stands, it is very much a symbol of the machine age. Its structure, too, is more important than its function.

Its hierarchy is very different from that of the family. Each higher level has a clear and demonstrable function of holding together the levels beneath it. You obey the boss because it is his or her **role** to instruct you.

The rational purpose of the corporation is conveyed to you through him. He has legal authority to tell you what to do and your contract of service, overtly or implicitly, obliges you to work according to his instructions. If you and other subordinates did not do so the system could not function.

The boss in the Eiffel Tower is only incidentally a person. Essentially he or she is a role. Were he to drop dead tomorrow, someone else would replace him and it would make no difference to your duties or to the organisation's reason for being. His successor might of course be more or less unpleasant, or interpret the role slightly differently, but that is marginal. Effectively the job is defined and the discharge of it evaluated according to that definition. Very little is left to chance or the idiosyncrasies of individuals.

It follows that authority stems from occupancy of the role. If you meet the boss on the golf course, you have no obligation to let him play through and he probably would not expect it. Relationships are **specific** (see Chapter 7) and status is **ascribed** (see Chapter 8) and stays behind at the office. This is not, however, a personal ascription of status as we see it in the family. Status in the Eiffel Tower is ascribed to the role. This makes it impossible to challenge. Thus bureaucracy in the Eiffel Tower is a depersonalised, rational-legal system in which everyone is subordinate to local rules and those rules prescribe a hierarchy to uphold and enforce them. The boss is powerful only because the rules sanction him or her to act.

Careers in Eiffel Tower companies are much assisted by professional qualifications. At the top of German and Austrian companies, which are typically Eiffel Tower models, the titles of professor or doctor are common on office doors. This is extremely rare in the USA.

Almost everything the family culture accepts the Eiffel Tower rejects. Personal relationships are likely to warp judgments, create favourites, multiply exceptions to the rules and obscure clear boundaries between roles and responsibilities. You cannot evaluate your subordinate's performance in a role if you grow fond of him or her or need their personal loyalty for yourself. The organisation's purpose is logically separate from your personal need for power or affection. Such needs are distractions, biases and intrusions by personal agendas upon public ones.

Each role at each level of the hierarchy is described, rated for its difficulty, complexity and responsibility, and has a salary attached to it. There then follows a search for a person to fill it. In considering applicants for the role the personnel department will treat everyone equally and neutrally, will match the person's skills and aptitudes with the job requirements and will award the job to the best fit between role and person. The same procedure is followed in evaluations and promotions.

We tested the influence of the **role** culture as opposed to the more **personal** culture by posing the following dilemma to managers.

> Two managers talk about their company's organisational structure.
>
> **A** One says: "The main reason for having an organisational structure is so that everyone knows who has authority over whom."
> **B** The other says: "The main reason for having an organisational structure is so that everyone knows how functions are allocated and co-ordinated."
>
> Which one of these two ways usually best represents an organisational structure?

Those nations most attracted to putting roles before persons, largely North American and north-west European, opt by large majorities for B. Here the **logic of subordination is clearly rational and co-ordinative**. In option A it is left unspecified. The organisation legitimates existing power differences.

The Eiffel Tower points to the goals to be achieved by the edifice, which is relatively rigid and has difficulty pointing in different directions. If, for example, the Eiffel Tower company needs to achieve goals inconsistent with hierarchical co-ordinated roles, say inventing new products, then its structure tends to impede achievement. On the other hand, it is well designed to renew passports or check insurance claims, where the rules are devised in advance and consistent treatment is legally required.

In one of our workshops the head of strategic planning in a major German company gave a one-hour presentation on his company's strategic planning. He spent 45 minutes on how his firm was organised and the remaining 15 on strategic issues. Over lunch I asked him why he had not wanted to give 60 minutes to strategic issues. "But I did," was his reply. For him, structure **was** strategy.

Thinking, learning and change

The way in which people think, learn and change in the role-oriented Eiffel Tower company is significantly different from similar processes in the family. For employees in the Eiffel Tower, the family culture is arbitrary, irrational, conspiratorial, cosy and corrupt. Instead of following set procedures which everyone can understand, and having objective benchmarks which employees agree to conform to, the family is forever shifting goal

Figure 11.4 The reason for organisation

Percentage of respondents opting for function rather than personality

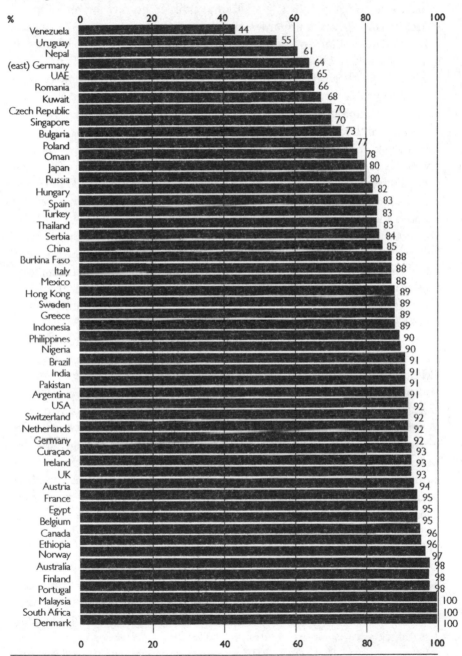

%	Country	Value
	Venezuela	44
	Uruguay	55
	Nepal	61
	(east) Germany	64
	UAE	65
	Romania	66
	Kuwait	68
	Czech Republic	70
	Singapore	70
	Bulgaria	73
	Poland	77
	Oman	78
	Japan	80
	Russia	80
	Hungary	82
	Spain	83
	Turkey	83
	Thailand	83
	Serbia	84
	China	85
	Burkina Faso	88
	Italy	88
	Mexico	88
	Hong Kong	89
	Sweden	89
	Greece	89
	Indonesia	89
	Philippines	90
	Nigeria	90
	Brazil	91
	India	91
	Pakistan	91
	Argentina	91
	USA	92
	Switzerland	92
	Netherlands	92
	Germany	92
	Curaçao	93
	Ireland	93
	UK	93
	Austria	94
	France	95
	Egypt	95
	Belgium	95
	Canada	96
	Ethiopia	96
	Norway	97
	Australia	98
	Finland	98
	Portugal	98
	Malaysia	100
	South Africa	100
	Denmark	100

posts or suspending competitive play altogether.

Learning in the Eiffel Tower means accumulating the skills necessary to fit a role and hopefully the additional skills to qualify for higher positions. In Eiffel Tower companies, people or "human resources" are conceived of as similar to capital and cash resources. People of known qualifications can be planned, scheduled, deployed and reshuffled by skill sets like any other physical entity. Manpower planning, assessment centres, appraisal systems, training schemes and job rotation all have the function of helping to classify and produce resources to fit known roles.

Change in the Eiffel Tower is effected through **changing rules**. With any alteration in the company's purpose must come changes in what employees are formally required to do. For this reason, the culture does not adapt well to turbulent environments. In theory, constant rule-change would be necessary but this would in practice bewilder employees, lower morale and obscure the distinction between rules and deviations. Change in an Eiffel Tower culture is immensely complex and time-consuming. Manuals must be rewritten, procedures changed, job descriptions altered, promotions reconsidered, qualifications reassessed. "Restructuring" or "rationalisation" tend to be dreaded words in Eiffel Tower cultures. They usually mean wholesale firings and redundancies. Such companies resist change and when it becomes inevitable suffer major dislocation as a consequence.

An American manager responsible for initiating change in a German company described to me the difficulties he had had in making progress, although the German managers had discussed the new strategy in depth and made significant contributions to its formulation. Through informal channels he had eventually discovered that his mistake was not having formalised the changes to structure or job descriptions. In the absence of a new organigram, this Eiffel Tower company was unable to change. Like the Dutch manager above who had similar problems in dealing with a French family company, his assumption was that once an intellectual decision had been agreed, instant action would follow. Both these managers came from task-oriented guided missile cultures themselves (see below).

Motivating, rewarding and resolving conflict

Employees of the Eiffel Tower are ideally precise and meticulous. They are nervous when order and predictability is lacking. Duty is an important concept for the role-oriented employee. It is an obligation people feel within themselves, rather than an obligation they feel towards a specific individual.

Conflicts are seen as irrational, pathologies of orderly procedure, offences against efficiency. Criticisms and complaints are typically channelled and dealt with through even more rules and fact-finding procedures.

The family and the Eiffel Tower in conflict

MCC, the company employing Mr Johnson, whose problems we have been following throughout this book, is broadly speaking a task-oriented company, and many of Mr Johnson's difficulties have arisen through clashes with colleagues whose expectations of companies are much closer to the family model. (The final instalment of Mr Johnson's story will be found at the end of this chapter.) Another example of what happens when these two models find themselves side by side is the story of Heinz, a manager from a large German multinational, experienced and outstandingly successful, who was selected to help a Colombian packaging material company to get out of the red. All stakeholders, the Colombian government included, acknowledged that modernisation and more professional management were needed. Heinz wanted to make the factory profitable and more efficient by introducing new production and quality standards.

The most important person in the company next to Heinz was Antonio, a Colombian, designated to take over Heinz's job after the German had completed his mission. After almost a year of working in Colombia, Heinz concluded that the activities in the factory had not improved significantly despite his best efforts.

The following are excerpts from a consultant's report (rewritten by Leonel Brug) in which Heinz and Antonio were interviewed separately.

Antonio's story. Antonio is very positive about Heinz's technical and organisational capabilities. The need to increase efficiency is undeniable and the production processes still need much work. Heinz is quite right on this score.

Antonio is, however, shocked by the way Heinz is trying to impose his methods and ideas on the Colombians. He describes this as turning them into robots; he is dehumanising the whole organisation.

He says Heinz seems obsessed with time and money. People hardly count at all. He yells at workers for taking longer breaks than they should, forgetting that the previous week they worked overtime without extra pay, without complaint and, of course, without thanks. He does not seem to realise that punctuality is not possible. We have people reporting for work who walked when the bus broke down and he shouts at them as they limp in at the gate. Antonio is amazed that they come to work at all.

There are two men who waded a river to get to work when the floods washed the bridge away and yet Heinz still wanted to dock their pay. Antonio refused to do this. He told Heinz: "Look, they have to **want** to come to work, to be appreciated here, or absenteeism will become far higher than it already is."

Heinz's story. Heinz explains that the factory was a real mess when he arrived. There was no order, no procedure, no discipline and no responsibility.

He complains that Antonio is always making excuses. Everything is a special case or an exceptional circumstance. He runs around like a wet-nurse trying to discover why the employees are unhappy or disturbed. He is forever telling Antonio to let them stand on their own two feet.

Employees think they can turn up to work when it is convenient for them, despite the fact that they know production cannot start until nearly all of them arrive. They wait for things to go wrong and then act as if they are making heroic gestures of self-sacrifice. He has told them repeatedly that he does not need them to stay late, he just needs them to get to work on time.

> "They have more colourful excuses than a tale of the Wild West. To hear them tell it they only come to work at all because they love us. And that they were late because their brothers missed an appointment or some bridge fell down or who knows what. We get 'scenes of village life' here every day."

Heinz explains that he has told Antonio that he does not want to bully employees or harass them, he just wants to keep to agreements, deadlines and schedules. He does not believe that is too much to ask.

In this example, it should be noted, Heinz represents a very sophisticated Eiffel Tower culture and Antonio quite an unsophisticated family one. In the hands of a sophisticated family culture, like many Japanese companies, the consequences could be different. Nor are cultures necessarily exclusive. Families can "take on" the exacting rules of Eiffel Towers and become formidable competitors. The finest combinations lie beyond stereotypes and simple contrasts.

The guided missile culture

The guided missile culture differs from both the family and the Eiffel Tower by being **egalitarian**, but differs also from the family and resembles the Eiffel Tower in being impersonal and task-oriented. Indeed the guided missile culture is rather like the Eiffel Tower in flight. But while the rationale of the Eiffel Tower culture is means, the guided missile has a rationale of ends. Everything must be done to persevere in your strategic intent and reach your target.

The guided missile culture is oriented to tasks, typically undertaken by teams or project groups. It differs from the role culture in that the jobs members do are not fixed in advance. They must do "whatever it takes" to complete a task, and what is needed is often unclear and may have to be discovered.

The National Aeronautics and Space Administration (NASA) pioneered the use of project groups working on space probes which resembled guided missiles. It takes roughly 140 different kinds of engineers to build a lunar landing module and whose contribution is crucial at exactly what time cannot be known in advance. Because every variety of engineering must work harmoniously with every other, the best form of synthesis needs to be discovered in the course of working. Nor can there be any hierarchy which claims that "A's expertise is greater than B's expertise". Each knows most about his or her part. How the whole will function needs to be worked out with everyone's participation. All are **equals**, or at least potentially equal, since their relative contributions are not yet known.

Such groups will have leaders or co-ordinators, who are responsible for sub and final assemblies, but these generalists may know less than specialists in each discipline and must treat all experts with great respect. The group is egalitarian because it might need the help of any one expert in changing direction towards its target. The end is known but the possible trajectories are uncertain. Missile cultures frequently draw on professionals and are cross-disciplinary. In an advertising agency, for example, one copywriter, one visualiser/artist, one media buyer, one commercial film buyer and one account representative may work on a campaign yet to be agreed by the client. All will play a part, but what part depends on the final campaign the client prefers.

Guided missile cultures are expensive because professionals are expensive. Groups tend to be temporary, relationships as fleeting as the project and largely instrumental in bringing the project to a conclusion. Employees will join other groups, for other purposes, within days or weeks and may have multiple memberships. This culture is **not** affectionate or mutually committed, but typifies the **neutral** cultures discussed in Chapter 6.

The ultimate criteria of human value in the guided missile culture are how you perform and to what extent you contribute to the jointly desired outcome. In effect, each member shares in problem-solving. The relative contribution of any one person may not be as clear as in the Eiffel Tower culture where each role is described and outputs can be quantified.

In practice, the guided missile culture is **superimposed** upon the Eiffel Tower organisation to give it permanence and stability. This is known as the matrix organisation. You have one (Eiffel Tower) line reporting to your functional boss, say electrical engineering, and another (guided missile) line of responsibility to your project head. This makes you jointly responsible to your engineering boss for quality engineering and to your project leader for a viable, low-cost means of, say, auto-emissions control. The project has to succeed and your electronics must be excellent. Two authorities pull you in different, although reconcilable, directions.

Thinking, learning and change

The guided missile culture is **cybernetic**, in the sense that it homes in on its target using feedback signals and is therefore circular rather than linear. Yet the "missile" rarely, if ever, changes its mind about its target. Steering is therefore corrective and conservative, not as open to new **ends** as to new **means**.

Learning includes "getting on" with people, breaking the ice quickly, playing the part in a team which is currently lacking, being practical rather than theoretical and being problem-centred rather than discipline-centred. Appraisal is often by peers or subordinates rather than by someone further up the hierarchy.

Change comes quickly to the guided missile culture. The target moves. More targets appear, new groups are formed, old ones dissolve. People who hop from group to group will often hop from job to job, so that turnover tends to be high, and **loyalties to professions and projects are greater than loyalties to the company**. The guided missile culture is in many respects the antithesis of the family culture, in which bonds are close and ties are of long duration and deep affection.

Motivating, rewarding and resolving conflict

Motivations tend to be **intrinsic** in this culture. That is, team members get enthusiastic about, identify with and struggle towards the final product. In the case of the Apple Macintosh, the enthusiasm was about creating an "insanely great machine". The product under development is the superordinate goal for which the conflicts and animosities of team members may be set aside. Unless there is high participation there will not be widespread commitment. The final consensus must be broad enough to pull in all those who work on it.

This culture tends to be individualistic since it allows for a wide variety of differently specialised persons to work with each other on a temporary basis. The scenery of faces keeps changing. Only the pursuit of chosen lines of personal development is constant. The team is a vehicle for the shared enthusiasm of its members, but is itself disposable and will be discarded when the project ends. Members are garrulous, idiosyncratic and intelligent, but their mutuality is a means, not an end. It is a way of enjoying the journey. They do not need to know each other intimately and may avoid doing so. Management by objectives is the language spoken, and people are paid by performance.

The incubator culture

The incubator culture is based on the existential idea that organisations are secondary to the fulfilment of individuals. Just as "existence precedes essence" was the motto of existential philosophers, so "existence precedes organisation" is the notion of incubator cultures. If organisations are to be tolerated at all, they should be there to serve as **incubators for self-expression and self-fulfilment**. The metaphor here should not be confused with "business incubators". (These are organisations which provide routine maintenance and services, plant equipment, insurance, office space and so on for embryo businesses, so that they can lower their overhead costs during the crucial start-up phase.)

However, the logic of business and cultural incubators is quite similar. In both cases the purpose is to free individuals from routine to more creative activities and to minimise time spent on self-maintenance. The incubator is **both** personal and egalitarian. Indeed it has almost no structure at all and what structure it does provide is merely for personal convenience: heat, light, word processing, coffee and so on.

The roles of other people in the incubator, however, are crucial. They are there to confirm, criticise, develop, find resources for and help to complete the innovative product or service. The culture acts as a sounding board for innovative ideas and tries to respond intelligently to new initiatives. Typical examples are start-up firms in Silicon Valley, California, in Silicon Glen in Scotland and on Route 128 around Boston. The companies are usually entrepreneurial or founded by a creative team that quit a larger employer just before the pay-off. Being individualist they are not constrained by organisational loyalties and may deliberately "free ride" until their eggs are close to hatching. In this way larger organisations find themselves successively undermined.

Cultural incubators are not only small innovative companies. They can be doctors in group practice, legal partners, some consultants, chartered surveyors, or any group of professionals who work mostly alone but like to share resources while comparing experiences. Some writers see the incubator as the organisational wave of the future. Others see the decline of Silicon Valley as evidence that this culture cannot survive maturity and is but a temporary phase in starting up an organisation from an ad hoc basis. Others point to the rarity of incubator cultures outside the "enclaves of individualism" in the USA, the UK and the English-speaking world.

Just as incubators have minimal structure, so they also have minimal hierarchy. Such authority as individuals do command is strictly personal, the exciting nature of their ideas and the inspiration of their vision leading others to work with them.

Incubators often, if not always, operate in an environment of intense **emotional** commitment. However, this commitment is less towards people per se than to the world-changing, society-redeeming nature of the work being undertaken. The personal computer will bring "power to the person", gene-splicing could save crops, save lives, rescue the economy and represents an odyssey into the unknown, wherein "the journey is the reward".

Incubator cultures enjoy the process of creating and innovating. Because of close relationships, shared enthusiasms and superordinate goals, the incubator at its best can be ruthlessly honest, effective, nurturant, therapeutic and exciting, depending as it does on face-to-face relationships and working intimacies. Because the association is voluntary, often underfunded and fuelled largely by hope and idealism, it can be the most significant and intense experience of a lifetime. But this is very hard to repeat or sustain, since the project no sooner succeeds than strangers must be hired and the founders' special relationships are lost. Incubators are typically limited in size by the leaders' "span of control"; it becomes hard to communicate spontaneously and informally with more than 75–100 people.

Thinking, learning and change

Change in the incubator can be fast and spontaneous where the members are attuned to each other. Roger Harrison[2] has likened the process to an improvising jazz band, in which a self-elected leader tries something new and the band follows if it likes the theme and ignores the theme if it does not. All participants are on the same wavelength, empathically searching together for a solution to the shared problem. But because a customer has not defined any target, the **problem itself is open to redefinition** and the solution being searched for is typically generic, aimed at a universe of applications.

American start-up companies with incubator cultures rarely survive the maturing of their products and their markets. This culture learns to create but not to **survive altered patterns of demand**. The "great designers" of the novel products continue to be the heroes of the company long after the focus has shifted to customer service and to marketing.

Motivating, rewarding and resolving conflict

Motivation is often wholehearted, intrinsic and intense with individuals working "70 hours a week and loving it" as the T-shirts at Apple Computer used to read in its earlier days. There is competition to contribute to the emerging shape of something new. Everyone wants to get his or her "hands on". There is scant concern for personal security and few wish to profit or have power **apart from the unfolding creative process**. If the whole succeeds there will be plenty for everyone. If it does not, the incubator itself will be gone. In contrast to the family culture, leadership in the incubator is **achieved**, not ascribed. You follow those whose progress most impresses you and whose ideas work. Power plays that impede group achievement will be reviled. Conflict is resolved either by splitting up or by trying the proposed alternatives to see which works best.

Which countries prefer which corporate cultures

As we have already said, these "pure types" seldom exist. In practice the types are mixed or overlaid with one culture dominating. Nevertheless in different national cultures one or more of these types clearly dominate the corporate scene, and if we list the main characteristics of the four types it becomes easy to refer back to the national cultural dimensions discussed in the preceding chapters. The following table shows how in the four models employees relate differently, have different views of authority, think, learn and change in different ways, and are motivated by different rewards, while criticism and conflict resolution are variously handled.

The original 79-item questionnaire used to compile our main database was not aimed at measuring the four corporate cultures, although it incidentally included the questions illuminating family and Eiffel Tower approaches described above (with results shown in Figures 11.2–4). Five years ago, however, United Notions – the centre for intellectual business studies – decided to start compiling a new database of corporate culture, using a similar approach. Sixteen questions were devised which deal with general concepts of egalitarianism versus hierarchy, degrees of formality, different forms of conflict resolution, learning, and so on. (Examples of these are in Appendix 2.) Respondents are asked to choose between four possible descriptions of their company, which are geared respectively to the power-priority of the family, the role-dominance of the Eiffel Tower, the task-orientation of the guided missile and the person-orientation of the incubator. This work is fairly new; the database currently totals 13,000 and we have significant samples for 42 countries. These show very marked distinctions. Figure 11.5 shows the results of totalling the responses to the whole questionnaire. This puts the highest scores for guided missile companies in the USA and the UK, and the highest for family companies in France and Spain. Sweden scores highest for incubators

Characteristics of the four corporate cultures

	Family	Eiffel Tower	Guided missile	Incubator
Relationships between employees	Diffuse relationships to organic whole to which one is bonded.	Specific role in mechanical system of required interactions.	Specific tasks in cybernetic system targeted upon shared objectives.	Diffuse, spontaneous relationships growing out of shared creative process.
Attitude to authority	Status is ascribed to parent figures who are close and powerful.	Status is ascribed to superior roles who are distant yet powerful.	Status is achieved by project group members who contribute to targeted goal.	Status is achieved by individuals exemplifying creativity and growth.
Ways of thinking and learning	Intuitive, holistic, lateral and error-correcting.	Logical, analytical, vertical and rationally efficient.	Problem-centred, professional, practical, cross-disciplinary.	Process-oriented, creative, ad hoc, inspirational.
Attitudes to people	Family members.	Human resources.	Specialists and experts.	Co-creators.
Ways of changing	"Father" changes course.	Change rules and procedures.	Shift aim as target moves.	Improvise and attune.
Ways of motivating and rewarding	Intrinsic satisfaction in being loved and respected. Management by subjectives.	Promotion to greater position, larger role. Management by job description.	Pay or credit for performance and problems solved. Management by objectives.	Participating in the process of creating new realities. Management by enthusiasm.
Criticism and conflict resolution	Turn other cheek, save others' faces, do not lose power game.	Criticism is accusation of irrationality unless there are procedures to arbitrate conflicts.	Constructive task-related only, then admit error and correct fast.	Must improve creative idea, not negate it.

and Germany for Eiffel Towers.

The reader, however, should interpret this cautiously. Smaller companies **wherever** located are more likely to take the family and incubator forms. Large companies needing structure to cohere are likely to choose Eiffel Tower or guided missile forms. Our database has relatively few respondents from smaller companies, so that these are under-represented. In France, for example, smaller companies tend to be family and larger companies Eiffel Tower. In the USA guided missile companies may dominate among large corporations, but the archetypal incubators are to be found in Silicon Valley, as they are in the UK in Silicon Glen.

Figure 11.5 **National patterns of corporate culture**

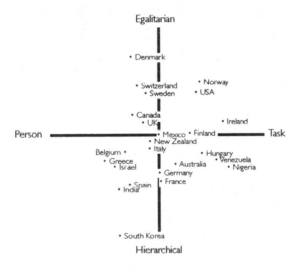

SUMMARY

We have defined four broad types of corporate culture, which are closely related to the national differences described in earlier chapters. Just as national cultures conflict, leading to mutual incomprehension and mistrust, so corporate cultures collide. Attempts to "dice" the family with a matrix can cause rage and consternation. Getting cosy with subordinates in the Eiffel Tower could be seen as a potentially improper advance. Asking to be put in a group with a special friend is a subversive act in the guided missile culture. Calling your boss "buddy" and slapping him or her on the back will get you thrown from the Eiffel Tower, while suggesting in an incubator that everyone fill out time-sheets will be greeted with cat-calls.

(If you really want to discover norms, **break them**; reading this chapter is intended as a less painful alternative.)

Yet the types exist and must be respected. Really successful businesses borrow from all types and ceaselessly struggle to reconcile them. We turn to this process in the last chapter. First, however, we should say goodbye to Mr Johnson.

Back in St Louis at the MCC management meeting Mr Johnson reported on the introduction of pay-for-performance. It had been resisted widely, and where it had been tried, in parts of southern Europe, the Middle East and Asia, early results showed it had failed. The meeting listened in silence. The atmosphere was distinctly cool. "Well," said the CEO, "how do you plan to cope with these problems, Bill? I'm sure we don't need the HR function to tell us that there are a lot of different people and opinions in the world."

Johnson had by now decided that he had nothing to lose, so he voiced a concern he had felt for many months. "I realise we make machines, but I sometimes ask myself if we are letting the metaphor run away with the organisation. These are people, not microprocessors or integrated circuits, which can be replaced if they don't work." "I wish we **could** operate more like a computer," interrupted the finance manager. "We hire quality people to do as we tell them, and function in ways they are trained. Either they do this or we get somebody else. What's wrong with that?"

The CEO was trying to calm things down. "I have to disagree there," he said. "I see this company as more of an **organism**. If you go to Barcelona and chop off heads, don't be surprised if the body dies. If we take out some subsidiary's right hand we can't expect it to work well in future. What I can't understand is why Bill can't get them to see that we're all one organism and that the hands and feet can't go off in all directions."

Suddenly all the exasperations of the last few months came to the surface. For a moment Johnson had thought that the CEO was supporting him, but it was the same old message: get the whole world to march in step with us.

"What **I've** been through in the last eight months is about as far from a smoothly running computer or a living organism as you could get. I'll tell you what it's really like, because I was reading the story to my kids. It's like that crazy croquet game in Alice in Wonderland where she has to play with a flamingo as a mallet, waiters bending over as hoops and hedgehogs as balls. The flamingo twists its head round to look at Alice, the hoops wander off and the balls crawl away. The result is chaos.

Other cultures aren't part of a machine, or the organs of a supranational body. They're different animals, all with logic of their own. If we asked them what game **they** are playing, and got them to explain the rules, we might discover when we aren't holding a mallet at all, or even get the hedgehog to go in the right direction."

Was Mr Johnson promoted, or given the job of overseeing the welfare of MCC pensioners? My guess is that he is running a small but fast growing consultancy somewhere, specialising in cross-cultural management.

References

1 Inzerilli, G. and Laurent, A., *The Concept of Organisational Structure*, Working Paper, University of Pennsylvania and INSEAD, 1979; "Managerial Views of Organisational Structure in France and the USA", *International Studies of Management and Organisations*, XIII, 1-2, 1983, pages 97–118.
2 Harrison, R., "Understanding Your Organisation's Character", *Harvard Business Review*, May–June 1972.

General

Hampden-Turner, C., *Corporate Culture*, The Economist Books/Business Books, London, 1991.
Handy, C., *The Gods of Management*, Souvenir Press, London, 1978.

12

TOWARDS INTERNATIONAL AND TRANSNATIONAL MANAGEMENT

This book has elucidated national differences, of which we have found a great many. So wide and pervasive are these variations that they would seem to confirm the doubt expressed at the beginning as to whether universal or general principles of "how to manage" were feasible or useful.

Yet the implications of the research presented here is that universals exist at another level. While you cannot give universal **advice** that will work regardless of culture, and while general axioms of business administration turn out to be largely American cultural axioms, there are **universal dilemmas or problems of human existence**. Every country and every organisation in that country faces dilemmas:

- in relationships with people;
- in relationship to time;
- in relations between people and the natural environment.

While nations differ markedly in **how** they approach these dilemmas, they do not differ in needing to make some kind of response. People everywhere are as one in having to face up to the same challenges of existence.

In this chapter we look at some of the specific problems faced by international management, in terms of structure, strategy, communications and human resources, and consider a common approach to their solution.

Our research methodology consists of stories, scenes, situations and questions which put two moral and/or managerial principles in conflict. It is the researchers who force the managers to prefer one over the other. In reality each of the managers whose reactions have gone to make up the database we have examined was explaining which was his or her first and which his or her second "foundation stone" in **building the moral edifice**. Some, for example, felt that you had to give priority to a universal rule (universalism) and behave in particular instances accordingly. Some felt that you had to give priority to your affection for particular people (particularism) and develop whatever universals you could out of such obligations. But few were actually rejecting the alternative solution out of hand, and as the figures show it is rare for any national result to be anywhere near 100% in favour of any priority. Almost all our problems, and their solutions, are recognisable all over the world.

There is another important respect in which all the world's managers are the same. Whichever principle they start with, the circumstances of business and of organising experience requires them to reconcile the dilemmas we have been discussing. You can only prosper if as many particulars as possible are covered by rules, yet exceptions are seen and noted. You can only think effectively if both the specifics and the diffuse wholes, the segments and the integrations are covered. Whether you are at heart an individualist or a communitarian, your individuals must be capable of organising themselves and your communities are only as good as the health, wealth and wisdom of each member.

It is crucial to give status to achievers, but equally crucial to back strategies, projects and new initiatives from people who have not yet achieved anything, in other words to ascribe status to them in hope of facilitating success. Everyone should be equal in their rights and opportunities, yet any contest will produce a hierarchy of relative standings. Respect for age and experience can both nurture and discourage the young and inexperienced. Hierarchy and equality are finely interwoven in every culture. It is true that time is both a passing sequence of events and a moment of truth, a "now" in which past, present and future are given new meanings. We need to accept influences from the depth of our inner convictions and the world around us. In the final analysis **culture is the manner in which these dilemmas are reconciled, since every nation seeks a different and winding path to its own ideals of integrity**. It is my position that businesses will succeed to the extent that this reconciliation occurs, so we have everything to learn from discovering how others have travelled to their own position.

Problems for the cross-cultural manager

We are not the first to note these differences. Geert Hofstede did so in his international samples of IBM employees,[1] as did Inzerilli and Laurent[2] in their research comparing Italian and French managers to those in the USA, Japan and Europe. As we tracked the experience of Mr Johnson of MCC from chapter to chapter, we found what these researchers have also noted, that favourite American solutions do not always solve the dilemmas of other nations. Since the USA has been the principal source of management theory, this is crucial information for all students of business practice.

For example, the matrix organisation is a very clever reconciliation of the need to be organised by discipline and function, and the need to respond to projects, products-under-development and customer specifications. But while this solves American, British, Dutch and Scandinavian dilemmas, it directly threatens and contradicts the family model described in Chapter 11, so that some Italian, Spanish, French and Asian companies will have to devise a different solution.

Similarly, Peter Drucker's management by objectives is a justly famous reconciliation of an American dilemma which has rightly been adopted by like-minded nations. The conflict between equality and hierarchy, and the individual and the community is reconciled by getting individuals to pledge themselves freely to fulfil the key objectives of the community and the hierarchy. Voluntarily negotiated contracts join the person to the group. That is good, but not so good for nations which regard the performance of individuals as part of the relationship with the boss and who attribute excellence to the whole family or relationship.

Pay-for-performance is similarly an attempted solution to the achievement–ascription dilemma. Why not ascribe status and financial rewards to employees in proportion to their achievements? Again, this has great appeal to those who put achievement first but none to those who put ascription first and seek to be the emotional "authors" of a subordinate's success. We discussed this problem in detail in Chapter 8, but it is so central to the issue that it will bear an additional anecdote here.

An American computer company introduced pay-for-performance in both the USA and the Middle East. It worked well in the USA and increased sales briefly in the Middle East before a serious slump occurred. Inquiries showed that indeed the winners among salesmen in the Middle East had done better, but the vast majority had done worse. The wish for their fellows to succeed had been seriously eroded by the contest. Overall morale and sales were down. Ill-will was contagious. When the bosses discovered that certain salesmen were earning more than they did, high individual performances also ceased. But the principal reason for eventually abandoning the system was the discovery that customers were being loaded up with products they could not sell on. As A tried to beat B to the bonus, the care of customers began to slip, with serious, if delayed, results.

Centralisation versus decentralisation
The main dilemma which those who manage across cultures confront is the extent to which they should **centralise**, thereby imposing on foreign cultures rules and procedures that might affront them, or **decentralise**, thereby letting each culture go its own way, without having any centrally

viable ideas about improvement since the "better way" is a local, not a global pathway. If you radically decentralise you have to ask whether the HQ can add value at all, or whether companies acting in several nations are worthwhile.

Decentralisation is easier under some corporate cultures than others. To decentralise you have to delegate. Of the four models described in Chapter 11, this can be done in the Eiffel Tower and the guided missile cultures but not so easily in the family model where the parent remains the parent. Stories are common of the difficulties that Japanese managers have in decentralising and delegating to foreigners. The family communicates by a kind of in-house osmosis of empathy and bowing rituals that foreigners cannot easily share. Policies are made on the telephone lines to Tokyo because the intimate understandings between Japanese insiders are very difficult to delegate.

As most of our case histories and anecdotes have shown, miscommunication is far more common than dialogue. Nevertheless, centralising and decentralising are, like all the other dimensions introduced in this book, potentially reconcilable processes. A biological organism grows to higher levels of order and complexity by being more differentiated and more integrated. The more departments, divisions, functions and differentiated activities a corporation pursues, the greater the challenge, and also the greater the importance of **co-ordinating all this variety**. As Paul Lawrence and Jay Lorsch[3] showed in the late 1960s, both over-centralised (over-integrated) and over-decentralised (over-differentiated) companies underperform to significant degrees. Differentiating and integrating need to be synergised or reconciled. The corporation with the best integrated diversity is the one which excels.

Group management is often fooled by a foreign subsidiary doing as it is asked by HQ, but essentially performing a corporate rain dance. The local managers know it will make no difference to the rainfall, but if HQ wants a list of everyone's qualifications and salaries to compare the two, they will provide one. Never mind that the qualifications have probably been invented to fit the existing salaries. When these perfect scores arrive HQ feels it is "in control" worldwide, but of course this is an illusion. The policy handbook says "we pay no bribes", but in many countries paid they will be. Relationships without presents are impossible.

The centralising–decentralising dilemma is often experienced as consistency versus flexibility of corporate identity. Is it more important for Shell to relate successfully in the Philippines by helping peasants to raise pigs or should the strategy of being an energy company be used to maintain continuity? In practice the pig farming has helped to prevent oil pipelines being blown up by communist insurgents. If you are anyway digging for oil in Nigeria, why not find some water too and build some desperately needed wells?

Examples of this kind show that the relationship between centralisation and decentralisation is a subtle one. It is not true that every differentiated activity takes you further from your core business simply because it is different. Water wells and pig farms may make all the difference between gaining business in less developed countries or losing it. It is **because we are all different that we have so much to exchange with each other**. In matters of culture, as in the relationship of the sexes, the difference can be the chief source of attraction. Italian design and Dutch engineering can lead to conflicts, as we have seen; they could also lead to a product made in heaven.

The ideal, then, is to differentiate in such a way as to make integration more effective, or to decentralise activities in such a way that an ever broader diversity gets co-ordinated by the "central nervous system" of your corporation. In matters of cultural diversity there is always a challenge, but where this challenge is met valuable connections result.

Quality not quantity in decentralisation

It is not a matter of **how much** to decentralise, but **what** to decentralise and what to keep at corporate HQ. A company that does not centralise information cannot cohere at all, but this does not mean that decisions cannot be made locally. Arguably technical specifications, for example the rules, standards and procedures by which oil refineries are operated, can be decided centrally, but what mix of products to refine could be decided nationally, close to customers' changing demands. Pricing may also be a local decision, sensitive to the proximity of competitors and the degree of overcapacity. Financing decisions are normally allocated centrally or locally according to their size. National companies often pay a standard overhead to headquarters and get legal, financial, planning and personnel services "free"; this arrangement tends to protect the role of centralised functions. You have to pay so you might as well use them. Alternatively HQ staff may provide consultancy services to national companies on request. Under this system, unnecessary staff services at HQ will shrivel on the vine if no one wants them, an arrangement which tends to favour decentralisation.

International and transnational companies

The issues of centralisation and decentralisation have been fully discussed by Christopher Bartlett and Sumantra Ghoshal in relation to their analysis of global versus multinational, and international versus transnational corporations.[4] As they define them, global and multinational companies are both essentially centralised, in that their subsidiaries relate to the head company or country, even if not necessarily very strongly, rather than to the other companies or nations in the group. For these companies there are unlikely to be many foreigners in the top management team, and the myth of the universal applicability of management techniques is likely to be strong. In contrast, in both international and transnational corporate structures there is a significant attempt to overcome the dilemma of centralisation versus decentralisation; each of these in its own way sets out to manage diversity and gain competitive advantage from being located in different countries with special capacities. This book is aimed at those who are already operating on international or transnational levels, or aspire to do so.

The two forms take different paths to the reconciliation of centralising and decentralising. The international corporation moves out influence from its centre to regions and nations, retaining a co-ordinative role, while the transnational corporation loses its centre in favour of polycentric influences from different parts of its network.

The **international** corporation, of which Shell, ABB, Ericsson and Procter & Gamble are examples, breaks with the notion that national organisations are spokes around a wheel. National organisations have legitimate relationships with each other based on what it is that the customer wants and the best source of supply within the international system. The HQ's role becomes not so much to instruct or to evaluate as to **co-ordinate**, to make sure that if one nation has embarked in a promising direction, other nations also learn from this. HQ facilitates this and possibly helps other nations to emulate the initiative.

International corporations are likely to have top management teams which are a microcosm of the whole system, with Germans, Dutch, French, Italian and Japanese executives at company HQ, where considerable businesses are located in those countries. These are not "delegates" or "representatives" in a foreign country, but full-time contributors to multi-cultural management so that, say, the Italian subsidiary has its cultural traits not only within but at the co-ordinating centre.

As corporations move from a multi-local to an international form, the HQ behaves **less like a policeman and more like a consultant**. Hence the Shell International Petroleum Company speaks not of an HQ but of central offices (divided between London and the Hague). It has no CEO or controlling centre but a committee of managing directors, each with local responsibilities in addition to central ones. Functional and geographical chiefs are called co-ordinators, their authority stemming from the fact that they know what several functions, regions or nations are doing.

The **transnational** corporation is polycentric rather than co-ordinated from the centre. It consists of several centres of specialised excellence which will exercise authority and influence whenever these are qualified to do so by the challenge confronting the organisation. Gunnar Hedlund, a Swedish professor, sees this as increasingly typical of some Swedish organisations such as IKEA and Ericsson, for example. Bartlett and Ghoshal regard transnationalism as an important future direction, rather than a reality, in which companies such as Philips and Matsushita are heading. Jay Ogilvy, an American academic, has spoken of heterarchies replacing hierarchies.[5]

All these predictions of the future form of the successful transnational imply a flatter corporate structure drawing on a multiplicity of points of expertise. Hence if a company was designing a new international sports car, the electronics might come from Japan, the engine and suspension from Germany, the design from Italy, the fibreglass shell from the Netherlands, the mahogany wood finish from Britain and the assembly might be done in Spain. National marketing departments will adopt different tactics to sell it, while exchanging experience and drawing upon each other's brand management expertise. Each element in the "value-added chain" or loop would exercise authority on the issue of its own cultural strength. Robert Reich, the American political scientist, has argued[6] that it does not really matter any more who owns the company, be they American shareholders, Europeans or Asians. What matters is where the greatest value is added in the transnational network. Countries will prosper or stagnate by the skills they inject into these "value chains". In the economy of the future, knowledge is king and influence flows from wherever that knowledge resides.

In the transnational company influence can be exercised by any nation on one or more others and can start at any point, accumulating value as it goes and "circling" to reconcile cultural strengths.

What is important about transnationalism is that it follows the circular reconciliations sketched at the ends of Chapters 3–10. The methodology of reconciliation is discussed in detail in Chapter 13.

You can join Italy's particularism to Germany's universalism, or join American individualism and inner-directed creativity to Japanese rapid communitarian exploitation of new products and other-directed skills of customer satisfaction. Where countries specialise in what they do best, the transnational circuits so formed could prove unbeatable. The remaining question is how the transnational organisation is to survive the complete atrophy of its centre.

Human-resource management in the future

The main preoccupation of our analysis of cultural differences has been under the general heading of human resources. In the recruitment of the senior managers of the future, large companies seem at present (recession apart) to be at some disadvantage. The notion that it is desirable to gain "power" by climbing high in large organisations is currently somewhat out of fashion; autonomy is more sought after, especially it would seem in north-western Europe, and the attraction to recruits of internationalism is more likely to lie in the experience, knowledge and investigation of multiple cultures. Recruits will want to plan their own careers in the international and transnational corporation of the future and some career "ladders" may look more like "walkabouts". Companies which succeed in reconciling the centralisation versus decentralisation dilemma will have learnt how to rotate their employees internationally (especially the high flyers), how to work in several languages and how to make decisions at many points on the globe and to spread their effects.

Once the scarce commodity of intelligent managers has been attracted, the future transnational will set out to give them further training in cross-cultural awareness, starting with learning how to recognise a cultural problem, which, as we have seen, is often unidentified; it is not a problem but "the stubbornness of south Europeans about incentive schemes". People who resist American universals are seen as traditional, unbusinesslike or even backward.

The growth of information

The Dutch author once gave a seminar in Thailand that saved a company $1.5m. It was not, alas, the result of any insights I imparted. A French executive sitting next to a Thai executive of the same company discovered that the latter was about to build a pilot plant which would duplicate something the French had just completed. This is indicative of the frequent failure of internal corporate communications.

The development of information technology, however, presents new problems. IT has its own curious forms of absolutism. Given the high capacity, high speed and high cost of computers, the impulse following their installation is to generate a great deal of information as quickly as possible thereby reducing the cost-per-byte.

To know everything statistical about your subsidiary before it has even discovered this itself is therefore much prized. I have heard of subsidiary companies called up during breakfast because of time zone differences with complaints that tin wastage rates in the canning plants are up 50%.

This approach can have disastrous consequences for intercultural communication, and militates against the development of international or transnational structures. The head of a national subsidiary is paid in part to use his or her discretion, free of oversight. If you seek a genuine cultural contribution from a foreign subsidiary you cannot check up on it daily. Information should go first and foremost to those whose operations it concerns, with a lag before HQ gets it. This gives time for local answers to be found and action to be taken.

A company will remain a centralised, directive, global organisation so long as information is used for power and advantage. Because information depends on input, it is easily distorted. Subsidiaries punished for not meeting their forecasts will lower the forecast next time. IT can give an illusion of control which does not survive closer examination.

In the international and transnational structures, national operating companies communicate because they wish to and because the parallel activities of other companies in nearby markets are opportunities and resources. The IT philosophy in these structures states that every national company is free to take major initiatives without prior consultation but should keep the network informed of its actions. It has local autonomy but no right to secrecy about the exercise of that autonomy after the fact. All interested parties must know what has been done. A good software for keeping networks informed is the highlight system. Any interested subsidiary or centralised function can tap into those activities which concern it. This allows for ad hoc project groups to take advantage of any number of converging lines of research or activity. The hallmark of the international or transnational structure is lateral connections between activities capable of being catalysed to the advantage of the whole network. Recall that in this structure subsidiaries connect to subsidiaries. Like hounds hunting for a fox, anyone may pick up the scent, bay loudly and have the others follow the new direction.

Software, moreover, may be more or less culturally compatible with how managers think. Diffuse ways of thinking and learning are often diagrammatic and configurative. Streams of words are more linear, specific and sequential. "Windows" allow for selective viewing of information by those interested. The shape of software needs to be a microcosm of the larger structure and consistent with it. There is software for scenarios of alternative futures, for creative connections between ideas, for alternative applications of key technologies and for spin-offs. There will in future be software to facilitate cross-cultural communication by comparing your individual responses to dilemmas with those of another culture.[7]

Implications for business strategy

Culture can all too easily put brakes on any movement to internationalise. Universalism tends to create global structures in which the values of the home country are celebrated worldwide. Individualism can produce multinational structures in deference to the individuality of each nation. Inner-directedness also contributes to global or multinational structures depending on whether the inner-direction is towards a parent company (a global structure) or a national group (a multinational structure).

Equality, other-directedness and achievement orientations will encourage internationalisation, and it is notable that both the Dutch and the Swedes, who display these attributes, are quite successful internationally. Family-style corporate cultures may work well in their countries of origin but be difficult to transfer overseas. Eiffel Tower cultures will be rejected in nations with family-style traditions, especially if the "universals" are foreign. Guided missile cultures also offend family feeling with their on-again off-again relationships and their "two fathers".

The principal implication for business strategy is a healthy respect for the "founding beliefs" of foreign cultures and the images they have chosen to create coherence. A "strange" culture usually has values neglected in ours and to discover these is to find lost parts of our own cultural heritage. Hence family-style cultures can remind us that work is not necessarily alienating, impersonal and self-seeking. We can benefit from such insights without putting our relatives on the payroll or feeling like children when the boss walks in. International and transnational structures allow us to **synthesise the advantages of all cultures while avoiding their excesses**. Families are quite capable of nurturing independence and encouraging achievement. Managing across cultures gives you more possible pathways to your goal.

The only strategic system open to a genuinely international company will be the system described by Michael Goold[8] as **strategic control**. Here strategy is neither laid down by the centre nor subject to strict financial parameters, but fed to the centre by national companies. They propose and the centre co-ordinates, criticises, approves and adds its own funds. What occurs is a multi-cultural negotiation.

An international or transnational structure greatly reduces its own powers unless it gives a free rein to certain national, cultural proclivities. Strategies tend to vary with national culture; hence inner-directed, universalistic, specific, achievement-oriented cultures, typically the English-speaking ones, talk as if they were engaged in military campaigns, saturating consumers with a withering hail of commercials and generally conquering and occupying markets. In contrast, outer-directed, particularistic, diffuse and ascription-oriented cultures, typically the Japanese and the "four little dragons", speak as if they were serenading customers before climbing into bed with them. They do not use the word "strategy" at all, although they clearly have a method of co-evolving with customers. Individualist cultures with a sequential view of time, like the USA and Britain, are usually short-term in their business strategies. Communitarian cultures with a synchronic view of time, like Germany and Japan, are typically long-term strategically.

An international or transnational structure which does not allow those willing to postpone rewards for several years from doing so could miss out on the secret of Asian and German economic strengths. Within the international or transnational structure a microcosm of international economic competition is going on. We would be foolish not to notice who is winning or why, and to fail to apply the lessons.

Local freedom to prioritise employment values

One interesting way of combining the universal values generated by head office with local flexibility and the impact of national cultures arises in assessment procedures. The head company makes a list of what is to be appraised, but leaves their priority to the national operating company. Shell, for example, until recently operated its HAIRL system of basic appraisal. This stands for Helicopter (the capacity to take a broad view from above), power of Analysis, Imagination, sense of Reality and Leadership effectiveness. We were interested to discover if these were equally important to various Shell operating companies and asked participants in several seminars to prioritise HAIRL for themselves. The results were are follows.

Netherlands	France	Germany	Britain
Reality	Imagination	Leadership	Helicopter
Analysis	Analysis	Analysis	Imagination
Helicopter	Leadership	Reality	Reality
Leadership	Helicopter	Imagination	Analysis
Imagination	Reality	Helicopter	Leadership

There is no inherent reason, it seems to me, why all nations should place equal weight on all values. If the Dutch want to stress realism so be it. They find most of the oil by drilling where it really is and not where they imagine it to be. Prioritising the values of assessment can tell us a lot about how cultures vary. It is the theme of this book that all cultures need to be both universalist and particularist, both individual and communitarian, both ascriptive and achieving, both inner- and outer-directed. Their difference lies in their priorities, where they "start". We have argued the essential **complementarity** of values. To post an individualist to communitarian Singapore can help to make that communitarianism more responsive to individuals and the reverse would be true of posting a Singaporean to the USA.

We should not forget that different priorities are not all equally successful. From studying different value priorities in different cultures come vital clues as to how we can better manage our own affairs.

Local freedom to reward

It is similarly possible to have a universal rule that "success must be rewarded commensurate with its size", yet leave the form of that reward up to the national company. Our case study of MCC conveyed that message. That company was unable to accept that while it could have a central philosophy of pay-for-performance it needed to decentralise its application. Managers around the world are in favour of the principle; the difficulty is that they all mean different things by pay and different things by performance. It is entirely reasonable that a person in a communitarian culture should seek to reward the team members for his or her own successful efforts. They get the money he helped generate, he gets the respect, affection and gratitude, which is not such a bad bargain. That the high performer in an individualistic society might like to attract rewards away from colleagues is also entirely reasonable. The solution is for communitarian and individualist cultures to give group rewards and personal rewards in accordance with their own judgments and results. After all, no culture pays salaries entirely as bonus for individual effort; part is always fixed, so we are talking about relative emphasis. In a truly international or transnational corporation **every nation would be charged with finding its optimal mix between personal and group rewards**, with more of that reward for successful operations.

If we do this we might be surprised. Do individuals in western cultures create because of extrinsic rewards like money, or because their peers encourage them? The answers could be instructive.

Hierarchical versus egalitarian pay structures could also be up to the national company. Relatively equal pay may improve co-operation. Relatively unequal pay may increase competition among employees. How much of each works best? The company should have a fixed ratio of its turnover to distribute as it sees fit. National companies might also be given the discretion to take lower salaries overall so as to reduce prices to customers, using a strategy of "increasing market share". The notion that everyone is motivated principally by money rewards needs to be challenged. Those willing to take long-term advantage of wage control strategies should be encouraged. Corporate cultures based on the image of the family may not care so much about wage levels. Those who work principally for each other's affection can be fiercely competitive on costs, as the Japanese have shown. Pay-for-performance tends to be expensive.

Especially when people are poor a group or communitarian orientation may be crucial for takeoff. A group bonus scheme used by Shell Nigeria, for example, was a water well and irrigation scheme for the town the employees lived in, which materially benefited their homes and neighbourhood besides raising their status in the community. Arguably such a scheme was far more valuable to individual employees than dividing the cost of the project between them and giving them the money instead.

The error-correcting manager

Other cultures are strange, ambiguous, even shocking to us. It is unavoidable that we will make mistakes in dealing with them and feel muddled and confused. The real issue is how quickly we are prepared to learn from mistakes and how bravely we struggle to understand a game in which "perfect scores" are an illusion, and where reconciliation only comes after a difficult passage through alien territory.

We need a certain amount of humility and a sense of humour to discover cultures other than our own; a readiness to enter a room in the dark and stumble over unfamiliar furniture until the pain in our shins reminds us where things are. World culture is a myriad of different ways of creating the integrity without which life and business cannot be conducted. There are no universal answers but there are universal questions or dilemmas, and that is where we all need to start.

References
1 Hofstede, G., *Culture's Consequences*, Sage, London, 1980.
2 Inzerilli, G. and Laurent A., "Managerial Views of Organisation Structure in France and the USA", *International Studies of Management and Organisations*, XIII, 1–2, 1983.
3 Lawrence, P.R. and Lorsch, J.W., *Organisation and Environment; Managing Differentiation and Integration*, Irwin, Homewood, Illinois, 1967.
4 Bartlett, C., and Ghoshal, S., *Managing across Borders*, Hutchinson Business Books, London, 1990.
5 Ogilvy, J., *Global Business Network*, Ameryville, California (personal communication).
6 Reich, R.B., *The Work of Nations: preparing ourselves for the 21st century*, Knopf, 1991.
7 Under development by the Centre for International Business Studies, Amstelveen, Netherlands.
8 Goold, M., *Strategic Control*, The Economist Books/Business Books, London, 1990.

13

RECONCILING CULTURAL DILEMMAS

As we have explained throughout the book, every country and organisation faces certain universal dilemmas. A nation's culture is expressed in the way people within it approach these dilemmas. This chapter explains how **transcultural competence** can be achieved by being aware of cultural differences, respecting them and ultimately reconciling them.

Awareness of cultural differences

An American CEO had exchanged customary, polite greetings with his Japanese opposite number, a ritual which the American felt had gone on far too long. They had at last come to the root of the problem and the Japanese president was being evasive, ducking all the straight questions and repeating that "with goodwill and sincerity" all such questions could be satisfactorily answered.

As part of the initial greeting ceremony the parties had exchanged *meishi* (business cards) and the American CEO, conscious of Japanese custom, had laid the cards on the table in front of him in the same pattern as the seating arrangement for the Japanese delegation. In this way he could call everyone by name, having a convenient reminder in front of him.

As the meeting grew more stressful and his impatience with evasive answers grew, he picked up one of the cards, absent-mindedly rolled it into a cylinder, unrolled it again and crossly cleaned his nails. Suddenly he felt the horrified eyes of the entire Japanese delegation on him! There was a long pause and then the Japanese president stood up and withdrew from the room. "We would like to call an intermission," the Japanese interpreter said. The American looked at the battered *meishi* in his hand. It was the one the Japanese president had given him.

This example aptly demonstrates the devastating effects which insufficient awareness of cultural differences may have. If the CEO had merely been following a long list of tips, or dos and don'ts, it is somehow unlikely that "don't abuse the *meishi*" would have been on the list. After all, there are thousands of possible mistakes.

But a **systematic** understanding of cultural differences would have enabled the CEO to have foreseen this pitfall and others. Had he remembered that the Japanese rarely answer directly, like to build a relationship before coming to the point, give their presidents very general duties, many of them ceremonial, so that they do not know the details, and regard *meishi* as symbolising the status of the person referred to, as well as the quality of the relationship being created, then he would never have dreamed of mangling someone's *meishi* while that person was watching!

Cultural awareness, then, is understanding **states of mind**, your own and those of the people you meet. You can never be fully informed, since there is an infinite range of potential errors, but our seven dimensions of culture provide us with a frame of reference for analysing ways in which people attribute meaning to the world around them.

One of the goals of cross-cultural training must therefore be to alert people to the fact that they are constantly involved in a process of assigning meaning to the actions and objects they observe. For cross-cultural training to be successful, it must not be limited to delivering more or less detailed information about other countries and cultures. If it is, even the most sophisticated model of cross-cultural differences will only enhance the particular stereotypes that the participants have about another culture. So if we are approached by participants after a training course with comments like, "Thank you, Dr Trompenaars, I already knew that I had difficulties working with the French. They are strange beings and you have proved it empirically. The information you just gave me proves that I am right," we know that something has gone wrong.

Increasingly, professionals in cross-cultural management, who seek to develop transcultural competence, sense the need to go beyond the defence of their own model. It is legitimate to have a mental model. We are all creatures of our culture. The problem is to learn to go beyond our own model, without being afraid that our long-held certainties will collapse. The need to win over others to our point of view, to prove the inferiority of their way of thinking, reveals our own insecurities and doubts about the strength of our identity. Genuine self-awareness accepts that we follow a particular mental cultural program and that members of other cultures have different programs. We may find out more about ourselves by exploring those differences.

The seven dimensions all indicate ways in which another culture may start from seemingly "opposite" premises. But this does not invalidate our own frameworks. It is simply a different approach from which we can learn. Milton Bennett, a cross-cultural researcher, has found that people encountering foreign cultures may **isolate** themselves and **separate** their norms and values from those of the foreign culture. But this only impedes self-awareness. Both sameness and difference tell us who we are: "I am like A, but *not* like B."

Respecting cultural differences

An initial step towards developing respect for cultural differences is to look for situations in our own life in which we would behave like a person from another culture. This is what helped a member of the purchasing department of a big European oil company who was negotiating an order with a Korean supplier. At the first meeting, the Korean partner offered a silver pen to the European manager. The latter, however, politely refused the present for fear of being bribed (even though he knew about the Korean custom of giving presents). Much to our manager's surprise, the second meeting began with the offer of a stereo system. Again the manager refused, his fear of being bribed probably heightened.

When he gazed at a piece of Korean china on the third meeting, he finally realised what was going on. His refusal had not been taken to mean: "let's get on with business right away", but rather: "If you want to get into business with me, you had better come up with something bigger." How embarrassing his refusal must have been for the Korean partner became clear to him when he remembered a similar situation in his own life. On one of his first dates with his wife, he had bought her a small present. But from the expression on her face, he could easily tell that it was not quite what she had expected. Remembering this made him accept the fact that the Korean partner was simply trying to establish a relationship and had no intention of bribing him. To avoid similar misunderstandings in future encounters with Korean partners, the manager decided to try to communicate that he, too, was interested in good relationships but that he felt no need to exchange expensive presents. (One alternative he might have come up with could have been to offer presents that were of little material value, but nevertheless signalled appreciation and interest.)

This story illustrates how we can learn to appreciate and respect behaviours and values different from our own. Thinking about situations in your own life might help you understand that behaviours that seemingly differ are often different only in terms of the type of situation in which you observe them, not in terms of their function. This will prevent you from prematurely valuing a behaviour as negative and, more importantly, help you understand what the other person is actually trying to do. In understanding the other's intentions, and in possibly signalling that you do understand those intentions, you take the first step towards developing a shared meaning with your partner.

Generally speaking, what is strong in another culture will also be present in some form in our own culture. We speak of "guilt cultures" and "shame cultures", for example: those which try to make us feel guilty for breaking rules, and those which demand public apologies and subject the miscreant to the hostile stares of their group, e.g. "loss of face". This is a significant difference between West and East: but who has never wished the ground would open up because of an excruciatingly embarrassing lapse?

Respect is most effectively developed once we realise that most cultural differences are in ourselves, even if we have not yet recognised them. For example, we often think that the Japanese are mysterious, even unreliable. You never know what they are feeling or thinking and they always say "yes", even when they are negative about something. But don't we have situations in which the same happens to us? If your own child has given a rather nervous and halting performance in her first solo in a school concert but must go on again after the interval, you might well say "Wonderful, darling" to give her confidence, even though you don't actually believe her performance was good.

Or suppose a minority employee who has been subject to discrimination in your company comes to see you in despair. You are worried that he might injure himself, sue the company or attack his supervisor. It is likely that you would work on re-establishing your relationship with this employee, gaining his confidence, *before* suggesting that he might consider alternative forms of behaviour. You would obviously be tactful and indirect in making these suggestions. You would be behaving in a "Japanese" manner, because the circumstances warrant it. But perhaps circumstances in Japan make the sense of self so vulnerable that one usually tiptoes around another person's sensibilities. If we assume that most Japanese have a frail sense of self, their behaviour makes very good sense! We would be wise to do the same when in Japan.

Consider another case encountered by a German engineer in South Africa. We all work for money and most of us have a sense of pride and duty in our work, but the money–duty continuum may be radically different in different cultures. The engineer gave his maid a Christmas bonus and she promptly disappeared for two months, since as she saw it she had no need to work. He was appalled. Of course we don't know her motives: she may have felt no obligation to an employer she disliked, but a sense of duty to an employer she did like. Or perhaps being a maid is only something she did in desperate circumstances. The engineer's wife concluded that she was "lazy", but such a judgment came from her own frame of reference.

To sum up, both awareness and respect are necessary steps towards developing transcultural competence. But even their combined power may not always suffice. In workshops, people often ask questions such as: "Why should only we respect and adapt to the other culture? Why don't they respect and adapt to ours?" We will come back to this question when we discuss reconciliation.

Another, perhaps more interesting problem is that of mutual empathy, a term employed by Milton Bennett. What happens when one person attempts to shift to another culture's perspective when at the same time the other person is trying to do the same thing?

Motorola University recently prepared carefully for a presentation in China. After considerable thought, the presenters entitled it "Relationships do not retire". The gist of the presentation was that Motorola had come to China in order to stay and help the economy to create wealth. Relationships with Chinese suppliers, subcontractors and employees would constitute a permanent commitment to building Chinese economic infrastructure and earning hard currency through exports.

The Chinese audience listened politely to this presentation but was quiet when invited to ask questions. Finally one manager put up his hand and said: "Can you tell us about pay for performance?"

What was happening here is very common. Even as we move towards the other person's perspective, they have started to move towards ours, and we pass each other invisibly like ships in the night. Remember that those Chinese who come to a presentation by a western company may already be pro-western and see western views as potentially liberating. This dynamic is especially strong when a country is small and poor. When a drug salesperson from a US company meets with the minister of health from Costa Rica, the former's salary may be ten times the latter's. This kind of encounter only hardens our prejudices: "See, they all want to be like us."

But foreign cultures have an integrity which only some of its members will abandon. In the Vietnam War the USA found that the genuine nationalists among the Vietnamese were very much tougher than their own opportunist allies. People who abandon their culture become weakened and corrupt. We need foreigners to be themselves if partnerships are to work. It is this very difference which makes relationships valuable.

This is why we need to **reconcile** differences, be ourselves but yet see and understand how the other's perspectives can help our own.

Reconciling cultural differences

Once we are aware of our own mental models and cultural predisposi-
tions, and can respect and understand that those of another culture are
legitimately different, then it becomes possible to reconcile differences.
Why do this? Because we are in the business of creating wealth and value,
not just for ourselves, but for those who live in different cultural worlds.
We need to share the values of buying, selling, of joint venturing, of working in partnership.

Take two companies, one in the Netherlands and one in Belgium. The
first was innovation oriented. The second relied on its strong traditional
reputation and the prestige ascribed to it by Belgian culture. The status of
the two companies was derived from achievement and ascription respectively. They could have quarrelled endlessly about their comparative
"worth", but they did not. Rather they jointly strove to establish a reputation for both innovation and quality which they then achieved.

There are ten steps which are useful in achieving reconciliation:

1   The theory of complementarity
2   Using humour
3   Mapping out a cultural space
4   From nouns to present participles and processes
5   Language and meta-language
6   Frames and contexts
7   Sequencing
8   Waving/cycling
9   Synergising and virtuous circling
10 The double helix

The theory of complementarity

The Danish scientist Niels Bohr proposed a theory of complementarity.
The ultimate nature of matter is manifested both as specific particles and
as diffuse waves. Nature reveals itself to us as a response to our measuring
instruments. There is no one form "out there", but forms which depend on
how we perceive them and how we measure them.

Throughout this book, all our seven dimensions have represented continua with two extremes. Universalism and particularism are not separate
but different, on a continuum between rules and exceptions. Things are
more or less similar to the rule, or more or less dissimilar and hence exceptional. You could not even define rules without also knowing what exceptions were. The terms are therefore complementary.

It is the same for all seven dimensions. The individual is more or less separate from the group. "Being by yourself" requires a group if the difference is to register. There can be no specific part without a concept of the diffuse whole. Directing yourself from inside outwards is necessarily in contrast to being directed from the outside inwards. To say that we seek to integrate our values and that all cultures look for integrity and reconciliation is a recognition that values are holistic to begin with.

Using humour

We become aware of dilemmas through humour, which signals an unexpected clash between two different perspectives.

Values taken to extremes often suggest that the opposite value is really present, rather than the proclaimed one: "The more he talked of his honour, the faster we counted our spoons." "Why does the ascent of the preacher's rhetoric in TV evangelism so often accompany the descent of his trousers?", the *New York Times* recently asked.

Corporations who announce that they "trust their people" may end up breaking into their offices at night and rifling their desks, because they cannot be seen distrusting them publicly but are secretly concerned about a spate of thefts. For the "lowdown" on what really happens in the corporation, look at the cartoons stuck on the walls of employees' offices. They are often incisive satires of the official line and reveal what the dilemmas really are.

Mapping out a cultural space

Another effective process for exploring dilemmas is to turn their "two horns" into axes to create a cultural space. We can map some or all of the seven dimensions on this cultural space. The map is constructed through either interviews or questionnaires. Issues mapped recently include:

> **A** Given the pluralism of local initiatives in Europe, is it possible to exercise any strategic leadership from US headquarters which is applicable to all the units concerned?
> (Universalism–particularism dilemma)
> **B** Given the obvious desirability of getting our best products on to the market according to the value of their achievements, is it possible to attain this while giving the autonomous R&D for high-potential products the space they need to mature?
> (Achievement–ascription dilemma)
> **C** Given the need for a quick response to very swiftly changing markets in the USA, is it possible to keep ourselves committed to a long-term vision developed at our centre in South Korea?
> (Short-term–long-term dilemma)

Respondents drew attention to the first three dilemmas in words para-phrased below:

A Universalism–particularism dilemma

● The markets in Europe could be served much better if our American HQ could only understand the particular needs we have over here.

● If the Europeans could only understand what it takes to become a truly global company.

● We know here in the USA very well what different markets need, but we need to co-educate them in order not to fall into the trap of having very happy clients but no margins for us. Economies of scale force us to limit our offerings.

B Achievement–ascription dilemma

● If we in R&D could get some more time to work out our very promising products without continuously being pushed by marketing, our products would be much better in the long run.

● You can't be innovative unless you are given some time to work things out. Customers need to leave you alone for a while.

● R&D people tend to deliver too late products which the market frequently doesn't need. In marketing we should be more responsible and give R&D strict guidelines and deadlines.

● In our company we should have more trust in what we are developing. It is good stuff. Let's go for it wholeheartedly.

C The short-term–long-term dilemma

● The Americans hinder our long-term achievements because of their drive for quarterly results. Our vision is often jeopardised by a quest for the quick buck!

● It seems like in the Far East and in Europe there are no shareholders. The ease with which they accept quarterly losses would be unacceptable in the USA.

Most of these remarks clearly show basic dilemmas that are inherent in cross-cultural debates. In intercultural encounters people frequently complain of excessive rivalry and an inability to harmonise the efforts of different units, representing different cultures.

Dilemma A can be mapped between the pluralism of local initiatives on the horizontal axis and the universal truth of HQ on the vertical axis (Figure 13.1).

Figure 13.1 **Dilemma A**

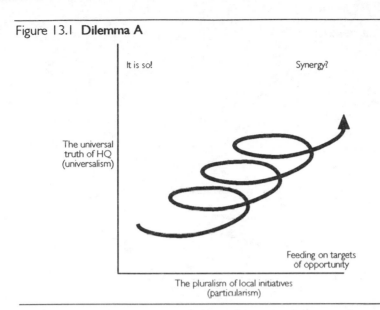

It is so!

Synergy?

The universal
truth of HQ
(universalism)

Feeding on targets
of opportunity

The pluralism of local initiatives
(particularism)

Dilemma B is between identification with customers' viewpoints on the horizontal axis, because it is the customer who buys the achievements of the product. On the other hand, R&D wants to be committed to the product by ascribing status to it, which allows its development without being hindered by clients' needs too early or too frequently (Figure 13.2).

Figure 13.2 **Dilemma B**

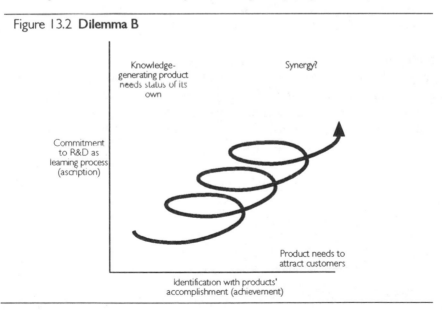

Knowledge-
generating product
needs status of its
own

Synergy?

Commitment
to R&D as
learning process
(ascription)

Product needs to
attract customers

Identification with products'
accomplishment (achievement)

Figure 13.3 **Dilemma C**

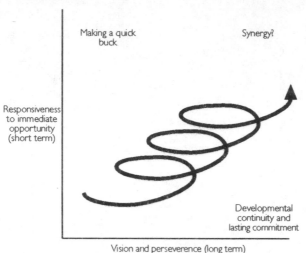

Making a quick buck

Synergy?

Responsiveness to immediate opportunity (short term)

Developmental continuity and lasting commitment

Vision and perseverence (long term)

Dilemma C is between short- and long-termism. On the one axis the market demands a quick response and US shareholders look for good returns every quarter. On the other axis we find the long term needs to be framed by a vision which allows the short term to have meaning (Figure 13.3).

The dilemma must be mapped before reconciling it, so that we and clients have a clear definition of what has to be reconciled. The remaining steps in the process show how genuine reconciliation can be attained.

From nouns to present participles and processes
A noun could be defined as "a person, place or thing". But a value is none of these and we get into difficulty when we use nouns like universalism or particularism, loyalty or dissent to describe the horns of a dilemma. We have done so in this book because it is the convention of the social sciences to make phenomena look and sound physical, but it is still misleading. So, as a step on the road to reconciliation, we shall turn all nouns into present participles, ending in -ing, which transforms them into processes. Thus:

Universalising–particularising
Individualising–communing
Specifying/analysing–diffusing/synthesising
Communicating neutrality–communicating emotion
Achieving–ascribing (status)
Directing oneself from inside–going with the flow of the environment
Sequencing time–synchronising time

Not all nouns can be made into present participles, but if we know what we want – to get rid of the "hard edges" and render the value as a process requiring the participation of people – then suitable words can be found. Since processes mingle in a way that things do not, we are now much closer to understanding that all seven dimensions are really continua, with a preponderance of one process at one end (yin) and a preponderance of the other process at the other end (yang). We have also softened the adversary structure of clashing nouns or "isms". This is what De Bono calls "water logic".

Language and meta-language

Since we are stuck with the structure of language, it is as well to consider how language achieves reconciliation. It does so by using a ladder of abstraction and putting one value (or horn of the dilemma) above the other, that is, by using both an object language and a meta-language and allowing them to dovetail.

Consider this famous quotation from Scott Fitzgerald:

"The test of a first rate intelligence is to hold two ideas in your mind at the same time and still retain the capacity to function. You must, for example, be able to see that things are hopeless, yet be determined to make them otherwise."

This might appear at first glance to be a contradiction, but it is not. Contradictions cancel each other out: they are meaningless. What the author has done here is to dovetail the two statements at different levels of language.

Meta-level	"be determined to make them otherwise"
Object level	"see that things are hopeless"

The object level is about things being hopeless. The meta-level is about the determination of the person who sees. The two statements are not contradictory because they do not apply to the same "things". The second is about the person seeing, not about the things seen.

This applies equally to our seven dimensions. We could say:

"The test of a first-rate manager is to hold two ideas in your mind at the same time and still retain the capacity to function."

You must, for example, be able to see that a **particular** customer request is outside the **universal** rules your company has set up, yet be determined to qualify the existing rule or create a new rule based on this case.

Meta-level	Determined to qualify rule or create new one

Object level	Particular request breaks existing rule

We could do the same for any of the seven dimensions. Take a small business unit which has enjoyed extraordinary success:

Meta-level	Ascribe importance to this strategy company-wide

Object level	Admire and reward this form of achieving

Top management has encouraged achievement in a particular unit and has ascribed universal importance to the strategy employed, so that other business units can benefit by emulating the particular achievement. Here both particularising and universalising, and achieving and ascribing have been reconciled.

Frames and contexts

In the previous example of language levels, you could say that the meta-level frames the object level:

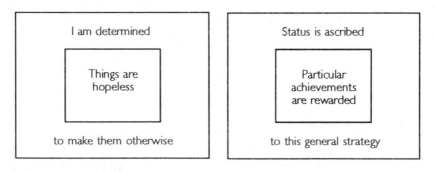

The usefulness of thinking in frame and contexts is that the latter contain and constrain the "picture" or the "text" within them. There is always a danger of people's value extremes "running away". "To see that things are hopeless" can lead to despair, unless framed by "a determination to make them otherwise". We might have concluded from the out-standing achievement of the business unit that top management should simply keep out of their way, but that would have prevented the organisa-tion learning from a local success.

The important thing to grasp is that text and context are reversible, as are the picture and the frame. We could focus on a very intelligent person and say: or we could say:

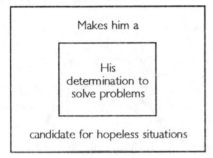

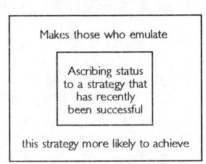

Sequencing

Values appear to clash and conflict when we assume that both must be expressed simultaneously. It isn't possible to be right and wrong, to uni-versalise and particularise, to be steered from inside and from outside at the same time. One obviously precludes the other.

But it is possible to go wrong and then correct, to particularise and then generalise, to observe outer trends and dynamics and then direct yourself at your objective. So a major element in reconciling values is to sequence processes over time.

Indeed one of the frames and contexts comments on what your present action is leading to: or:

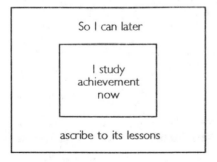

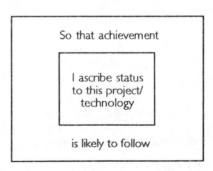

Waving/cycling

Have you every stopped to wonder what happens to our values if, instead of assuming they are things (i.e. colliding billiard balls), we assume that they are wave-forms? Common sense assumes values to be like coins, jewels or rocks. We could take the view that they are like water waves, electromagnetic waves, sound waves, light waves etc. This makes a great deal of difference.

Consider the cycle of sleeping and waking, which looks like Figure 13.4.

Figure 13.4 **Sleeping and waking**

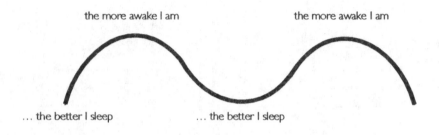

the more awake I am

the more awake I am

... the better I sleep   ... the better I sleep

Or consider music on various frequencies (Figure 13.5).

Figure 13.5 **High- and low-frequency sound**

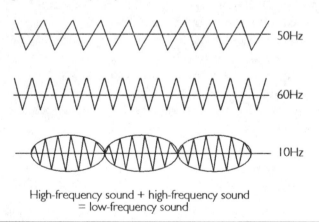

50Hz

60Hz

10Hz

High-frequency sound + high-frequency sound
= low-frequency sound

If we have two different frequencies, 50Hz and 60Hz, these combine to form a beat frequency of only 10Hz, because a low-frequency wave has been created by harmonising the two waves. The high-frequency sound is now "within" the low-frequency beat. If values are like sound waves, no wonder their harmony (what south-east Asians call *wa*) can be more beautiful still.

If the wave-form is a legitimate expression of values and if the values alter-

Figure 13.6 **Process of continuing improvement**

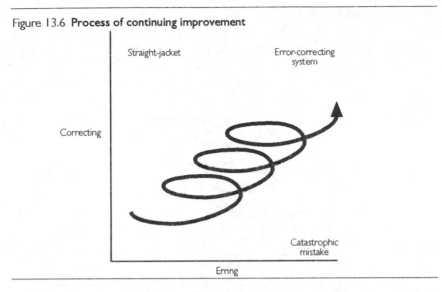

nate like sleeping and waking, relaxing and exciting, erring and correcting, then we can draw the wave-form between the axes as in Figure 13.6.

Here we first err, then correct, then err again, then correct again and so on. The entire process is called an **error correcting system**. We avoid both catastrophic mistakes (perhaps by using simulation) and the straight-jacket of never making a mistake. Arguably if we want to learn fast, many small errors which are corrected might be the best way. "Error", of course, is relative. If we call the bottom 35% of our performance "errors", we will go on improving. If we call only 5% "errors" we may come to ignore them or hush them up.

The notion of learning by error correction is so important that we include this idea in all our dilemmas, especially the seven dimensions. Suppose that we were to create a wave-form between universalising and particularising. It might look like Figure 13.7.

This is a diagram of how particular exceptions are encountered and noted before encompassing them within changed or reformed rules. No scientific law can ignore mounting anomalies. No legal statute can survive massive opposition. No corporate procedures can fail to account for a growing number of exceptions. In all such crises the old rules must be reformed or new ones created. The point is that rules must be open to refutation if we are to improve them. Nor can we properly appreciate what is unique and outstanding unless we know what the common standards are.

We have retained the idea of error correction by rendering our wave-form as a cycle. This assumes that we will periodically get things wrong and have to make a second "try" or circuit before improving on both axes.

Figure 13.7 **Generating new rules and reforming current ones**

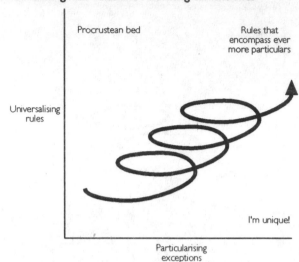

Synergising and virtuous circling

An important test of optimal reconciliation which includes both ends of the values continuum, in even greater harmony, is the criterion of synergy. The word comes from the Greek *sunergos*, meaning "to work with". When two values work with one another they are mutually facilitating and enhancing. Thus ascribing importance to a major project with France Télécom makes it more likely that your working group will be inspired to achieve that project. That your company has recently been seen to be achieving the project makes it far more likely that senior management will ascribe great importance to it in next year's strategy deliberation. The virtuous circle looks like Figure 13.8.

Synergy is also present in nature. Steel alloys for jet engines are immensely stronger than the strength of all their components combined. The molecular chain in the alloy is simply a stronger structure.

The double helix

Finally we come to our model of models: DNA, the double helix molecular structure (Figure 13.9). Let us make it clear that we are using this as a metaphor, not trying to borrow the mantle of biological science. But then most, if not all, of the social sciences are based on metaphors. Since cultures are alive we have consciously borrowed from the life sciences.

The double helix model helps to summarise the steps to reconciliation. The ladder of protein synthesis has four rungs. We have a ladder of values

Figure 13.8 **A virtuous circle between ascribing and achieving**

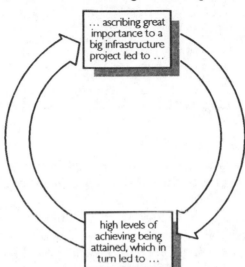

... ascribing great importance to a big infrastructure project led to ...

high levels of achieving being attained, which in turn led to ...

synthesis with seven rungs. The twisted ladder is full of **complementarities**. When the "pairs" come together unexpectedly it can be **funny**. We can use the uprights on each side of the ladder as cultural space for **mapping**. The twisted elements of the ladder constitute a growth **process**. Each twist of the spiral speaks the **language** of growth and contains coded instructions. Each turn of the helix is framed and **contextualised** by the helix within and around it, containing and constraining. The process is **sequential**. It constitutes **waves and cycles**, with synthesis producing growth and **synergy**.

In short, the double helix helps summarise all nine processes by which values are reconciled.

Figure 13.9 **The double helix of reconciliation**

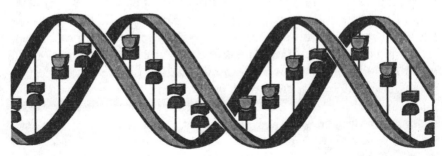

14

SOUTH AFRICA:
THE RAINBOW NATION

So far this book has concentrated on national cultural differences. In this chapter we discuss the differences found *within* one of the most pluralist societies in the world, South Africa.

The Dutch author remembers offering a kindergarten in the Netherlands a Shell-sponsored annual donation of 5000 Dutch florins, about US$2500. It was a scheme whereby Shell sponsored the charitable concerns of its own employees. The kindergarten operated in a poor immigrant community. Its board refused the money because it saw it as tainted by Shell's connection to South Africa. In this regard, it sided with the African National Congress (ANC) and sacrificed a small grant to poor domestic immigrants. As this example shows, not all dilemmas are easily solvable. Some divide the world, divide communities and split our own hearts.

Happily things have changed in South Africa and a man has been brought to power who has the creativity, courage and grandeur to reconcile cultural opposites. He is an extraordinary example of African humility. Whether his example and vision will be enough to heal decades of injustice remains to be seen. Some people rise above oppression, most do not. South Africa's future remains in the balance.

One of President Nelson Mandela's prime goals seems to be reconciliation, to unite the variety of cultures in South Africa around one major cause: a free and democratic nation in which bloodshed and conflict define the past, not the future. After his inaugural speech he has been very clear about his strategy. The white population, Afrikaaners and English-speaking whites, are seen as an essential component in South Africa's future economy. Furthermore, Mandela has done his utmost to convince foreign investors that reconciliation between races can be the basis of stability in South Africa. Afrikaaners received a presidential guarantee that their language and culture would not be attacked in revenge for the past. And it should not be forgotten that some prominent Afrikaaners, like former Vice-President Frederik Willem de Klerk, came of age after the introduction of apartheid and began to question the very basis of the system they inherited from their predecessors. The transition to black rule has not resulted in a bloodbath and it was achieved by black and white together.

The Truth and Reconciliation Committee, under Archbishop Desmond Tutu, was given the task of investigating the human rights violations of the Apartheid years. This process will result in an amnesty being granted to those who fully confess. Although some people fear that making public details of the excesses will stir up bitterness, this approach is a unique effort to find a path to reconciliation.

In the context of President Mandela's call for a productive way of reconciling cultural differences, the Centre for Intercultural Business Studies recently accepted an invitation from its namesake and South African partner. In close co-operation with Louis van de Merwe, president of CIBS South Africa, we mapped the cultures in South Africa according to our seven-dimensional model. The results confirmed that South Africa can be seen as a microcosm of the world. Not only black Africans from a variety of backgrounds, language, ethnicities, tribes etc. but also white people, European descendants and a variety of Asian cultures, can be found in this fascinating continent. Colonial cultures were not able to suppress the indigenous African cultures. The country has been forced to experiment with new forms of living together based on a variety of backgrounds, and this is also true in business. Here reconciling principles are put to an extreme test.

Dilemma mapping in South Africa

Africa is culturally diverse, not simply among blacks and whites but also among the various language groups within the black community as well as between rural and urban black and white communities. We divided our sample into eight groups by language group as follows and drew mainly on economically active, therefore urban, respondents.

Language group	Universalism–particularism	Individualism–communit.	Neutrality–affectivity	Specificity–diffuseness	Achievement–ascription	Inner–outer directedness
Afrikaans	89	58	70	70	61	72
English	92	72	57	72	65	67
Zulu	78	51	65	75	58	60
South Sotho	70	42	54	70	58	48
North Sotho	71	68	53	51	41	60
Xhosa	38	73	36	84	58	61
Tsonga	71	22	45	58	55	49
Tswana	40	52	61	78	63	65

Universalism–particularism
The law has played a major part in apartheid policies in recent decades. It

is not surprising, therefore, that English and Afrikaans South Africans favour universal laws with minimal exceptions. More surprising is the strong support for universalism in the Zulu community, contrasted with the strong support for particularism and exceptions to the law among the Xhosa community in which the African National Congress is strongly represented.

Of course, the universalism favoured by Zulus is not the same universalism favoured by the English and Afrikaaners, which helps explain the separatist strategy of KwaZulu-Natal province, which sets its own laws for its own people and which for many years collaborated with the apartheid regime in murdering members of the ANC. The Zulus are traditional warriors with a strict military code. Their 78% score on universalism contrasts sharply with the 38% of the Xhosa and the Tswana known for their high flexibility in unanticipated situations. Even today Zulus are found in security, police and military occupations, while the Xhosa are the negotiators, legislators and mediators.

Individualism–communitarianism

English South Africans are the descendants of immigrants who left their countries for a lone trek into what they considered to be a wilderness. It is therefore not surprising that they compare with Americans on individualism (72%). They are substantially more individualist than the Afrikaaner community (58%), a language group specialising in political rather than economic power, originally Boer farmers who fought fiercely against British domination. Afrikaaner people have always had a more collective identity, a feeling that their culture would disappear unless tenaciously defended against the whole world. The "Voortrekkers" took to their wagons to avoid British rule, but eventually had to fight.

Interestingly, the Xhosa are highly individualist too, which may explain the appeal of Nelson Mandela to the western world. He was a prisoner of conscience and has kept his dignity in the tradition of Henry David Thoreau and the great dissenters. There are highly communitarian groups, the Tsonga, the South Sotho and to a lesser extent the Zulus. Black South Africans are also communitarian in their tactics, if not their temperament, with a stronghold on trade unions and the ability to mobilise crowds. Any group which constitutes a majority of the population can advance its cause by collective representations.

Neutrality–affectivity

One of the most potentially dangerous, even explosive, differences is between the white Afrikaans community and the black Xhosa and Tsonga tribes. The latter are extremely exuberant and affective in their behaviour,

with strong body language, including dancing on the balls of the feet in a ritual step. In contrast, the Afrikaaners reveal very little feeling, are taciturn,
serious and controlled. The problem is that such marked contrasts in
behaviour lend themselves to stereotyping. The exuberant black becomes a
"savage" menacing civilisation. The controlled white becomes a "cold,
uncaring" person. As each side faces off against each other, each becomes
more of a caricature, hugely over-excited, increasingly blocked emotionally.
The excesses drive the other to further excess as each tries to make up for the
lack in the other. The end may come neither with a bang nor a whimper, but
with Xhosas erupting in rage and Afrikaaners freezing into icicles of rigidity.

Specific–diffuse

There are no notable differences along this dimension. This does not mean,
however, that all groups share the same orientation. Some black South
African groups combine diffuse features, such as the importance attached
to good and deep relationships, and putting the whole and visions before
analyses and facts, with more specific features, such as a very direct way of
relating, and attaching great interest to principles and a consistent moral
stand, demonstrated by the success of indigenous Christian churches
among the black population in South Africa. English South Africans tend
to combine specific features such as putting analyses and facts before the
whole and visions, with diffuse features such as a more indirect style of
communication. These different mixtures of diffuse and specific features
may cause conflict, but may also be seen as conducive to reconciliation.

Achievement–ascription

Differences here are significant and consistent, but not large. The English,
especially, define themselves by economic achievement. The Afrikaaners
who, until recently, had friends in government are also achievement oriented, but slightly less so. All black Africans with the exception of the
Tswana are more ascription oriented, with the North Sotho most pro-
nounced. But overall, achievement is the dominant pattern. This may be a
temporary phenomenon, since opportunities have been opened up quite
recently and hopes may still be running high. It may also reflect substan-
tial changes taking place within urbanised populations. In any event, differences are not large enough to cause serious trouble. South Africa wants
to become the achieving society of Africa. There is no lack of motivation,
although there may be a serious lack of education and opportunity.

Inner versus outer directedness

We might have expected black Africans to be fatalistic, supernatural and outer directed, partly as a consequence of colonialism and apartheid, during which period any attempt to become masters of their own destinies was severely curtailed. In contrast, the minority white regime would have had the experience of influencing the activities of millions of voteless blacks. They would be overwhelmingly inner directed.

However, the differences are not as sharp as we might have expected. True, the Afrikaans speakers, who were long the arbiters of apartheid, are the most inner directed, with the English who made their way in commerce second, but the Tswana, once again the exceptional group, come close behind, as do the Xhosa and the Zulus. Here we think we can see the pattern of a successful struggle for liberation. Asserting your freedom and finally winning it is an exercise in inner direction, and it is not surprising that the Xhosa, who spearheaded the ANC, score among the highest in inner direction, with the Zulus third among blacks.

To a very real extent South Africa's struggle for human rights was played out in front of a western audience. It is not surprising, therefore, that its doctrines were those of personal struggle, with those most impatient of injustice rising to leadership positions through personal courage and inner-directed defiance, which gave a lead to less bold spirits. It was "moral theatre", but like Gandhi's struggle in India it was designed to appeal to western democratic traditions in which the human spirit revolts against injustice. It was western sanctions which finally brought the apartheid regime to the ballot box. Asian economies like Japan played little part. Mandela and his followers aimed for North American and European support and they won it. This strongly influenced the whole culture of the liberation struggle.

Looking to future development in Southern Africa, it is this inner directedness which might provide the early indication of high potential for developing an entrepreneurial economy which could become the locomotive that moves the sub-Saharan region forward towards an "African miracle".

Comparing African and western mental models

Where are the gaps widest between the western mental model and that in South Africa? Where does the society threaten to come apart? Where are the opportunities for creative synergy and reconciliation of dilemmas?

If we examine the data we can see that the three widest gaps are in universalism–particularism, especially that between whites and the Xhosa and Tswana; individualism–communitarianism, to which the Xhosa are exceptions (we can expect strong trade union pressure for wage rises since individualists also use voluntary associations to get their way); and a very large gap between the neutrality of whites, especially Afrikaaners, and the affectivity of blacks, especially the Xhosa. We can map these three bifurcations within our cultural space and describe what might happen if they became lop-sided, top-heavy, compromised, adversarial, defensively avoidant or synergised. The cultural space would look something like Figure 14.1.

Figure 14.1 **Mapping the bifurcations**

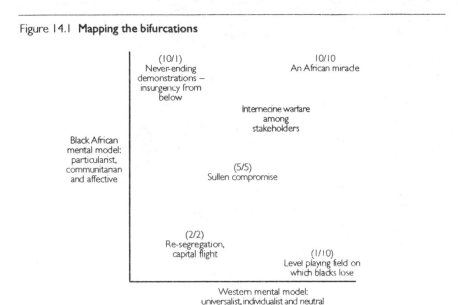

What white-dominated business is trying to do is to create the conventional image of the level playing field (1/10). For obvious reasons – less education and skill, less universalism and individualism – blacks are likely to lose in such a contest, a situation which the political majority will find intolerable. They are likely to resort to a "freedom struggle" which will take the form of never-ending demonstrations and insurgency from below, will tend to cripple industrial relations and is likely to frighten off investors. The struggle could end in a sullen compromise 5/5, in re-segregation and capital flight (2/2) or in domination of either the demonstration mode or the level playing field mode, i.e. 10/1 or 1/10. Worst of all, this split could trigger an internecine war among stakeholders in which the government, corporations, unions, shareholders and the community all try to grab the others' shares instead of working together to create wealth. The dispute may be fed by black insurgents clashing with ultra-neutral Afrikaaners, as thousands of "victorious" workers are told that international investors are withdrawing all funds, leading black governments to seize the assets of "rogue corporations" – which will only dry up any further investment.

It is not difficult to create a vicious circle from such events (Figure

Figure 14.2 **A vicious circle**

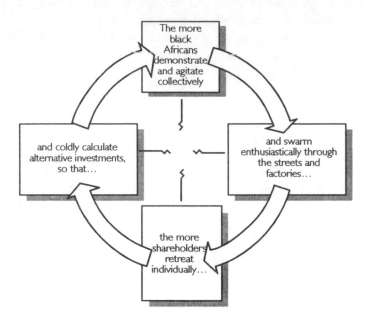

14.2). But it is also possible, if difficult, to generate a virtuous circle that spirals towards synergy (Figure 14.3).

There is probably a residue of goodwill towards South Africa's ascent from domination. People may want to invest there, yet fear personal losses if they do. The virtuous circle reconciles collective aspiration with individual rewards, black African enthusiasm with the calculating mode of capital markets, continuing law and order with a place in the sun for particular people seeking a better life. The helix would wind between the two dangerous extremities, as in Figure 14.4.

We succeed in avoiding both the illusion of the level playing field on which black Africans fail, and the non-stop demonstrations triggered by this failure. Instead we create an economy which is genuinely fair and level because the values of all eight cultures have been reconciled, and where black Africans have joined together to create the rules by which they will operate and be assessed.

There are encouraging signs of a growing faith in reconciliation in South African business, such as the adoption of *bosberaads* in which former enemies meet and debate their differences; the establishment of the National Economic Development and Labour Council (NEDLAC: a forum

Figure 14.3 **A virtuous circle**

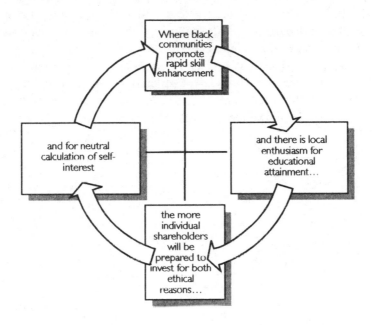

Figure 14.4 **Helical development**

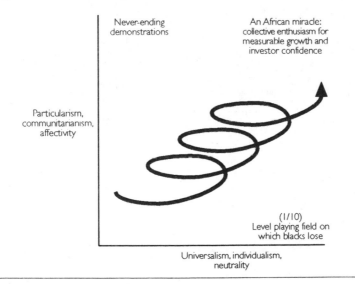

in which representatives of organised business, organised labour, government and socially excluded groups negotiate to try to reach consensus on social and economic policy) and the new Labour bill that provides for the creation of workplace forums that facilitate a shift from adversarial collective bargaining to joint problem solving and participation.

Acknowledging that South African culture has a triple heritage, from African society, Europe and Asia, all of which have a key role to play, might lead to the evolution of a unique new "rainbow management" style and contribute to the generation of a South African economic miracle.

15

GENDER, ETHNICITY AND FUNCTIONAL DIVERSITY

As well as differences between nations, there are also differences in the way in which men and women approach dilemmas. This chapter discusses those differences, and goes on to consider gender, ethnic and functional diversity within the USA, often described as a cultural 'melting pot'.

Gender differences worldwide

Figure 15.1 gives profiles of gender differences worldwide based on interviews with male and female managers. At first glance these are disappointing since differences are small. But this, in itself, is highly significant.

Why are the male and female scores so close? The women we studied were trying to make their way as managers in a predominantly male world and trying to escape the stereotypes with which women often find themselves labelled. If you were a woman in such an environment, would you adopt professionally neutral behaviour, or easily burst into tears? The truth is that the way to the top in any organisation is to adopt its most salient values and eschew its least salient. If anything, women in North America and north-west Europe need to work harder than men to show they are achieving individuals, measuring themselves by specific criteria and by universal yardsticks.

That said, some differences do exist, mostly on issues where stereotypes are weaker. Women are consistently more outer directed than men, feeling less personal control over the direction of their lives, and they are much more synchronic in their relationship to time, telescoping past, present and future and doing things simultaneously or in parallel rather than in sequence. We suspect this difference may remain because there are no stereotypes around synchronicity as there are, for example, around female intuition (diffusion). Hence no conscious effort is being made to live up to masculine values of sequential thinking. Women admit to being slightly more emotional than men, but even women are trying not to be emotional. If we isolate American scores, American men admit to show-

Figure 15.1 **Gender profiles**

World samples	Male	Female
Universalism–particularism	66	64
Individualism–communitarianism	50	52
Neutral–affective	59	56
Specific–diffuse	71	72
Achievement–ascription (of status)	60	61
Internal–external (control)	62	54
Time orientation past/present/future	1.28/1.93/2.76	1.23/2.03/2.70
Sequence–synchronicity	5.7 (low)	4.4 (high)

English-speaking democracies and NW Europe	Male	Female
Universalism–particularism	70	73
Individualism–communitarianism	53	56
Neutral–affective	59	57
Specific–diffuse	71	72
Achievement–ascription (of status)	60	61
Internal–external (control)	62	54
Time orientation past/present/future	1.25/1.90/2.76	1.07/2.04/2.85
Sequence–synchronicity	6.2	5.1

Latin cultures (South America, southern Europe, Caribbean)	Male	Female
Universalism–particularism	63	61
Individualism–communitarianism	45	46
Neutral–affective	56	53
Specific–diffuse	66	67
Achievement–ascription (of status)	52	51
Internal–external (control)	61	55
Time orientation past/present/future	1.39/1.89/2.68	1.34/2.01/2.61
Sequence–synchronicity	5.7	5.4

Asian cultures	Male	Female
Universalism–particularism	59	54
Individualism–communitarianism	37	39
Neutral–affective	64	62
Specific–diffuse	60	56
Achievement–ascription (of status)	48	43
Internal–external (control)	51	43
Time orientation past/present/future	1.06/2.08/2.83	1.12/2.13/2.66
Sequence–synchronicity	5.7	4.8

ing more emotion: it is now politically correct to do so.

There is some evidence that the French want their women to be different, while Americans want their women to be the same. The American female manager is more individualist than the male, the French female significantly less individualist. One might ask whether organisations should seek to promote women because they are "just as good" as men, or because they are "significantly different" and they want the benefit of that difference. These are two good but very different reasons for promoting women.

Clearly there is no such thing as a "female culture" in the middle and upper reaches of major corporations where our work has been done. This is because we have not yet been able to look at situations where women form a critical mass and make the rules of the corporation. Nor is there a "female culture" globally. Nearly all our female respondents were outnumbered, some heavily. There could and will be a female culture when sufficient numbers join certain corporations and set their strategies. The Body Shop, for example, is a largely female culture and is almost certainly different from male-dominated corporations.

But we must also be wary of expecting that women managers in the West would uphold the "weaker", less popular end of the value dimensions, i.e. be particularist not universal, diffuse not specific, ascriptive in getting status from their husbands and not achieving personally, warm rather than cold etc. If men specialise in being tough and women specialise in being tender, the oppression of tenderness by toughness will not cease. Women do not play "soft" roles in US corporations because they know they would lose if they tried! They would be seen as less "American" and hence central to cultural life. Theirs is certainly a wise precaution.

However, we must not forget the emphasis on reconciliation in earlier chapters. The point is not to be tough or tender, but to be tough on problems and tender with people; not to choose between rules and particular exceptions, but to make sure that the exception proves the rule, the community nurtures its individuals and ascribed values are achieved. The importance of women in the workforce is that, provided they are not exploited, they are capable of revealing values different yet complementary to those of men, thereby creating a synthesis of values. A strategy for both men and women is to learn to command all the value dimensions, to be individualist enough to generate a group which develops individuals, to be universalist enough to cover all particulars, yet to realise when an exception is so crucial that only a new universal will suffice.

Diversity in the USA

Recently the Society for Human Resource Management (SHRM) asked the Centre for Intercultural Business Studies in Amsterdam and the Ruth Institute (Philadelphia) to co-operate in conducting a survey among (potential) participants of its annual national conference in Orlando in 1995. More than 1000 participants responded to a 60-item questionnaire developed in order to measure basic cultural differences. The main conclusions can be summarised as follows.

Ethnic diversity exhibits far greater differences than gender, perhaps because women can more easily approximate men (and vice versa) than black Americans, Hispanics, American Indians and Asian Americans can approximate Caucasians. Moreover, ethnic groups go home to their own kind. Men and women tend to go home to each other.

A voluntary association of HR specialists is significantly different from American managers as a whole. The function you play in a corporation or your willingness to confer with those from other organisations fulfilling the same function would appear to generate a diverse culture and sub-group within US business. Our SHRM sample was significantly more concerned with groups and teams (communitarianism), more concerned to base their achievements on who they were, i.e. women, native Americans, blacks (ascription), more diffuse, i.e. in the multiplicity of relationships, more externally controlled by the needs of clients and more synchronic in conceiving of time.

This resonates with the judgment that HR activities in the USA are one of the places where the counter-cultural advocates of the early 1970s found a working home, and that people in such a role have a distinctive outlook shaped by the cultural rebellions of the 1960s and early 1970s. Much of the ad hoc radicalism of these times was influenced by sympathy for oppressed minority groups, concern for the environment and about injustice to women and so on. HR initiatives are one way of pursuing such goals without disruption or loss of income.

We might also note that the number of ethnic minorities with a middle-class lifestyle and a good job was probably higher in this sample than among US business as a whole. Problems with black, Hispanic, Asian or native American workforces are often dealt with by hiring a supervisor or HR specialist from the ethnic group concerned, so that cultural conflicts can be resolved at managerial levels. In short, SHRM respondents constituted a cultural mosaic with minority group members not only more senior and more numerous than in US business culture at large, but more assertive and influential. Ethnic group members had reason to believe that they represented to management the cultures from which they came.

All such considerations probably contributed to the differences we found and the tendency of minority group members to remain true to their traditions. We will go through the seven dimensions in turn. Figure 15.2 summarises the first six.

Figure 15.2 **Diversity within the SHRM conference**

Ethnic group	Universalism–particularism	Individualism–communit.	Neutral–affective	Specific–diffuse	Achievement–ascription	Internal–external
Black/African	51	52	35	45	52	43
Native American	41	43	62	32	48	22
Asian/Pacific Islander	43	29	71	29	56	34
White/Caucasian	65	71	44	67	78	69
Hispanic	63	62	32	34	61	61
Other	58	47	39	45	55	46

Universalism–particularism

You will recall the car accident that we discussed in Chapter 4. On the responses to this dilemma differences were relatively small. HR conferences largely share the USA's high universalism, although by a significantly smaller margin: 91 to 95. Men and women are identical, both seeking to succeed or otherwise according to a common set of rules. Caucasians and Native Americans tend to pull up the universalist scores. Black Americans, Asians and Hispanics tend to pull these down, with a minority espousing particularism and exceptionalism, believing perhaps that the "level playing field" is not as fair to those of their race as is commonly supposed. In Figure

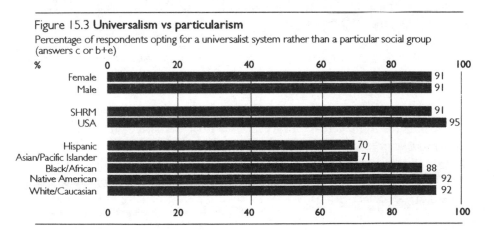

Figure 15.3 **Universalism vs particularism**
Percentage of respondents opting for a universalist system rather than a particular social group (answers c or b+e)

15.3 we can see the percentage of respondents who would consider that their friend had no right to expect any help in court after the accident, and those who would allow them some right but not lie in court.

However, even among Hispanic and Asian minorities there is no major challenge to the US legal system and the need to serve it by truthful witness, even where people of your own ethnic group are facing punishment. The question used was about the traffic accident and refusing to cover up the fact that your best friend was speeding. Asians and Hispanics within the USA are closer to the score of South-east Asia, Spain and Latin America, but only halfway there. They are clearly divided between American universalism and the greater particularism of their traditional culture.

The group versus the indiviual

Each of us must decide what we owe ourselves and what we owe the groups which raised us, educated us, employ us. Do we start with what "I want" or do we consider our obligations? 1000 US managers answered the following question:

> Two people were discussing ways in which one could improve the quality of life:
>
> **A** One said: "It is obvious that if one has as much freedom as possible and the maximum opportunity to develop oneself, the quality of one's life will improve as a result."
> **B** The other said: "If the individual is continuously taking care of his/her fellow human beings the quality of life will improve for everyone, even if it obstructs individual freedom and individual development."
>
> Which of the two ways of reasoning do you think is usually best, A or B?

Here, in contrast to universalism-particularism, the contrast between SHRM and US managerial culture as a whole is massive. Only 55% of human resource professionals at this conference chose the individualist option, compared with 79% of US managers generally, a difference of 24% – larger than that between most national cultures. This is probably a result of the social conscience that motivates much HR work and the desire to develop the careers of minority aspirants. It is of interest that Caucasians are more socially oriented than Hispanics, perhaps defining them-

Figure 15.4 **Individualism vs communitarianism**
Percentage of respondents opting for individual freedom

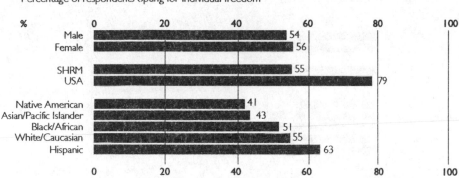

selves as "change agents" for a more inclusive society. Native Americans and Asians are more socially than individually oriented. Females are marginally more individualist than males, perhaps fearing that they will be taken advantage of if they are too altruistic.

Female individualism is characteristic of the USA. In most other countries men are significantly more individualist. Female "liberation" has been defined in the USA as making it in a male competitive arena. Hence women tend to score even more like men.

To show or not to show our emotions

There are good reasons for showing our emotions – how else can other people keep us happy and know what we want? But there are also good reasons for emotional restraint and neutrality: for reserving our feelings for very important occasions, not making demands, not ruffling feathers, being attuned to soft signals. There is no "better way". Cultures have conventions about how much or little you show and draw their conclusions about your mood, pain and pleasure accordingly. We asked the following question:

> Please indicate the degree to which you agree or disagree with the following statement (a = strongly agree; b = agree; c = undecided; d = disagree; e = strongly disagree):

> In retrospect I very often think I have given away too much in my enthusiasm.

We can see from Figure 15.5 that among HR professional men showing more emotion is considered good – 54 report wearing their hearts on their

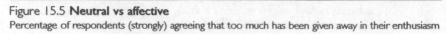

Figure 15.5 **Neutral vs affective**
Percentage of respondents (strongly) agreeing that too much has been given away in their enthusiasm

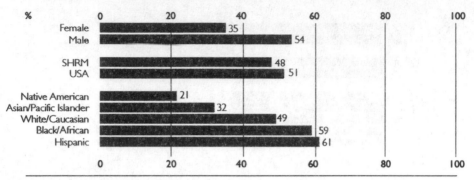

sleeves. They are improving their EQ (emotional quotient) and showing the sensitivity practised by facilitation. Good HR men should be "in touch with themselves". Women eschew affectivity in much larger numbers: 65% choose neutrality, only 35% affectivity. They probably calculate that for them to succeed the stereotype of "hysterical woman" must be left even further behind. Once again, this shows American women on a different path to women in most of the rest of the world, who admit to being more affective than men.

Among ethnic minorities, Hispanics judge themselves as too excitable by the norms of their US culture, closely followed by black Americans. Asian Americans and Native Americans are emphatically neutral and rarely give themselves away. HR professionals as a group may also be fighting the "touchy-feely" stereotype. They are less affective than US managers as a whole.

How far do we get involved?

Closely related to whether we show emotions in dealing with other people is the degree to which we engage others in specific areas of life and single levels of personality, or diffusely in multiple areas of our lives and at several levels of personality at the same time.

In specific-oriented cultures a manager segregates the task relationship she or he has with a subordinate from other dealings. But in some cultures every life space and every level of personality tend to permeate all others.

Ethnic differences are evident under the headings of specificity and diffuseness. The range is illustrated by responses to the following situations:

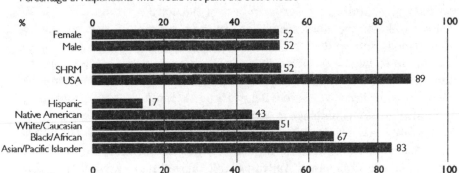

Figure 15.6 **Specific vs diffuse**
Percentage of respondents who would not paint the boss's house

A boss asks a subordinate to help him paint his house. The subordinate, who doesn't feel like doing it, discusses the situation with a colleague.

A The colleague argues: "You don't have to paint the house if you don't feel like it. He is your boss at work. Outside he has little authority."
B The subordinate argues: "Despite the fact that I don't feel like it, I will paint the house. He is my boss and you can't ignore that outside work either."

In specific societies status is confined to the job in hand, not to situations in general. If I meet my boss in the bowling alley where he is a novice and I am a champion, I will treat him like the novice he is, not rudely but realistically. Back at work, he instructs me.

The scores on this question are summarised in Figure 15.6. The really extraordinary difference is between US managers as a whole – 89% of them reject the boss's diffuse authority and its influence beyond the workplace – and SHRM members, only 52% of who reject diffuse thinking. What makes SHRM members so different? Why do they have a strong tendency to diffuseness even in a situation as seemingly open and shut as this one?

One reason might be that HR management is not, in fact, a specific function or task within corporations, in the way that sales, R&D and finance are. HR personnel are responsible for employees in whatever department they work. There is no part of the organisation where human processes operate where HR's remit does not run. They may be called in and consulted on any human problem affecting the company. Because their authority is diffuse and crosses boundaries, so does the way they think.

Once again there is no male–female divide on this topic. A small majority would decline to paint their boss's house, but 48% of both genders would agree. Minority group members of SHRM are even more diffuse in their thinking. We have seen that "human resources" pervade every department, but so does being black, being Asian, being an American Indian and being Hispanic. In so far as being a minority person is a problem, that problem diffuses everywhere and the solution – non-discrimination – diffuses everywhere too. Being Hispanic is not simply a problem in accounting, but a challenge in general for that person in all departments.

Minority groups also bring their own cultures to the USA. Hispanics and Asians come from more diffuse cultures like Mexico, Puerto Rico, Columbia, the Philippines, Taiwan etc. It takes time to assimilate and it may not be wise to try. Highly cohesive ethnic groups, Japanese Americans and Jews, have been among the most successful in the USA and they have generally kept their cultures intact.

Is high status earned through achievement or ascribed?

All societies give certain members higher status than others, signalling that unusual attention should be focused on such people and their activities. While some societies accord status to people on the basis of their achievements, others ascribe it to them by virtue of age, class, gender, education, position, project and posture. Hence the curator of a museum, surrounded as she is by beautiful things, has taste, refinement and sensibility ascribed to her. It is, in contrast, hard to say what she has achieved – perhaps a successful exhibition – but her association with the museum is probably stronger. In contrast, a star salesman of aluminium siding is identified by his sales record and the bonuses he earns. Status comes, if at all, from his success at selling and very little else. Status is thus either achieved by success at some task or calling, or ascribed to people because the culture they live in likes what they are.

Achievement-oriented cultures justify their hierarchies by claiming that senior people have "achieved more" for the organisation; their authority, justified by skill and knowledge, benefits the organisation.

Ascription-oriented organisations justify their hierarchies by "power-to-get-things-done". This may consist of power over people and be coercive, or power through people which is participative. There is a high variation within ascriptive cultures and participative power has well-known advantages. Whatever form power takes, it is intended to advance the values to which status has been ascribed, and so help the organisation realise its vision through managers who personify it.

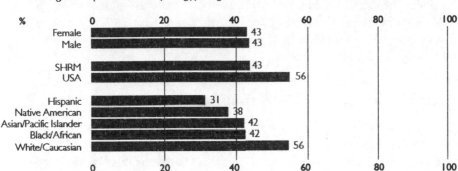

Figure 15.7 **Achievement vs ascription**
Percentage of respondents who (strongly) disagree that men and women are treated differently

Ascribing cultures tend to following characteristics that "naturally" evoke admiration, i.e. older and wiser people, those with dignity and presence, beautiful and elegant women, highly qualified experts, and those running projects thought to be of natural importance: the Headstart Programme, the Peace Corps, the Equal Opportunity Commission.

Within HR doctrine there is also a strong current of opinion that minority group members must accept their ethnicity, i.e. as being black, Asians, Native or Hispanic Americans. In order to do this, ascription would need to be placed first: "I am a black American and achieve as a black American, holding open the door to fellow blacks and acting as a role model for them."

It is commonly believed among HR professionals that without this ethnic identification the success of minority members merely reinforces the dominant achievement ethos, so that successful blacks, Hispanics or women are used to prove that no further assistance is needed for those groups. The best of them will achieve on their own.

This may help explain the much higher achievement ethic among American managers in general than among HR professionals attending the conference. The scores are shown in Figure 15.7 in response to the statement, "In our society men and women are treated significantly differently."

Those who thought that treatment was significantly different would attribute this to ascriptive norms; those who denied this difference would attribute women's lower pay and position to their non-achievement, a fair and logical consequence. The figure above shows the extent to which "different treatment" was rejected. 43% of both men and women regard the opportunities of men and women to achieve to be roughly equivalent. Women do not complain more than men about difference in treatment, perhaps because at least some women are confident of achieving and see this as their route to the top, rather than by protesting against inequality.

However non-whites complain of discrimination (against women) in far larger proportions than do Caucasians or American managers in general. 69% of Hispanics, 62% of Native Americans and 58% of black and Asian Americans see the "playing field" as not level for women and almost certainly not level for themselves.

Control or be controlled: American belief in inner-directedness

An important dimension concerns the idealised relationship between humans and the environment. Cultures with an organic view of nature see human beings as immersed within, and hence as part of, the larger eco-system. To survive we "go with the flow", adapt to natural forces and allow ourselves to be outer directed.

In contrast, other cultures have a more mechanical view of themselves as controlling, mastering and subjecting nature, as one might plough a field or clear a forest and harness natural laws to do one's bidding. Such a view is inner directed and "puts you in the driver's seat", to quote an Avis advertisement. Roger Bacon declared that "knowledge is power". Through scientific advances we demonstrate to each other that nature can be predicted and controlled: we even "master" business administration and "call the shots".

The American psychologist Rotter,[1] working in the 1960s, developed a scale designed to measure whether people had an internal locus of control, typical of more successful Americans, or an external locus of control, typical of relatively less successful Americans, disadvantaged by their circumstances or shaped by the competitive efforts of their rivals. Outer-directed persons tend to bewail their "bad luck" and cry foul.

We used the questions he devised to assess our 1000 US managers' relationship with natural events. The answers suggest that there are some very significant differences here between geographical areas. These questions all take the form of alternatives; managers were asked to select the statement they believed most reflected reality. The first of these pairs was:

A Becoming a great success is a matter of hard work; luck has little or nothing to do with it.
B Getting a good job depends mainly on being in the right place at the right time.

Figure 15.8 shows the percentage of respondents who chose the answer A, i.e. the inner directed. These scores are very much in line with what we find elsewhere in the world – males believing that much more of

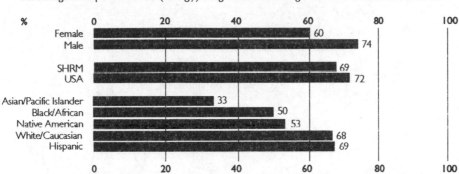

Figure 15.8 **Internal vs external control**
Percentage of respondents who (strongly) disagree that becoming a success is a matter of hard work

their destiny is in their own control. Females seem to be significantly more "outer directed".

HR specialists are somewhat less inner directed than US managers as a whole, 68% to 72%. Perhaps they experience the necessity of having to consult widely and "grow" people rather than direct them. Perhaps they had been consulted on cases of injustice to minorities. Yet the difference is small. Female HR personnel are considerably more outer directed: 60% to 74%. Women may feel that their careers depend very much on being liked and on unknowable responses from men. Hispanics are marginally more inner directed than Caucasians, a reflection possibly of the macho tradition of the irresistible man. But Asians and native Americans, like most of the cultures from which they come, are preponderantly outer directed (65%) and this may be more a matter of aesthetics than of oppression, of being in harmony with the universe.

Ethnic minorities tend to be criticised whatever they do: for being "too pushy" if inner directed, or "too passive" and quiet if outer directed. Women are also caught in this trap. Being stereotyped as gentle "by nature", they easily offend men if they are inner directed or assertive. Even in HR positions they feel generally less secure and more at the mercy of outside events and unforeseeable contingencies. This may be a realistic reflection of their lower pay and seniority.

How is time organised in the USA?

If only because managers need to co-ordinate their business activities, they require some kind of shared expectations about time. Just as different cultures have different assumptions about how people relate to one another, so they approach time differently.

Figure 15.9 **Past, present and future**

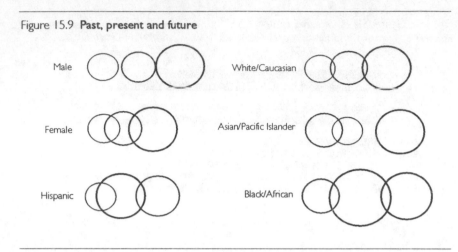

This orientation is about the relative importance a culture gives to the past, present and future. St Augustine pointed out in his Declarations that time as a subjective phenomenon can vary considerably from time in the abstract. In its abstract form we cannot know the future because it is not yet here, and the past is also unknowable. We may have memories, partial and selective, but the past has gone. The only thing that exists is the present, which is our sole access to past or future. St Augustine also wrote: "The present has, therefore, three dimensions: the present of past things, the present of present things and the present of future things."

The question asked was Tom Cottle's circle test (see page 126).

While the difference in the relative size of circles was not significant for men and women, the degree of overlap was. Indeed it is the most startling contrast in this chapter. Men think sequentially, past, present and future as passing us in a straight line like a train or the progress of a digital watch. Women think of past, present and future as synchronised and merged within the mind as interactive, parallel processes. Perhaps women have been free to deviate so widely from men in this respect because no negative stereotypes have been brandished to bring them into line.

This particular characteristic of female mental processing is not a topic of reproach or ridicule; we have not yet discovered the extent of its ramifications. But it does suggest that American women, at least, have an integrative capacity and orientation not exhibited by most men, and it raises the interesting question as to whether they may not be more adept at dilemma reconciliation, i.e. getting the two ends of our various dimensions to work together. Certainly this will be our next hypothesis for testing. Women, subject to demands from men and children, may simply be more adept at responding to simultaneous inputs.

We can also see from the circles diagram that women most resemble Asian Americans in their orientation to time and indeed the cultures of Japan and south-east Asia generally. In the light of very high scores on satisfaction for North American women posted to south-east Asia and Latin America and recently reported by Nancy Adler,[2] we may be witnessing a coincidental meeting of the minds and a possible advantage in utilising women overseas.

There is a tendency for ethnic groups subject to the most discrimination, blacks and Hispanics, to regard the present as most important. This may reveal a strong desire to "make it" now and an impatience with slow emancipation. But without further investigation we cannot be sure.

Functional diversity

Although not as strong as international differences, differences between functional areas are still quite significant and dominant.

A manager at the Dutch multinational Philips once told us that in the 1980s it was known as a company with outstanding research and development activities (patents in small audiocassettes, Video System 2000 and basic compact disc technology are just a few examples) and a quite impressive marketing and sales operation. Despite these excellent credentials Philips was close to bankruptcy in some crucial business areas in the early 1990s. The problem, according to this Philips manager, was that functional discussions of manufacturing, marketing and R&D were not well co-ordinated.

Consider western medicine. It seems to work quite well within medical specialties, but with over 1000 known atrogenic (doctor-caused) diseases, many patients turn to holistic medicine (homeopathy etc.), despite the fact that the efficacies of such practices are not confirmed. What are called "side effects" in western medicine are the displacement of symptoms from one speciality to another.

The whole pattern of western cultures shows greater emphasis on differentiating functions than on integrating them. We hear much of the "division of labour", but too little about its integration.

United Notions uses workshops to highlight functional differences. In one case we use a large chemical company which has had problems launching a new product, owing to miscommunication between functions. Some typical comments from three functions illustrate the problem:

> **Marketing:** If manufacturing would just once get their act together, we could serve our customers so much better and more quickly. In manufacturing they take too much time to readjust their set-ups.

R&D: Marketing people in general and their salesforce in particular sell before the products have been tested properly. They do the quick and dirty stuff and we get the blame if it is not up to standard.

Manufacturing: Both R&D and marketing have no clue about what our problems are. We are continuously put under pressure from both sides to speed up. When we don't have a technical problem it is a social one.

Marketing: Of course we put the system under pressure. If we didn't, it would take forever for R&D and manufacturing to get their act together.

Manufacturing: Why don't we create cross-functional taskforces? It is just a lack of communication. Often R&D and marketing have information we don't get.

R&D: In order to be innovative we need to be left alone for a while. Too often we are asked to repair things on existing products. In order to be first in the market we need to push our technology.

Most people will recognise these comments. The occurrence of these cross-functional tensions partly depends on the type of organisation and the way it is structured. Our research shows that there might be deeper cultural reasons for miscommunication across functional teams. These tensions were examined within our US sample, in order to avoid influences by nationality. Further research, however, indicates that these tensions hold across nationalities. Consider Figure 15.10, which shows some significant differences.

Figure 15.10 **Functional diversity**

Function	Universalism–particularism	Individualism–communit.	Neutral–affective	Specific–diffuse	Achievement–ascription	Internal–external
HR	78	42	56	67	54	52
Manufacturing	63	52	54	78	72	59
Finance	76	51	62	76	63	62
R&D	74	52	60	66	78	69
Marketing	53	61	57	79	82	80
Legal	79	56	62	72	55	65
Administration	64	32	72	75	80	49
Public affairs	53	81	58	92	38	42

Universalism–particularism

The highest universalist scores are found among legal, financial, R&D and HR managers. Following the rules is an obvious point of departure even for HR people. For them it looks like a counter measure against too many particularist demands by the workforce.

On the other extreme, we see the significantly more particularist public affairs, manufacturing and marketing (including sales) scores are apparently more stimulated by the particular case than the universal rule coming from R&D, legal affairs and finance.

This is one of the main challenges that need to be reconciled in western business. The universal truth of legal and R&D people needs to become the foundation for marketing and salespeople to adapt to the particular needs of the market.

Individualism–communitarianism

We would expect a very individualist score for marketing and a group-oriented score for HR, manufacturing and administrative job holders. This indeed is confirmed. The highest individualist score, however, is found among those in public affairs. Finance, R&D and legal represent average scores.

Neutrality–affectivity

Our data indicate that the most neutral of functional cultures are found in R&D and finance, and expressive employees are not surprisingly found in marketing (in particular sales) and production functions. The most neutral people seem to be found in the administrative functions. This is partly explained by the fact that the highest percentage of female participation is found in this job category. As discussed earlier, female administrative staff need to avoid falling into the male trap of considering that only good professionals go for a heart attack rather than showing emotions.

Specificity–diffuseness

On the specific side the top scores are in marketing, manufacturing and public affairs, while HR and R&D are quite diffuse in their approach. This is confirmed by the fact that the latter seem to be at one with their clients (HR) and ideas (R&D). If you attack them this is seen as a personal confrontation that involves some loss of face. Marketing people tend to be much more open to brainstorming, where they might chunk your brain into pieces, but no problem: "next brain!"

Achievement–ascription
In the orientation of status we see the highest achievers among marketing and production people, while status seems to be more connected to ascribed criteria like formal titles and other personal backgrounds such as age, gender etc. in legal, HR and public affairs.

Internal–external control
Although marketing scores have been very similar to those of sales people, for internal/external orientation we see marketing people at the extreme of internal control, while sales people score at the extreme end of the external orientation (score 41). Marketing is joined by R&D on the inner-directed side, while administrative workers join sales and public affairs in other/outer directedness. Legal, finance, public affairs and manufacturing scores are average. This is not surprising if we see the essence of selling products as empathising with clients' needs. Marketing, on the other hand, is more distant from the actual client and analyses market segments, product/market combinations and "grids" in preference to reality.

Time orientation
The last dimension relates to time. Very interesting differences are found here. We can see from Figure 15.11 that people from marketing share a predominant future orientation combined with a past that is best ignored. In R&D we see a fairly large future combined with a relatively small present and again a fairly large past. It seems that R&D is about recreating the corporate future through the experiences and knowledge accumulation of the past. Administrative and public affairs staff share a relatively dominant present orientation with a relatively small future. These last two functional groups also share a sequential approach, as is reflected in a fairly low overlap between the circles they drew. Problems are perceived to be current and need to be solved now, or even better yesterday. HR people seem to be the most balanced in terms of time orientation and combine this balance with a large overlap frequently expressing synchronicity.

Diversity in industries

While ethnic groups and functions show significant differences, so do industrial groups (see Figure 15.12). As with the other cultural groups, these are the result of frequently recurring problems and dilemmas that are solved almost automatically. It is not surprising that a group of banking people have a different time orientation to that of an employee of a

Figure 15.11 **Past, present and future**

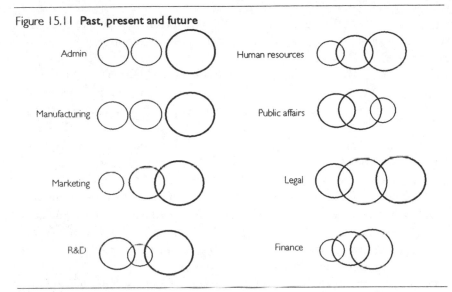

high-tech firm. And would you expect a bank culture to nurture an ascribed status system more than a culture in the textile industry?

One of the most universalist cultures is found in pharmaceuticals and transportation equipment (would you like them to ignore the rules?). Does it come as any surprise that individualism tends to be high in academia and the tobacco industry, while government and mining tend to be more oriented towards the group?

Some remarkable differences are found in universalism and particularism. People in health (hospitals etc.), academia and pharmaceuticals score on the very universalist side of the scale, while people in detergents, tobacco and textiles seem more to ride the particular wave.

Individualism seems to be very well developed in industries where it might help obtain better products and services, such as in academia. The fact that oil companies, and motor, metals and chemical industries are more communitarian in orientation is explained by the importance of shifts in their production facilities. Teamwork is the name of the game.

The health professions, the clothing industry and mining seem to be more expressive in emotions than their colleagues in the motor, transportation equipment, computer and electronics industries. No comments are necessary here since it seems self-explanatory.

Would you like a government official who deals with your car taxes to be well informed about the planning of utilities in your neighbourhood? And if you are developing a microchip in the electronics industry, would you have as broad a scope as those who work in a refinery? Obviously you would expect different orientations. We observe diffuse orientations in health, aerospace, detergents and the oil industry, while specificity seems very popular among government and the electronics, telecommunications and food industries.

In analysing the way different industries accord status, we find high achievers in transportation equipment, aerospace, food and government, while mining, textiles, health and detergents seem to favour ascribed status.

Differences in loci of control are very significant. Inner-directed cultures are not surprisingly found in the food, computer, aerospace and car industries, while other/outer-directed cultures seem to be more successful in detergents (marketing driven), mining, health and government.

Finally, we observe significantly different time orientations. Some are obvious. In interpreting the circles we find very past-oriented tobacco, health and textiles industries. The computer, aerospace and telecommunications industries seem to be occupied by the present, which in view of their fast-changing environments can be a very reasonable orientation. The cultures that seem to need a future-oriented approach are detergents, transportation equipment and the motor industry: lower in technology but higher in the need to plan for the future.

Figure 15.12 **Industry diversity**

Industry	Univ.–part.	Ind.–comm.	Neut.–aff.	Spec.–diff.	Ach.–asc.	Int.–ext.	Past	Present	Future
Construction	25.0	69.9	56.4	44.4	25.0	36.2	1.5	2.0	2.1
Telecomms	44.2	46.2	63.0	25.0	55.5	41.6	2.2	2.0	1.8
Bank/finance	60.1	65.0	56.4	53.9	51.6	41.6	2.2	1.9	2.0
Government	63.6	37.4	75.0	57.2	75.0	25.0	2.0	2.0	1.8
University	56.7	55.4	45.5	57.2	55.5	56.8	2.3	1.9	2.1
Aerospace	60.1	46.2	49.2	60.6	75.0	61.6	1.9	2.1	1.9
Beverages	53.3	55.4	41.6	35.6	43.9	56.8	2.2	1.8	2.0
Chemicals	50.2	50.7	56.4	35.6	25.0	56.8	2.0	2.0	1.9
Clothes/dress	47.1	37.4	25.0	38.5	28.8	33.4	2.2	2.1	1.7
Computers	53.3	50.7	49.2	57.2	59.4	51.9	1.9	2.1	1.9
Electronics	50.2	69.9	66.2	41.4	51.6	54.3	2.0	1.9	2.0
Food/drink	41.3	75.0	59.8	47.5	59.4	61.6	1.9	1.9	2.0
Metal	38.6	50.7	41.6	60.6	51.6	44.2	1.7	1.9	2.1
Mining	67.3	69.9	33.5	75.0	75.0	49.3	1.7	2.1	2.0
Motor vehicles	41.3	29.0	45.5	71.3	51.6	75.0	1.9	1.8	2.1
Petroleum	41.3	46.2	37.6	50.7	25.0	36.2	2.2	2.0	1.8
Pharmaceuticals	63.6	50.7	59.8	47.5	55.5	56.8	1.9	2.0	2.0
Detergents	36.1	29.0	37.6	53.9	36.3	41.6	1.7	2.1	2.0
Toys/sports	75.0	25.0	37.6	47.5	51.6	61.6	1.9	2.1	1.9

Database mining

To try to settle the question of where value differences originated, we looked at eight potential sources of difference: country or national culture, type of industry, religion, job or function, age of respondent, different corporations, educational level and gender. We then measured the relative amount of variety (low entropy) between those in that classification and the database as a whole. For example, how much difference is associated with being a woman, working in the energy industry, being a Protestant, being a US citizen? Is one's national culture the most or the least important of these variables? The importance of different classifications is in inverse proportion to their entropy. Rank orders are given for each classification.

Figure 15.13 **Variety in value differences**

Entropy	Universalism– particularism	Individualism– communit.	Neutral– affective	Specific– diffuse	Achievement– ascription	Internal– external	Time
Lowest	Country	Country	Country	Country	Country	Country	Country
	Industry	Religion	Industry	Industry	Industry	Industry	Industry
	Religion	Industry	Job	Religion	Religion	Job	Religion
	Job	Education	Religion	Age	Job	Religion	Education
	Age	Age	Corporate	Gender	Age	Gender	Job
	Corporate	Gender	Age	Education	Education	Age	Age
	Education	Job	Gender	Job	Corporate	Education	Gender
Highest	Gender	Corporate	Education	Corporate	Gender	Corporate	Corporate

National culture of origin is the most important difference for every dimension. Religion looms large for universalism, individualism, specificity and achievement. The Protestant religion, for example, treats the bible as "the law of God", codified instructions for salvation. It invites individuals to work for their own salvation, to offer God their work and to eschew all but the most specific and unadorned religious symbols. Type of industry is also important. Are you in a continuous process manufacturing system or customising complex services for particular clients? Job or function is moderately relevant, but gender, eduction, age or corporation show very small differences overall.

Such findings should not be misinterpreted. What they mean is that being female or male is not now being used as a competitive advantage for a company, not that a company founded and run mostly by women will not find such an advantage in the future. Low scores on corporate differences do not mean that corporate culture is unimportant, only that, on average, differences are not systematic and tend to cancel each other out.

No sooner do we change the circumstances than important differences start to appear. Cultures tend to appear and disappear from our horizon, depending on circumstances. Any difference, even the smallest, could become very important as the search for competitive advantage continues and pathfinders are imitated.

Religion, ethnicity and other variables may also combine, so that American Jews, for example, are more likely to enter law, medicine, social science, the media, universities and garment-making than are other ethnic groups. By becoming a majority or significant minority in certain key jobs and industries, these various cultures reinforce certain key values common to them all. Our data mining may only show that large patterns, national cultures, are more salient than smaller cultures, people of a particular age cohort or job description. The larger patterns are able to organise more values more consistently.

GENERAL CONCLUSIONS

It must be emphasised that the data we have been discussing are averages of a variety of scores within a certain national group. This and the previous chapter have considered some of the causes of this intra-cultural variety. We have found that ethnic differences within societies such as South Africa, and to a lesser degree the USA, can be as big as international differences.

We have also analysed other potential sources of major differences within national samples, such as gender, age, hierarchical level, industrial and functional background. We can indeed conclude that national differences in value orientations are a major source of cultural diversity, but that other factors do account for a large portion of the diversity we find within a national culture.

The factors which account for the greatest variance in our dimensions of culture can only be determined by sophisticated statistical analyses. Further information on the methods used can be obtained from United Notions (see Appendix 3).

References
1   Rotter, J.B., "General expectations for internal versus external control of reinforcement", *Psychological Monograph*, No. 609, 1966, pages 1–28.
2   See *Competitive Frontiers*, Nancy Adler (ed.), Basil Blackwell, Oxford, 1994.

APPENDIX 1

EXAMPLES FROM THE 16 QUESTIONS
USED TO MEASURE CORPORATE CULTURE

Question 9 Criticism

In your organisation, criticism:

a) is aimed at the task, not the person;
b) is only given when asked for;
c) is mostly negative and usually takes the form of blame;
d) is avoided because people are afraid of hurting each other.

Question 11 Conflict

In your organisation, conflict:

a) is controlled by the intervention of higher authority, and often fostered by it to maintain power;
b) is suppressed by reference to rules, procedures and definitions of responsibility;
c) is resolved through full discussion of the merits of the work issues involved;
d) is resolved by open and deep discussion of personal needs and the values involved.

Question 13 Hierarchy

In your organisation, hierarchies:

a) are redundant because each person is working for their own professional development;
b) are necessary because people have to know who has authority over whom;
c) are determined by the power and authority of the people involved;
d) are relevant only if they are useful for getting the task done.

Responses

The possible responses to these relate as follows to company models.

Question 9
a) Guided missile
b) Family
c) Incubator
d) Eiffel Tower

Question 11
a) Family
b) Eiffel Tower
c) Guided missile
d) Incubator

Question 13
a) Incubator
b) Family
c) Eiffel Tower
d) Guided missile

APPENDIX 2
THE TROMPENAARS DATABASE

Peter Woolliams, Professor of Systems Management,
University of East London, UK

This appendix summarises aspects of the development and analysis of the research database assembled by Trompenaars which underpins the main text. It is based on responses to his cross-cultural questionnaire instruments. The principal interest here is to review the data from the perspective of the level of national cultures, although extensive analysis of individual variations or variations through management function, industry sector, religion and gender are also available. For a comprehensive review and detailed data and statistical analysis, research monographs are available from United Notions.

The primary purpose of the Trompenaars database is to help managers structure their cross-cultural experiences in order to develop their competence for doing business and managing across cultures. In seeking to enhance the estimates of the average characteristics of managers in a given national culture, considerable efforts have been made to extend the size of the samples, reduce measurement errors and maintain homogeneity. Suggestions and issues identified in reports of the analysis of the earlier and smaller database described by Smith *et al.*[1] were given priority.

The raw data set comprises some 50,000 cases from over 100 countries. By restricting the analysis to managers from multinational and international corporations faced with internationalising their operations, some 30,000 comparative valid cases can be selected drawn from 55 countries. This represents a sample size of nearly three times that of the previous reviews. Analysis of the variety reveals functionally equivalent sets, since nearly all the selected managers were pursuing similar ends. However, it should be noted that the whole approach was not to seek an orthogonal dataset typified by classical market research. In the latter, a sample is targeted with the minimum number of cases to cover each attribute (country, gender, age etc.). But this presumes we know what attributes to measure in advance and also has practical difficulties, e.g. where does one find a young female Arab senior manager working in a Gulf country? Trompenaars therefore adopted the approach of collecting a larger dataset with extensive internal variety that enables a deductive analysis through data mining to be performed.

Work was also undertaken on improving the language of the questionnaire to make it more transparent across cultures and more acceptable where value systems and integrity are challenged. Cluster analysis was used to examine whether highly correlated items do in fact cluster around the concepts being tested. Validating interviews and cognitive mapping were also applied. Exhaustive quantitative analysis was applied to assess the validity of alternate questions and combinations of questions at both the 'world level' and ecological (country level).

Each of Trompenaars' dimensions is a scale based on a combination of finite alternatives to each of a series of finite alternatives which therefore generates a combinatorial (binomial) rather than normal distribution. However, the central limit theorem suggests parametric methods may be applied to this non-parametric data in view of the large sample sizes. While this was accepted for convenience, analysis was also performed on a strict exact tests basis as a precaution. In fact, the latter shows the distributions to be leptokurtic (even more closely clustered than for a normal distribution).

Some authors have misinterpreted the origin of Trompenaars' rationale for these scales and derived incorrect conclusions therein. Thus Hofstede[2] only used a subset of the data from individual questions or averages rather than in the weighted combination of these questions that provide scale values for each of Trompenaars' dimensions. Saying that 65% of US managers chose the universalistic option when answering a question is not what Trompenaars means when he asserts that the typical US managers can be placed 65% along the universalistic–particularistic scale. Trompenaars combines responses from different questions to give a scale along each dimension, not a polarised bimodal measure at each end. These combinations are chosen and have constantly been redefined so as to maximise the discrimination between countries along each scale. The individual questions show not only high validity but also high reliability. Responses to component questions are by design not perfectly correlated within the scales. If they were, only one question would be required for each dimension!

Cronbach's alpha test of reliability was applied to questions and combinations of questions. In some cases, and especially for corporate culture, questions were successively modified or removed where such change produced an increase in alpha. For each scale alpha was maximised and the final design has the performance shown in Table A1.

The scale for the time dimension which is based on the circles test required different treatment. With the wide diversity of diagrams, the aim was to identify common factors or underlying themes or cultural concepts which the respondents were trying to express. Thus the search was to find an algorithmic relationship with the co-ordinate system of their drawing and quantitative scales that could serve as the basis of cross-cultural discrimination.

Table A1

	Scale variety	Alpha
Universalism–particularism	216	0.71
Individualism–communitarianism	64	0.73
Specific–diffuse	25	0.63
Neutral–affective	243	0.75
Achievement–ascription	1024	0.64
Internal–external	1024	0.71
Time		0.74

As a result of extensive trials, it was concluded that three factors could be discerned which owed their origin in the degree to which the circles overlapped, touched or were separate and to the relative sizes of the circles. Earlier hand drawings were assessed visually. More recently, where the circles are drawn by the respondent directly on a computer screen, the scales were derived directly from the co-ordinates by integrating the area subtended at the base and the relative position of the centre of gravity. Thus a scale from 100 (maximum overlap=synchronic culture) through to 0 (no overlap=sequential culture) was derived. A second scale assessed the relative component of past, present and future orientation. A third scale could also be derived which measures a 'time horizon' (short-term thinking and planning vs longer-term thinking and planning). In many ways, these scales suffered fewer problems than the other dimensions based on forced text questions.

The scales for corporate culture were examined, reviewed and treated to the same degree of rigour to derive components with the following reliabilities:

Table A2 Cronbach's alpha

Role culture	0.79
Task culture	0.75
Person culture	0.63
Power culture	0.74

In some situations, the set of scores on each dimension scales were subjected to a parabolic transform function to account for skew and kurtosis. This has the effect of maintaining the sequence and relationships between country scores, but makes the distribution more symmetrical for the purposes of presentation.

In addition to applying statistical tests of validity and reliability and reporting orientations along each cultural dimension, other types of analysis were performed to support the postulates and frameworks on which this book is based.

In particular, non-parametric data mining was used to investigate the variety within the data as well as investigating dimension reduction with factor analysis. This sought to ask two key questions:

1 What is the relative importance of each attribute (age, gender, religion, country, job function)?
2 How many dimensions of culture are required to explain the variety in the data?

Relative importance of attributes

For this discussion, the model can be considered in the following form (for each dimension):

dimension score =
$c_1 \times$ country + $c_2 \times$ age + $c_3 \times$ religion + $c_4 \times$ gender + c_5... etc.

It is tempting to 'throw' established statistical techniques at the data to identify possible coefficients (c_1, c_2, c_3 etc.) using correlation and partial-correlation analysis or factor analysis. Some other authors have often done just that with their own more limited data sets or incomplete or extracted sets of the earlier data that have previously been published. This has been especially true of researchers with primarily a statistical mindset rather than open-minded inquirers or students with a genuine interest in trying to contribute to the debate and frameworks of cross-cultural analysis.

On examination of the data, it should be noted that these parametric methods are not strictly appropriate. Many of the data items are simply categories (nominal data) such as gender, religion or management function. Classical statistical non-parametric methods are not readily available for this particular problem and certainly none is included in industry standard statistical software. While analysis of variance and (categories) conjoint analysis can help with questionnaire design and testing, it cannot produce the analysis required here.

In order to explore the data set it is therefore appropriate to apply a different body of mathematics which is appropriate for this cause. Recent developments in relational database technology, database mining methods and knowledge elicitation (expert systems) come to the rescue.

The basic principle is to find the relative importance of the various attributes in determining the goal attribute. The first step is to normalise (arrange) the data to the so-called third normal form in separate tables (as would be required for representation in a relational database).

For the full database, the amount of entropy for each attribute can be computed. This gives a measure of the uncertainty of classification of the goal by each attribute. As the entropy increases, the amount of uncertainty gained by adding each attribute increases. However, the quest is to find how much information there is when the value(s) of any particular attribute is (are) given. This can be found simply by weighting occurrences.

To explain the total variety, it would be necessary to use the same variety as there are cases. This is the same as saying that 30,000 respondents are all individuals and 30,000 attributes are required to describe them. Alternatively, one could use one attribute with 30,000 values (such as name!) to identify them uniquely. In the above parlance, 'name' has the highest information content and lowest entropy. However, this is not the aim. Recall that Trompenaars is seeking to develop a model based on a number of dimensions (attributes) that help structure managers' experiences. The analysis attempted here is intended to support this aim by exploring the relative importance of different attributes rather than containing the total variety within the data set as an ideological statistician may prefer.

'Country' is confirmed to have the lowest entropy of classification and thus this corresponds to the least uncertainty. In other words, 'country' has the highest information content and thus 'country' is the major contributor in explaining the cultural orientation on the dimensions. Manager function, for example, has a smaller contribution. These computations support and justify the emphasis throughout this book on analysis at the ecological (country) level rather than that of individual respondent. The results of this analysis are further discussed in Chapter 15.

How many dimensions?

This is more difficult to answer because it partly depends on why the question is being posed.

A fundamental issue to consider is whether all the seven dimensions of the model are required and whether each is measuring a different aspect of culture. Culture is a construct that is derived from these individual dimensions, but are these dimensions themselves (orthogonal) individual? Perhaps there are alternative and simpler models of culture, such as:

culture = c_1 × (inherited characteristics)
c_2 × (acquired characteristics) ....equation i); or

culture = c_1 × (relationships between people)
c_2 × (relationship with nature)
c_3 × (relationship or orientation to time) ....equation ii)

In the former case one would only need two dimensions (and to determine the coefficients c_1, c_2), or three dimensions for the latter model. Thus possible inter-relationships between the dimensions need to be explored.

Table A3 shows the correlation between the dimensions. One can start the analysis with the use of parametric models by invoking the central limit theorem. If the correlations between the dimensions are zero then they are individually and uniquely measuring a different aspect of culture. Using the average country scores from the database shows values which are not zero but are all less than 0.5. Bartlett's sphericity test can be used to consider the hypothesis that the correlation matrix is an identity matrix (i.e. the diagonals are 1 and the off-diagonal elements are 0). Thus the chi-square of the transformation of the determinant of the correlation matrix is computed. This value is not low and therefore the hypothesis that the correlation matrix is an identity matrix should not be rejected.

Table A3 **Correlations between dimensions**

	unpa	indcom	spdi	neaf	achasc	intext
unpa	1.0000	.1269	.4669	.1209	.4223	.4013
indcom	.1269	1.0000	.4236	.0697	.4397	.2753
spdi	.4669	.4236	1.0000	-.0239	.4006	.4678
neaf	.1209	.0697	-.0239	1.0000	.2177	-.0444
achasc	.4223	.4397	.4006	.2177	1.0000	.4976
intext	.4013	.2753	.4678	-.0444	.4976	1.0000

Thus further probing is required to investigate whether there is any significance in the small off-diagonal correlation coefficients. However, Bartlett's test is strictly only valid for ratio data from a multivariate normal population and the Trompenaars data is only intended to indicate ordinal/ranked measurements of cultural components and country averages are being discussed, not individual responses. If individual cases are taken, much lower cross-correlations are found. This in itself may be sufficient to explain the small off-diagonal correlations here.

The partial correlation coefficients are a further indicator. If the dimensions share common factors, then again the off-diagonal correlation coefficients should be small when the linear effects of the other dimensions are controlled. Table A4 shows that the off-diagonal partial correlation coefficients are again small, but not zero.

Table A4 **Partial correlations**

	unpa	indcom	spdi	neaf	achasc	intext
unpa	-1.00000	-0.33034	0.28868	0.04792	0.45555	0.05059
indcom	-0.33034	-1.00000	0.55267	0.08339	0.22835	-0.03604
spdi	0.28868	0.55267	-1.00000	-0.18283	0.18540	0.15654
neaf	0.04792	0.08339	-0.18283	-1.00000	0.26277	-0.16338
achasc	0.45555	0.22835	0.18540	0.26277	-1.00000	0.34040
intext	0.05059	-0.03604	0.15654	-0.16338	0.34040	-1.00000

A better insight into the source of these small effects can be gained from computing the Kaiser-Meyer-Olkin (KMO) index.[3] This statistic compares the observed correlation coefficients to the partial correlation coefficients. If the sum of the squares of the partial coefficients between all dimensions is small compared to the sum of the squared total correlations, then the KMO will be close to 1. The small value of KMO indicates that correlation between the dimensions cannot be explained by the other variables. This is further evidence to support the need for all of the cultural dimensions.

One can also use factor analysis to seek a smaller number of factors that can be used to represent the relationship between the dimensions of culture. The goal is to represent culture parsimoniously – that is, a desire to express culture with as few indicators (factors) as possible. If one can reduce the number then not only is simplification achieved but new insights may arise. Ideally, the new factors should be interpretable because it would then be possible to derive the model of interest based on the constructs sought, rather than simply those that can be measured (the raw dimensions). Thus:

1   Can the not so directly measurable aspects of culture be extracted from the observable dimensions?
2   Can original data be explained by a model similar to equation i) or equation ii) above?
3   Are the observed correlations due to the sharing of common factors?

The KMO index above indicates that factor analysis is likely to be unsuccessful. Further, factor analysis is not simply multiple regression. The aim is not to try to express culture as a combination of dimensions but to combine dimensions into higher order factors that are not known in advance. However, the objective of factor analysis is to reduce the number of dimensions required to explain the data. Obtaining fewer factors by factor analysis does not mean that the seven-dimensional culture model is invalid or that the number of dimensions should be reduced. If the correlation coefficients had been higher, one might have expected to be able to extract valid factors because the inter-relationships between the dimensions would have been due to the presence of these factors.

For the sake of completeness, principal components analysis can also be considered. Linear combinations of the observed dimensions are taken to estimate possible factors. The first component is the combination that accounts for the largest amount of the variance in the database. Successive components explain progressively smaller portions.

Table A5 shows the Eigen values for each factor. Having attempted to represent culture with two factors (similar to equation i), this only explains some 50% of the variance and either seven replacement factors or all the original dimensions are required to account for the variance (cultural diversity). A scree plot data also reveals this. This result is not surprising, since both Bartlett's test[4] and the KMO index both indicated that there were unlikely to be underlying simpler factors.

Table A5: Eigen values

achasc	41.3% (cumulative)
indcom	52.5%
intext	76.6
time	85.7
neaf	92.7
spdi	97.3
unpa	100.0

Factor matrix and rotations

Again, little or no benefit is revealed, nor is any underlying model that justifies using these new factors rather than the original dimensions. If the rotation had achieved a simple structure, clusters of the dimensions would occur either near the ends of each axis or at their intersection. As expected, it is found that the original dimensions are widely scattered in the factor space.

Thus it cannot be concluded from the above discussion that fewer cultural dimensions can usefully explain the variance in the data. This could have been expected simply on the basis of the low correlations given above. However, further probing was undertaken with an open mind and to contribute to the debate. In addition, the question set is not ipsative (independent) because some questions are used for more than one scale and factor analysis does not correct for this in-built correlation.

One might also wish to reject the above discussion on the basis that the data collected is not genuine multivariate (ratio) normal data. If the data is ordinal or non-parametric, then one should really use non-metric (MDS) multidimensional scaling rather than factor analysis to probe variety reduction. Here the original data has to be transformed into a matrix of cultural differences. Thus it is necessary to compute (for each country, for each dimension) the **difference** between each case and all other cases. Normally this is obtained by computing the Euclidean distance (square of the differences) to obtain a measure of dissimilarity. In the MDS model, each country is represented in multidimensional space and arranged so that the distances between all pairs of cases (countries) is based on these differences – countries that score similarly on universalism–particularism will be closer together etc. As with factor analysis, if the aim is to seek to reduce the number of dimensions it may be possible to take combinations of cultural dimensions that cluster together, i.e. are measuring the same thing. It is necessary to assume that the data is always symmetric (the difference between the US and Japan is the same as the cultural difference between Japan and the US) and the analysis must be repeated for each dimension. Thus full (RMDS) replicated non-metric multidimensional scaling algorithm (after McGee[5]) is required which applies the analysis of dissimilarity to each (cultural) dimension simultaneously. The plot of the RDMS stimulus co-ordinates produces a scatter plot with the dimensions spread between the axes. If the cultural dimensions were components of common factors, then the RDMS plots would show the dimensions more significantly clustered. Thus the same conclusion is reached by applying this non-parametric assessment, namely that the model of culture cannot simply be reduced to one or two new dimensions.

Finally, agglomerative hierarchical clustering should also be reviewed. Here the aim would be to try to form groups of countries with similar cultural orientations. However, it should be remembered that cluster analysis is a subjective rather than analytical technique. When group (cluster) membership is known, discriminant analysis can be applied. Here group (cluster) membership is not known, so again Euclidean distance is resorted to. Classically, the countries which are most similar would be clustered, then the next and so on. By transposition, attempts are made to cluster the cultural.

Only very weak clustering can be found. Again, this derives from the very weak correlation coefficients discussed above. The **sequence** of clustering shows a possible and interesting aspect, namely that there is more variety in ACHASC than the other dimensions. This has some face validity too. When two people first meet, the initial first greeting is either 'Hi ! I'm Mr US, and I'm a lawyer', or 'I'm Sheik Haasam, and I'm the brother of El Refaie'. Does this confirm that on meeting someone we run our built-in survival program (shall we flee or fight?), and that who we are or what we do is the first thing we need to know about our assailant? As discussed elsewhere, in business applications other dimensions may have a higher priority in establishing the first point of cross-cultural communication.

In commenting on Trompenaars earlier work, Hofstede's[2] exclusive use of parametric analysis is surprising. He should have used non-parametric methods such as correspondence analysis or homogeneity analysis for performing optimal scaling. However, all of these procedures are designed to set out to achieve dimension reduction rather than to identify the number of dimensions required to explain the variety in the original data. Saying that the data can be summarised as two or three statistical derived factors is not the same as claiming that Trompenaars' seven-dimensional model is not supported by his data or that fewer than seven dimensions are required. In particular there is the case of 'outliers'. Although, as Hofstede claims, responses to some of Trompenaars' questions may correlate for many countries and therefore these dimensions might be combined, the separate dimensions are required for many specific cases (such as the Gulf countries, ignored by Hofstede) because for these countries they do not correlate. Thus for G7 countries compared to GCC (Gulf countries), different dimensions are required to explain these inter-country differences compared to the intra-G7 country differences.

Thus we may conclude in answer to the rhetorical question that, although fewer dimensions may be used to explain some of the data, in practice they are all required to explain the full diversity across the globe. In different practical situations (e.g. making comparisons between any two particular cultures), we can select those dimensions which best discriminate the two cultures. And let's remember that in the same way that gender correlates with height, just because two dimensions correlate is not the same as saying that they are measuring the same construct.

Further research

The Trompenaars database is one of the largest and richest sources of social constructs. Research is continuing to refine the instruments (particularly to avoid polarised dilemma options), to extend the number and variety of subcases and to apply further methods of analysis such as neural networks. Access to the data is offered to bona fide researchers and to client companies with particular interests or needs. Again, the reader is referred to the research monographs for comprehensive treatment of the summary presented here.

References

1 Smith, P.B. 'Appendix' to *Riding the Waves of Culture*, 1st edition, Nicholas Brealey Publishing, 1993; Smith *et al.*, "National cultures and values of organisational employees", *Journal of Cross Cultural Psychology*, vol. 27, 2, March 1996.

2 Hofstede G., "Riding the waves of commerce", *International Journal of Intercultural Relations*, vol. 20, 2, pp.189–98, 1996; Hampden-Turner, C. and Trompenaars, F. "A response to Hofstede", *International Journal of Intercultural Relations*, vol. 22, 4, pp.189–98, 1997.

3 Kaiser-Meyer-Olkin (KMO) index, see Kaiser, H., "Factor Analysis", *Psychometrika*, vol. 30, pp. 1–14, 1965.

4 Bartlett's test: *ibid.*, pp. 1–14.

5 McGee, "Multi-dimensional scaling, *Multi-variate Behavioural Research*, vol. 3, pp.233–48, 1968.

APPENDIX 3
TROMPENAARS HAMPDEN-TURNER
INTERCULTURAL MANAGEMENT GROUP

The mission of Trompenaars Hampden-Turner Intercultural Management Group (previously known as the Centre for Intercultural Business Studies (CIBS)/United Notions) is to help improve the global effectiveness of organisations through best practice training, consultancy and publishing in cross-cultural management. Established in the Netherlands in 1987, it has been at the forefront of the movement recognising that managing the complexity and ambiguity in a turbulent and heterogeneous environment and actually benefiting from the vast opportunities presented by cultural variety are major challenges.

Trompenaars Hampden-Turner Intercultural Management Group has branch offices in Japan, Singapore, South Africa, UK and USA. Since 1991 Intercultural Management Publishing (IMP) has produced and distributed a range of business books, videos, training materials and interactive media.

The basis of our approach is the 7D-Model, described in this book, which provides a framework for discussing real business differences by reference to how people from different cultures, who cope every day with the dilemmas of operating internationally, tell us they would respond to practical choices. This is supplemented by the extensive experience of our trainers and consultants in working and managing in cross-cultural environments.

One benefit of using such a model is that we can establish a shared vocabulary and method for discussing and resolving cultural differences. Our programmes are highly interactive, using case studies, simulations, anecdotes, research data and the personal experiences of the trainers and participants to build a high level of involvement. All participants complete and receive feedback on questionnaires to identify their own cultural orientation. We focus on the development of skills to deal with real business issues. Discussions of each of the dimensions of culture are oriented towards the needs of the group, but tend to include implications for managing or being managed, working together, building relationships, team working, negotiating and communicating with people from other cultures.

Products

Our Culture Compass Country Series® covers a range of printed and electronic products on specific country profiles. The core is a module where users can process their own culture map based on their scores on the cross-cultural questionnaire. Once users know their profile, they can compare it with the average profile (from our database) of the country of choice. They will receive special feedback on what the comparison means for them personally when doing business with people from the other country.

Currently versions for the USA, Japan, India, France, China, the Netherlands, Korea, Germany, Austria and Sweden are being developed. The culture compass also allows users to place the general cultural information within the context of their own organisation.

Trompenaars Hampden-Turner Intercultural Management Group also provides Welcome to Anywhere country briefings based on the material in the Culture Compass.

More information

Trompenaars Hampden-Turner Intercultural Management Group
A.J. Ernststraat 595-d
1082 LD Amsterdam
The Netherlands
Tel: +31 (0)20 301 6666
Fax: +31 (0)20 301 6555
E-mail: info@unotions.nl
Website: www.unotions.nl

INDEX